AF519854

# Life Skills and Teacher's Stress

# Life Skills and Teacher's Stress

Edited by
**Dr. G. VISVANATHAN**
Professor, Department of Education,
Annamalai University, Tamil Nadu
and
**Dr.S.K.PANNEER SELVAM**
Assistant Professor, Department of Education
Bharathidasan University, Tamil Nadu

RANDOM

**RANDOM PUBLICATIONS**

**NEW DELHI (INDIA)**

**Life Skills and Teacher's Stress**

---

ISBN 978-93-5111-314-0


Published in 2014 in India by
**RANDOM PUBLICATIONS**
4376-A/4B, Gali Murari Lal, Ansari Road
NewDelhi-110 002
Phone : +9111-43580356, 011-23289044
E-mail: randomexports@gmail.com; sales@randompublications.com; info@randompublications.com

*Type Setting by :* Shah Computer Graphics, Delhi-110094
*Digitally Printed at*: Replika Press Pvt. Ltd.

# Contents

# I

# Importance of Adult Education

Education is an instrument of social change and development in a society is based on technology and science. It is the education that determines the means of prosperity and level to which it can be achieved. It also helps the adult learner to improve his standard of living through participation, in various developmental programmes. Many such programmes have been specially designed to improve the lot of poor and the deprived sections of the society. Most of the adult learners usually belong to these sections of society. Due to illiteracy and lack of appropriate skills, they cannot take benefit of these programmes. Education enables individuals to actively participate in the developmental programmes, so that not only their socio-economic and political conditions are improved but also the national progress and prosperity are enhanced as a whole. To quote the Teheran Report (1965) "Literacy teaching should be resolutely oriented towards development and should be an integral part not only of any national education plans but also of plans and projects for development in all sectors of the national life". This means that literacy programmes should be linked with all development plans of the country, whether these are economic, social, political or cultural in character. V.K.R.V. Rao, in his book 'Education and Human

Resource Development' (1966) stated, "Without adult education and adult literacy, it is not possible to have that range and speed of economic and social development which we require nor it is possible to have that quality or tone to our economic and social development that makes it worthwhile in terms of values and welfare. The relationship between illiteracy and under development is manifold and can be summarized that :

- in the modem world, an illiterate person is circumscribed in playing his full potential role in the economic development of his country.
- he cannot participate fully and meaningfully in the social, civic, cultural and political activities of his country.
- he is forced to live a marginal existence.
- he cannot achieve his individual liberation and realize self-actualization.
- and he is highly vulnerable to exploitation and oppression.

Adult education, has, therefore, has to play a significant role in social, economic and political development of a country. In the social sphere, an ignorant man is not in a position to enjoy the comforts of life. The modern world is adding a lot to the welfare of the man but he can enjoy it only if he is knowledgeable and well informed. Adult education envisages to raise a desire for change, to face challenges, fight dogmatism, fatalism, exploitation, superstitions and forces of status quo and march towards modernisation.

Adult education is thus, a tool for developing critical social consciousness. It also include collective mobilization for social transformation, critical review of the action carried out, replanning of future action and re-evaluation of the previous diagnosis of social reality, national and international studies have also established that there is close relationship between literacy and other indicators of quality of life. It was found that .the countries where illiteracy is high, per capital income is low, infant mortality rate is high, life expectancy is low, undernourishment is a serious problem, communicable diseases are widespread and number of persons below the poverty line is much more. It is therefore evident that adult education is important for social development because it helps in bringing positive effects on illiterates and dispells their misgiving about various superstitions, dogmas, child marriages, education of girl child, dowry, etc.

Adult education embraces all forms of educative experiences needed by men and women according to their varying interests and requirements. It denotes the entire body of organized educational processes whereby adults develop their abilities, enrich their know-ledge, improve their technical or professional qualifications and bring about changes in their attitude and behaviour.

Adult education is increasingly being seen in its totality. Liveright and Hagood proposed that "adult education is the process whereby persons who no longer (or did not) attend school on a regular and full time basis undertake sequential and organised activities within a conscious intention about changes in information, knowledge under-standing or skills, appreciation and attitudes, or for the purpose of identifying and solving personal or community problems".

Bertelsen bas simplified the definition of adult education as "any learning experience designed for adults irrespective of content, level and methods used".

According to UNESCO, "the term adult education denotes the entire body of organized educational processes, whatever content, level and method, whether formal or otherwise, whether they prolong or replace initial education in schools, colleges and universities as well as in apprenticeship; whereby persons regarded as adult by the society to which they belong develop their abilities, enrich their knowledge, improve their technical or professional qualifications and bring about changes in their attitude or behaviour in the two fold perspective of full personnel development and participation in 'balanced and independent social, economic and cultural development. Adult education embraces all forms of educative experiences needed by men and women according to their varying interests and requirements, at their differing levels of comprehension and ability and in their changing roles and responsibilities throughout life".

## CONTINUING EDUCATION PROGRAMME

Total Literacy Campaigns have resulted in a positive change in attitude, a new confidence among the learners to upgrade their skills and adopt it for individual development, and eventually for social action in India. The enthusiasm and confidence generated among the learners in the districts which have successfully completed both the Total Literacy Campaign, as well as the post-literacy phases, clearly points towards the need to sustain the education process and to provide learning opportunities on a continuing basis. The literacy skills acquired by the neo-literates need to be further reinforced and widened so as to enable them to fully play the crucial role for their own personal, social and economic upliftment and for the development of the country.

Continuing education is an indispensable aspect of the strategy of human resource development and of the goal of creation of a learning society. Many of the third world countries and the developing countries are now recognizing that socio-economic planning alone is not enough and that the human resource development is a key enabling factor in development. All these countries are aware that education and human resource development will play a key role in the 21$^{st}$ century. What is more significant is the realization that expansion of formal education alone, which is only a small component of lifelong learning, cannot lead to human resource development. Formal education as an instrument of human resource development is not really effective in remedying the structural inequalities in the society. Continuing education, which provides a second chance to those who missed formal education and is responsive to learners' needs, directly addresses itself to structural inequalities. Only continuing education can bring about full development of human resources. Since continuing education is the opportunity to engage in lifelong learning, it is now emerging as the main component of the broader view of education as a whole. Continuing education includes post-literacy for neo-literates and school dropouts for retention of literacy skills, continuation of learning beyond elementary literacy and application of this learning for improving their living conditions. Continuing education goes beyond post-literacy. It includes all the learning opportunities all people want or need outside of basic literacy education and primary education.

## Objectives

The main objectives of the scheme and the activities aimed under it include the following:

1. Providing facilities for retention of literacy skills and continuing education to enable the learners to continue their learning beyond basic literacy.
2. Creating scope for application of functional literacy for improvement of living conditions and quality of life.
3. Dissemination of information on development programmes and widening and improving participation of traditionally deprived sections of the society.
4. Creation of awareness about national concerns such as national integration, conservation and improvement of the environment, women's equality, observance of small family norms, etc., and sharing of common problems of community.
5. Improvement of economic conditions and general wellbeing as well as improvement of productivity of organizing short duration training programmes, orientation courses for providing vocational skills and by taking up linkage activities for establishing direct linkage between continuing education and development activities.
6. Provision of facilities for library and reading rooms for creating an environment conducive for literacy efforts and learning society.
7. Organisation of cultural and recreational activities with effective community participation.

**Beneficiaries**

The beneficiaries of continuing education programmes would include the following :

The neo-literates who complete the functional literacy / post-literacy courses under total literacy / post literacy or other programmes :

(a) School dropouts;

(b) Pass-outs of primary schools;

(c) Pass-outs of non-formal education programme; and

(d) All other members of the community interested in availing opportunities for lifelong learning.

## Functions of Continuing Education Centres

As mentioned above, the principle objective of establishment of continuing education centres is to serve as a window or a focal service point where diverse kinds of continuing education programmes and activities are taken up to provide opportunities for life-long learning to all sections of the population. The functions of continuing education would be include:

### (i) An Evening Class

For upgradation of literacy and numeracy skills to be organized for 3-4 hours once a week. The learners would have the option to come for an hour or so at the time of their convenience on that day.

### (ii) A Library and Reading Room

For which books would be purchased from the non-recurring and recurring provisions; copies of old journals will be maintained and useful booklets relating to development programmes will be published by concerned agencies. Wall papers and newspapers, appropriate for adult learners, information and entertaining journals, developmental literature, etc., would also be available.

### (iii) A Charcha Mandal (Discussion Group)

For discussing on common problems, this forum could be utilized for quality of life improvement and individual interest programme.

### (iv) Training Programmes

Simple and short duration relating to such subjects as health and family welfare, new developments in agriculture and animal husbandry, conservation of energy, improved chulha, etc. Continuing Education Centres may also help the local youth to benefit from various vocational training programmes. Income generation programmes, which helps participants acquire or upgrade vocational skills and enable them to conduct income generating activities.

### (v) Sports and Adventurous Activities

The stress being on indigenous sports, walking excursions, cycling trips in groups, etc. If savings are available, visit by bus to development projects could also be arranged.

### (vi) Recreational and Cultural Activities

Particularly traditional and folk forms of art, rural theatre, puppetry, etc.

### (vii) An Information Window

For securing information, on various developmental programmes, information and material suitable for neo-literates may be procured from the concerned developmental agencies.

### (viii) A Communication Centre

Where community radio, audio cassettes player-cum-recorder may be provided (in the Nodal Continuing Education Centre only).

## 2. A BRIEF DESCRIPTION OF DIFFERENT SKILLS

Skill is defined as a practiced ability or expertise in a given ability. It is a system of behaviour that can be applied in a wide range of situations. Basically there are two types of skills. They are hard skills and soft skills.

### Hard Skills

Hard skills are those skills required to perform the functions of a specific job work or a specialized task. These skills are the technical abilities gained through education and practical hands-on application. For example, a machinist must have the skills, knowledge and know how to read technical diagrams and to shape metal as per the exact specifications, using a variety of equipment. A civil engineer, for example, should be skilful enough to plan, design, estimate, and execute construction of a building or dam; a doctor should develop the skills of diagnosing, operating and treating patients. Similarly, an adult education continuing education worker should be skillful in planning, organizing the learning activities and teaching according to the level of learners. Hard skills are acquired through learning over a period of time. The skills are quantitative in nature, which can be seen in terms of grades and percentages. These skills are also comparable and can be measured. Generally these skills are acquired through training and education programmes. A degree, diploma or a certificate confirms that the relevant abilities necessary to perform a particular job have been sufficiently mastered. Hard skills are vital to secure employment. Technical competence is a prerequisite to any mode of employment. However, hard skills alone might not be sufficient to survive successfully in today's world.

## Soft Skills

Besides hard skills, soft skills, also called human skills, are also important. In contrast to hard skills, soft skills are generally interpersonal competencies, a diverse range of abilities and are more difficult to define due to their subjectivity. This makes them difficult to measure. Employees looking for that extra edge crave for training that teaches them how to stand out with personal, as opposed to practical qualities. Soft skills includc: Listening skills, Communication skills, Team building skills, Leadership skills, Problem-solving skills, Time management skills, Negotiation skills, Conflict management skills, Assertiveness skills, Feedback skills, Counselling skills, Presentation skills, and Mentoring skills.

For an individual or an employee, the importance and value of soft skills, though hard to quantify, are immeasurable. Dealing with difficult peers or co-workers, negotiating office dynamics, and having the ability to listen and solve problems are some of the examples of soft skills. In today's uncertain economic times, the person who has the ability to interact with people is likely be the one who will succeed. With the ever-increasing use of e-mail as a communication tool, written skills are crucial to career development and growth.

## Soft skills are very important

- to handle interpersonal relations
- to take appropriate decisions
- to communicate effectively
- to have good impression and impact
- to gain professional development

Relationships play a vital role in human life, and one of the keys to successful relationships is development of soft skills. A continuing education worker who has interpersonal problems and has difficulty in taking decisions, suffers from lack of soft skills. Hence, a continuous renewal of soft skills through teaching and training of the continuing education worker is essential. This will make their dealings effective and successful.

Soft skills can enhance the career mobility of a person and increase the chances of success in getting the job he she wants. They are essential for a continuing education worker to develop so that he she can cope with different situations.

A continuing education worker with effective soft skills can manage a wide range of learners as well as management's expectations with fairness, tact, and understanding, with an eye on organizational goals. Good soft skills are critical while dealing with difficult colleagues, underachievers, leaders and the like.

**Interpersonal Skills**

An individual's ability to survive effectively in his / her group depends on the manner in which he / she maintains the relations with the group members. It encompasses the whole gamut of individual's approach to group living through a set of learned behaviour. Interpersonal relations include a wide range of human needs and individuals share these skills for their promotion and progress. Interpersonal skills are concerned with the ability to relate to others in a socially appropriate, meaningful way. They are a set of skills that enables one to get along well with others. These skills are also related to working on teams, teaching others, leading, negotiating and working well with people from culturally diverse backgrounds. Though interpersonal skills are related to communication skills, they are more specific about individual behaviours. They include cooperating, sharing, listening, participating, leading and respecting others. Interpersonal skills enable continuing education workers to work well with others to get a work done.

Interpersonal skills in a global sense can be defined as those skills that we employ when interacting with people. This definition is not very informative. However, since it really indicates what skills are used for rather than what they are, it is rather like defining an aeroplane as something that gets you from one country to another. Thus interpersonal skills could be understood as the learned and controlled skills required for the people to communicate, interact and behave in a particular social way in particular situations to obtain or maintain reinforcement from their environment.

## Team Work

A team will be highly effective, if the group of individuals work together with commitment to reach a common goal. Teamwork is referred to as 'any work that is accomplished through cooperation and coordination of individuals'. Whether it is of office or house, teaching or research, play or planning, all require team spirit for better outcome and performance. Thus, teamwork is an integral part of human life. 'Working in a team' requires certain minimum essential qualities among its members such as collaborative, communicative, disciplined, enthusiastic attitude and above all 'team spirit'. Without these the team wok cannot be strengthened and promoted.

The amount of work to be accomplished in today's work environments has increased about as fast as the technological advances have permitted. Since the work to be done is often complex, requiring the expertise of several individuals, teams are formed to meet deadlines, project requirements and budgets, etc.

Employers greatly value employees who can work effectively in teams because they can

- o Contribute efficiently to the organization's goals,
- o Complete complex projects rapidly, and
- o Respect other team members' thoughts and opinions.

Working in a team involves a delicate balance of personality, expertise, and co-operation. For a team to function, everyone must keep the best interests of the project, the organization, and the team in mind.

## Negotiating

We negotiate within our organizations, for example with colleagues and team members. The skill of negotiating can be applied universally for seeking a promotion, loan, or simply buying a vehicle. Webster's dictionary defines negotiation as 'to deal with some matter or affair that requires ability for its successful handling'. Negotiating is an act of discussing an issue between two or more parties with competing interests with an aim of coming to an agreement. It means contracting through the use of either competitive or other than competitive proposals or discussions. It is a dialogue between two or more people in order to arrive at an agreement that meets the needs of those involved without sacrificing anyone's priorities. It involves :

- o the process of reaching an agreement by conferring or discussing.
- o the transfer of rights in a negotiable instrument by endorsement and delivery.

  Almost all negotiations are characterized by four phases :

- o Preparation,
- o Opening,
- o Bargaining, and
- o Closing

Preparation involves information gathering – knowing the state of the issue, being aware of the pros and consequences, being aware of any current dealings and so on.

The opening phase of a negotiation involves both sides presenting their starting positions to one another. It usually represents the single most important opportunity to influence the other side. The aim of bargaining phase is to narrow the gap between the two initial positions and to persuade the other side that the case is so strong that they must accept less than they had planned. In order to do this one should use clearly thought out, planned and logical debate. The closing of a negotiation represents the opportunity to capitalize on all of the work done in the earlier phases. In large scale negotiations each of these phases is normally tackled sequentially. However, in small scale negotiations, it is quite common for these phases to merge possibly into a single unstructured process. In such a case, a good understanding of the logic that underpins the four-phase approach can guide us, even when we are negotiating smaller deals.

The process of negotiation depends on the following factors :

- o The goals and interests of the parties;
- o The perceived interdependence between the parties;
- o The history that exists between the parties;
- o The personalities of the people involved; and
- o The persuasive ability of each party.

**Empathy**

Success in life depends on getting along with other people and having them on our side. Empathy and being caring is the key factor in trying to win people over to our side. Empathy is defined as the ability to communicate and lead by understanding others' thoughts, views, and feelings. We usually empathize most easily with the people who are close to us personally, such as family, friends, classmates, colleagues or neighbours. We also empathize more easily with those who are like us or have shared similar experiences. In general, if we truly pay attention to what other people are saying, it means that we are empathetic to them. We become personally involved in their feelings and thoughts in order to better understand who they are and what they want or need, and to know how to respond to whatever message they are trying to get across.

Each of us practises empathy to a certain degree. The skill of caring and empathy allows us to build bridges between others and ourselves. These skills allow us to cross the apparent wide gaps between different backgrounds and perspectives, which are unique for human beings.

The following features of caring and empathy help us to develop interpersonal relations:

When empathy is highly developed, human beings become more human. Being a leader, building friendships, solving problems, encouraging teamwork, running effective meetings, or helping others-all are dependent upon empathy. It includes : truly listening to other people conveys a sense of caring; with the ability to care and empathize, we humans show greater sensitivity towards others; empathy helps us to understand others from a position within ourselves; it helps us communicate with others and heightens our sense of acceptance as a person; and people with highly developed empathy skills seem to have many friends.

Thus with the proper use of caring and empathetic skills, understanding, cooperation, and mutual success can be improved to a great extent.

## Qualities of Leadership

The qualities of leadership are vision, passion, self-sacrifice, confidence, and role-modeling.

The most basic and important quality of leadership is vision. The ability of the leader to connect people together with an idea is called vision. It is a desired set goal, which the leader communicates to motivate the followers to work in that direction. Vision means the leader and followers taking a journey into the unknown. It is a complex task that requires the ability to identify needs and opportunities, define the purpose or task into words, derive concrete goals from that vision, and engage the members of the group in the process of shaping the vision. Leaders frame statements of vision, visionary actions, set goals, motivate, build conceptual architecture aid predict future. Vision, therefore, depends on creativity and intellectual drive. Leaders simply do not run the community but plan and prepare for the future of the community. The vision must be clear, realistic and attainable. Vision is said to have a real value only when the outcome is seen in the form of the changes in behaviour, which is to be evaluated.

### Passion

This is a bit different than vision, but it isn't distinguishable. Passion refers to a strong inclination. It is a powerful feeling or emotion. Leaders who live with great enthusiasm are passionate people. For example, Mahatma Gandhi had passion for bringing independence to India through non-violence whereas Subash Chandra Bose had a passion to attain the same through violence. A leader who is effective is a person with a passion for a cause, which is larger than them. Gandhi had a passion for simple living and all through his life he maintained simplicity. In the same way, Dr. Ambedkar had a passion for the eradication of 'untouchability'. A leader will dream to build a better society. A leader without passion cannot always make the right decisions and implement them. Thus, a leader without passion for a cause will lower himself / herself.

### Self-Sacrifice

Self-sacrifice is said to be one of the important qualities of leadership. Self-sacrificing leadership is mostly associated with moral development, faith in a higher authority and a sense of self-actualization, A true leader is one who is willing to sacrifice his own comforts, resources, family, reputation and even his future to not only achieve the goal but also for the welfare of his followers. His desire is fuelled by a cause higher than himself. For example, Jesus Christ, in order to bring glory to God was prepared to lay down his life. Potti Sriramulu sacrificed himself for the separation of Andhra Pradesh from Madras.

### Confidence

Despite the great vision and passion that a leader has, it is difficult to implement the vision into action if he has no confidence. No change can occur without any action. Though the leader can generate good ideas, yet he has to identify his / her followers or employees with bright ideas. Leaders should act with confidence. Confidence in leaders is drawn from a basic sense of respect that leaders have for themselves and for other people leaders should ask for feedback, comments, and advice from group members. A confident leader is one who shows genuine interest in listening to the group members and conducts debates on key issues. To develop confidence, leaders should be aware of their own personal pattern and assess their own performance. They should also encourage the group members to be more of themselves.

Successful leaders are endowed with self-confidence. They also disclose and share their failures with their core teams so as to initiate a learning process. They learn from their mistakes. The leader who lacks confidence may not only find difficulty in diagnosing different situations but also in coping adequately with these situations. These difficulties lead to failure in performing certain functions. For example, a leader with low self-confidence will often exercise close supervision over followers, which may lead to resentment from the workforce. The leader who lacks confidence may delay decisions or in worse conditions take no decisions at all. Such a leader, for example, on many occasions makes decisions that compromise the morale of the followers. Leaders perform various functions like motivating, confidence building, planning, coordinating, decision-making, interacting, negotiating, time-management, mentoring etc.

## Interacting

Interacting is the quality of a leader where he/she often projects his/her ideas into activities, which excite people to share their views and ideas. The way in which a leader communicates and shares ideas, opinions and feelings with others is interacting. How do you typically share your ideas, feelings, and thoughts with others? For example, are you comfortable in large groups of people? In team situations? Or do you prefer to work on your own? Being aware of how you talk to and work with others can help you understand how you prefer to network with those with whom you work and live. In an interaction session, a leader develops fresh approaches to long-standing problems and opens issue to new options. A leader interacts with others, to evoke expectation and establish specific desires and objectives, which determine the direction of a group/organization. The leader can motivate his/her followers by interacting with them. The leader clarifies the doubts of the followers by interacting with them, and this ultimately would result in better performance. He can understand the problems of the followers while performing the tasks and suggests solutions. The effective communication skills and sound knowledge that the leader possesses make the interaction effective. Through his/her knowledge, a leader can convince others. The result of this interaction influences the group members to think about what is desirable, possible and necessary.

## Time Management

The only thing, which cannot be changed by man, is time whatever the position the man holds, one cannot stop time, cannot slow it down, nor can he speed it up. One cannot get back the time. Nothing can be substituted for time. Leaders have numerous demands that are to be completed within a limited time. Yet, to be effective, a leader manages time. The ability to schedule time to complete the task is known as time management. If we analyze how we are spending our time, we can find the time wasted. If we implement some time saving methods, we will gain valuable time.

The following are examples that show how people waste their time:

- Indecision makes us to think about the work, worry about it, and put off the work.

- Inefficiency makes us to rush and implement the task instead of planning, analyzing and implementing.
- Procrastination makes us not getting things done when they need to be done.
- Unrealistic time estimates.
- Poor organization, poor planning and lack of contingency plans.
- Ineffective meetings, which yield no result.
- Doing urgent rather than important tasks.
- Lack of understanding priorities, standards, policies am procedures

  Time Management is a set of tools, which allow the leader to :
- Eliminate wastage of time by managing the decision-making process.
- be prepared for meetings that have a purpose, a time limit, and include only essential people.
- Ignore unnecessary workloads.
- Monitor progress of a project.
- Allocate time based on the importance of the task.
- Ensure that long term projects are not neglected.
- Establish deadlines for personal goals and for the group / organization goals.
- Establish daily, short-term, mid-term, and long-term, priorities.
- Know when to stop a task, policy, or procedure.
- Maintain accurate calendars and abide by them.
- Delegate everything possible and empower subordinates.
- Set time to accomplish high priority tasks.
- Set aside time for reflection.
- Use checklists.
- Adjust priorities as a result of new tasks.

The leader saves the time and puts it into effective use.

**Creativity**

- Creativity is the ability to imagine or invent something new. It is the ability to generate new ideas by combining, altering, or reapplying existing ideas.

- o Creativity as an attitude is the ability to accept change and novelty. It is a willingness to have fun with ideas and possibilities, a flexibility of outlook, the habit of enjoying the good, while looking for ways to improve it. Creative individuals do not have fixed attitudes.
- o Creativity as a process continuously improves the ideas and solutions by making gradual alterations and refinements to the already existing work of a creative person.
- o Creativity as exploration looks beyond the boundaries of our normal thinking and experience.
- o Creativity never makes something from nothing i.e., creativity makes us simply notice in a way where its potential is being recognized or adds value to our lives or work i.e., a new product / a new service (library on wheels)/ a new system (IT systems) / theory or design / art etc.
- o Creativity in relation to a person is a talent for imaginative creation.
- o Creativity is universal i.e., it is not confined to any individual, groups, caste, age, location or culture. Every person is capable of demonstrating creativity to some degree.
- o Creativity is natural endowment as well as acquired through the influence of the cultural background, experiences, nurturing etc. Thus, creativity is exploring, finding something new and using it for better living. This suggests that there are different ways to be creative.

## Teaching

"Teaching" involves a highly personal relationship to the learner. It must deal with his emotional and spiritual development quite as much as with his intellectual development because the child tends to react emotionally to teachers and teaching. It is mistake to think of teaching as limited to instilling subject matter, assigning tasks, examining and giving rewards and punishments.

Teaching as the art of assisting another to learn. It includes "Providing information (instruc-tion) and of appropriate situations, conditions or activities designed to facilitate learning." The world Book Encyclopedia, describes it as "the process by which one person helps others achieve knowledge, skills and aptitudues", and the little

Oxford Dictionary gives the following under the word "teach". "Impart knowledge or skill, give instructions or lessons, instill and inspire with." The provide inspiration is in the affective domain in terms of Blooms taxonomy. In an extensive way S.K. Mitra further referred in his National Lectures about the term "Teaching", as was defined by Bage, as an art of "inter-personal influence aimed at changing the ways in which other persons can or will behave." Ryans defines teacher behaviour as "the behaviour, or activities, or persons they go about doing whatever is required of teachers, particularly those activities which are concerned with the guidance or direction of the learning of others" and Skinner defines teaching as the arrange-ment of contingencies of reinforcement." Now these definitions show that teaching is generally considered in three different ways :

1. It is imparting knowledge or skills;
2. It is doing anything and everything that may lead to learning; and
3. It is a special act of influence

and finally he defined teaching as a series of acts carried out by a teacher and guided by the formulation of teaching task in a formalised instructional situation".

The National Education Association (N.E.A.) Division of Field service has suggested eight criteria as follows: A profession. (1) involves. activities essentially intellectual, (2) commands a body of specialized knowledge. (3) requires extended professional preparation, (4) demands continuous in-service growth, (5) affords a life career and payment membership, (6) sets up its own standards. (7) exalts service above personal gain; and (8) has a strong clearly knit professional organization.

It may be said that at the present time, teaching has many characteristics of a profession and a few characteristics of a skilled trade. There, yet remains much to be done to bring the occupation upto the level which will mark it as a true profession in every sense. It is true that people lose their jobs or at a least miss out on promotions very often not for back of competence in vocational skills out rather because of inability to get along with others.

A teacher is one who imparts knowledge to the pupils. When a teacher is doing or helping someone else to learn, he or she is teaching. It is also important to keep in mind that the quality of teaching is directly related to the quality and the value of learning that is taking place in his students. Further, there is no best way to teach. What a teacher should do at a particular moment is not something that can be determined from any scientific formula. Successful teachers, like other artists develop their own ways of getting the results they seek.

Among the teachers, the last category would highly be limited and perhaps majority of them would come in the first category and the rest of the teachers may come under the remaining two categories.

Parameswara (1987) identified general characteristics of the teachers are as follows : (1) Good judgement, discretion, foresight, etc., (2) self-control, calmness, poise, dignity, etc., (3) Considerateness, courtesy, sympathy, tact, etc., (4) Enthusiasm, alertness, antmation, etc., (5) Cheerfulness, pleasantness, sense of humor, etc., (6) Adaptability, (7) Interest in profession, pupils and community, (8) Honesty, (9) Co-operation, helpfulness, loyalty, (10) Refinement, good taste, modesty, etc., (11) Forcefulness, courage, firmness, independence etc., (12) Carefulness, accuracy, thoroughness, (13) Health, (14) Attractiveness, personal appearance, (15) Leadership, initiative, self-confidence, (16) Industry, patience, perseverance, (17) Neatness, cleanliness, (18) Scholarship, (19) Dependability, (20) Originality, resourcefulness, (21) Promptness, punctuality, (22) Open mindedness, (23) Progressiveness, ambition, (24) Fluency, and (25) Thrift.

**Evaluation**

Evaluation is a recent scientific concept and more comprehen-sive than mere measurement. It takes into consideration with quantitative changes in the total being. In the words of Prof. James M. Bradfield, "Evaluation is the assignment of symbols to phenomena in order to characterise the worth of value of a phenomenon, usually with reference to some social, cultural or scientific standards.

Evaluation is a process of collecting evidence and using it to judge the degree of goodness or worth of the entity being evaluated for various types of decision making. In education, it is a study designed to determine the effectiveness of instruction in respect of an individual, a group of children or the school programme itself, taking into account the subjective opinions and qualitative changes as well as objectives and quantitative changes. It is an integral part for making teaching more effective.

Monitoring and evaluation are considered supplementary to each other and it is seen that the objective of both is not to 'prove' but to 'improve' the programme. Monitoring is a process of watching periodically the progress of adult education with a view to identifying its strength and weaknesses for taking corrective measures in the implementation of adult education programme more effectively. Evaluation is a more comprehensive, development-oriented and dynamic concept and consists of a systematic process for checking carefully the different aspects of the programme and improving them at different stages.

Monitoring and evaluation can be used effectively for taking remedial measures for improving and strengthening a programme of adult education. Every project would have to work out mechanism for operationalizing, monitoring and evaluation, so that they become in-built and processes for continual programme redesign and modification.

Evaluation is a relatively new technical term introduced to designate a mere comprehensive concept of measurement than is applied in conventional tests and examination. This emphasis in measurement is upon single aspect of subject-master achievement or scientific skills 311d abilities but the emphasis in evaluation is upon broad personality changes and major objectives of an educational programme. These include not only subject-matter achievements but also attitudes, interest, ideals, ways of thinking, work habits, personal and social adaptability.

The modem concept of evaluation denotes at least three different dimensions of evaluation: (a) "the evaluation attempts to measure a comprehensive range of behavioural objectives rather than the mere knowledge of subject-matter; (b) in modern evaluation, a variety of evaluation instruments are used depending upon the availability and applicability of the instruments and the skill of the teacher in using them. Some of these instruments are tests, essays, questionnaries and the interviews; (c) the evaluation includes integrating and interpreting various aspects of behaviour into a whole or into an inclusive picture of an individual, or a class of students, as may be required. The term evaluation, thus, means measurement of selected knowledge, skills, attitudes and even values for finding behavioural changes in the students.

**Scope of Evaluation**

The first element emphasizes the need for the clarification of what to evaluate. The clearer the perception and understanding of the specific entity being evaluated, the greater are the chances for ensuring validity and reliability of evaluation.

The second element involves a process of Judgement. This in fact is that result of evaluation. Sometimes evaluation cannot be totally valid, reliable and objective due to certain inherent limitation. Hence, the degree of goodness determined through such an evaluation process remains an estimation so that decisions should be made with due caution. The effort should then be to' optimise dependability of Judgment by adopting suitable evaluation techniques or their combinations which should help in reducing the error to a minimum level.

The third element refers to the collection and use of evidence through relevant information and other forms of data in order to arrive at a dependable Judgement. That is why there is a need to consider various technical aspects in the overall process of evaluation such as identification of data sources, adoption of sampling procedures where needed, application of different techniques and instruments for data collection, methods of data analysis both qualitative and quantitative, and interpretation of data.

The fourth element is closely connected with the evidence and its interpretation which should yield a clear result about the degree of goodness or worth of an entity being evaluated.

Finally, the evaluation result is to be used for varied types of decision making, such as improving a programme, revising a text book. increasing or decreasing the total length of time for literacy learning.

## Types of Evaluation

### (i) Formative and Summative Evaluation

As the terms suggest, the former is at the stage of development while the later is end of the programme evaluation. The advantage with formative evaluation is that it is important and process-oriented. With regard to the adult learners, formative evaluation could be used to judge the progress made by the learners, It could be formal or even informal or incidental. The formative evaluation diagnosis the ongoing process of the problems and difficulties and to re-build the same, while the summative evaluation diagnoses both the positive and negative aspects of the overall programme and finds the reasons behind them at the end of the programme.

### (ii) Norm-Referenced and Criterion Referenced Evaluation

These terms are also known as content referenced and self--referenced evaluation. These relate to the nature of reference point that is used for evaluation. In norm or content referenced evaluation the norm itself is the reference point. For example, if an evaluation instrument is administered to a group, a norm can be developed on the basis of results obtained. Thus, in a literacy test, an average score can be obtained that becomes a norm for the group to which the test is administered. The performance of each learner of the group could then be judged on the basis of this norm. In norm reference evaluation, the reference point emerges from the group itself.

On the other hand, in the case of criterion or self-referenced evaluation, the reference point emerges from one's earlier performance. Thus a test could be administered to an individual before the programme begins and the same test could be administered either mid-way or at the end of the programme. The difference between the two would determine the gain score.

## 4. AN OVERVIEW OF SUCCEEDING CHAPTERS

In the Second Chapter, the Review of related Literature is presented. Chapter Three deals with Statement of the Problem, Objectives and Hypotheses whereas Chapter Four concentrates on Methodology. In Chapter Five, Analysis of Results is presented. Chapter Six deals with Summary and Conclusions, Implications of the Study and Suggestions for Further Research.

# II

## Review of related literature

Research is systematic and creative activity to discover new facts and to obtain a more adequate solution of the problems. It is a continuous process and a professional area like adult education needs not only research studies but also a research tradition. There is a greater need to strengthen continuing education centres and to delineate strategies to strengthen the continuing education workers by inculcating right attitudes, values and skills. The possession of life skills is more expected on the part of the continuing education workers and it is essential to identify what constitutes life skills and its association with continuing education centres. Not many efforts are made to identify the life skills among continuing education workers. The studies conducted by White (1950), Aker (1962), Perace (1966), Oxford (1969), Cass (1971), Knox (1971), Cobley (1976), Grabowski (1976), Tripathi (1977), Malakondaiah (1980), Aikara and Herniques (1982), Yesanna (1986), Kusum Vir (2000), Mastan (2005), State Resource Centre for Adult Education, Hyderabad (2007) throw some light on the skills needed by the continuing education workers. The expereinces of Charles J. Margerison (1996), Wallace and Masters (2006) and Van Luis, S.R. (2007) in human resources management are presented due to their relevance to the study. The details of the studies are as follows :

## STUDIES RELATED TO QUALITIES OF INSTRUCTORS / CONTINUING EDUCATION WORKERS

According to White (1950), competencies appropriate for adult educators are as given below :

- To gain a better understanding of the basic needs which cause adults to participate in educational programmes.
- To gain a clear insight into the changing interests of adults in vocations, religion, family, leisure time activities, health and other areas of life.
- To increase ability to apply psychological principles to the selection of objectives.
- To acquire techniques for relating the programme more closely to the needs and the interests of adults.
- To become more skillful in recognising community needs and resources that are important to adult education programmes.
- To develop a better understanding of the kinds of educational methods most suitable for mature persons.
- To become familiar with procedures for 'keeping up' with new developments and material for adult education programmes.

Aker (1962) based on his study listed 23 types of behaviour patterns which are considered as adequate competencies for determining the achievement of educational objectives by instructors. They are as given below :

- Helps people to control and adjust to change rather than maintain the status quo.
- Intelligently observes and listens to what is being said or done and uses this information guiding his respondents.
- Selects and uses teaching methods, materials and resources that are appropriate in terms of what is to be learned and in terms of the needs and abilities of the individual learner.
- Helps his client to acquire the ability for critical thinking.
- Provides an atmosphere where adults are free to search through trial-and-error without fear of institutional or

interpersonal threat.

- o Identifies potential leaders and helps them to develop their potentials and capacities.
- o Makes use of existing values, beliefs, customs and attitudes as a starting point for educational objectives.
- o Is actively involved in continuous study that will increase his professional competence.
- o Understands the role of adult education in society and is aware of the factors and forces that give rise to this function.
- o Actively shares, participates and learns with the learners in the learning experiences.
- o Helps adults to actively set their goals and provides a variety of means and opportunities for intensive self-evaluation.
- o Identifies and interprets trends that have implications for adult education.
- o Has clearly defined his unique role as an adult educator and understands his responsibility for performing it.
- o Arranges learning experiences so that learners can integrate theory and practice.
- o Is effective in building a teaching team among leaders and group members.
- o Uses the process of appraisal to evaluate programmes, and to help clarify and change objectives.
- o Is creative and imaginative in developing new programmes, and believes that innovation and experiment are necessary for the expansion of adult education.
- o Makes use of the contributions of all group members through the utilization of individual talents and abilities.
- o Works with teachers, parents and beneficiaries to assist them in developing motivation, attitudes, understanding, and skills necessary for lifelong learning.
- o Objectively presents contrasting points of view.
- o Assumes the initiatives in developing a strong rational perception of importance and essentiality of continuing education.
- o Identifies when the communication process is not functioning adequately or when it breaks down.
- o Recognises and critically evaluates scholarly works by investigators in adult education and related fields.

Pearce (1966) lists the characteristics of effective instructors of adults, based on the opinions collected by him from a sample of students, teachers and administrators. The list covers characteristics like flexibility, patience, practicability, creativity and ability to develop and maintain self-confidence of adult learners to reach the goal.

The study of Oxford (1969) has identified certain ideal qualities of adult education instructors. They are : (a) fair dealings, (b) sense of humour, (c) fondness for knowledge, (d) ability to speak and communicate well, (e) liking for people who are informal, (f) uses lesson plans, (g) counsels students, (h) a good listener, (i) an enthusiastic teacher, (j) uses varied methods of teaching, (k) carefully observes, (*l*) knows students' interests, (m) has neat appearance, (n) uses visual aids, (o) stimulates discussion, (p) raises questions, (q) knows sources of information, (r) considers individual differences, (s) teaches well to students, (t) suggests further study, (u) has confidence in students, (v) is well prepared, (w) motivates learning, and (x) maintains interest in the subject.

Cass (1971) through his study on materials and methods for adult literacy programmes found that a successful teacher of adults, establishes personal relationship with each individual, builds his / her instruction around the needs and goals of the individuals, selects methods, techniques and the skills the learners need in their daily activities, and provides them with suitable learning experiences.

Knox (1971) reviewing twenty studies on adult education teachers came to the conclusion that a gap is always found between average and outstanding teaching. According to him the difference will be found in experience, knowledge of subject matter, familiarity with teaching methods, time spent on preparation and his or her personality to get along with adult students. From the description of the findings of the studies, it appears that the terms 'qualities', 'characteristics' and 'attributes' are used to describe more or less the same type of factors associated with effectiveness of adult education instructors.

Cobley (1976) defined qualities among effective adult education instructors, namely : fairness, sense of humour, desire to acquire more knowledge, good speaking and communicating ability, concern towards learners interests and individual differences, interest in the use of various methods of teaching and in stimulating discussion.

Characteristics of successful instructors in non-formal education programme as given by Tripathi (1977) were : ability to establish rapport with learners, respect for adult learners, ability to draw a curriculum to meet the environment needs of the learners, flexibility in approach, ability to motivate learners and exhibition of leadership qualities.

Grabowski (1976) identified ten competencies necessary for effective adult educators. They are as described below :

- Understands and takes into account the motivational and participation patterns of adult learners.
- Understands and provides for the needs of adults in learning.
- Is well versed in the theory and experiences in the practice of adult education.
- Knows the community and its needs.
- Knows how to use the various methods and techniques of instruction.
- Possesses communication skills, including listening.
- Knows where to locate and how to use educational materials.
- Has an open mind and provides an atmosphere that allows adults to pursue their needs and interests.
- Is able to appraise and evaluate programmes.

Characteristics of an effective instructor, according to Malakondaiah (1980) were : mutual co-operation with learners, capacity to organize the adult education centre successfully, knowledge of the subject, good eloquence, honesty, respect for moral values and ability to understand adult learners.

Aikara and Herniques (1982) found that majority of the instructors covered by the survey participated in the adult education programmes of the area had good teaching experience and obliged the request / order from certain persons, whom they respected.

Yesanna (1986) conducted a study of certain factors relating to the instructors effectiveness in the adult education programme. The results revealed that factors like communication skills, interest in teaching, co-operativeness, knowledge in the subject matter, moral values, learners' activeness were related to effectiveness of instructor.

Kusum Vir (2000) identified the skills and competitions required for continuing education workers for inclusion in training programmes to enhance their competencies. As outlined, the skills and competencies required for continuing education workers were as follows :

**i) Understanding of adult psychology and principles of adult learning**

The most important skill required for a continuing education worker is to understand adult psychology and principles of adult learning. Teaching an adult is entirely different from teaching a child, because adult is an experienced person who has already gone through a wide experience of life. Therefore, the psychology and method of teaching an adult differ from teaching a child. The continuing education worker has to apply altogether a different approach in teaching the adult learner.

**ii) Guiding skills and competency to motivate neo-literates / community**

Continuing education worker must possess the skill and competency to motivate and guide the neo-literates / community members about the importance and utility of continuing education in their lives. He / she should be able to make them aware of the programmes of continuing education centre, as well as, benefits of learning new things and acquiring new information at continuing education centre. He / she should be able to encourage them to continue their learning.

**iii) Planning skills and competency to schedule programmes of Continuing Education Centre**

Continuing education worker should be able to plan the programmes well in advance and prepare a weekly/month wise schedule of activities and display them at the centre. For this, following points may be taken care of :

(a) Continuing education worker should plan the programmes / activities of continuing education centre in consonance with the beneficiaries/local community.

(b) Continuing education centre activities should be planned in the light of the objectives of continuing education scheme.

(c) While planning the programmes, the convenience of the beneficiaries should be taken into consideration with regard to the timings and venue of the programme.

### iv) Organisational Skills

Organisational skills would include the following :

a) Organising books, broadsheets, newspapers and other supplementary material at continuing education centre and display these materials for the benefit of beneficiaries.
b) Organising library / reading room and making proper sitting arrangement, light arrangement etc.
c) Organising groups for conducting various continuing education activities.
d) Competency to organise equivalency programmes, income generation programmes, quality of life improvement programmes etc., as per the requirements of neo-literates and local needs.

### v) Discussion skill and competency to articulate

Continuing education worker should be able to organise Charcha Mandal / discussions at continuing education centre. For this, following competencies are required.

a) Selecting the topics for discussion.
b) Making everyone participate in the discussion.
c) Giving proper direction to the discussion considering particularly their background and level of learning.
d) Utilising local festivals and occasions for the discussion.
e) Taking care of time and controlling friction or bustle during the discussion.
f) Recording the new information obtained during the discussion.

### vi) Teaching Skills

Continuing education worker should be well acquainted with the adult teaching technique of Improved Pace and Content of Learning (IPCL) and should have good understanding of the method of teaching primers. He/she should also be competent in utilising audio-visual aids for the purpose.

### vii) Group-dynamics Skills

Continuing education worker should have group dynamics skills, so as to form separate groups of people for different continuing education programmes, like equivalency programme, quality of life improvement programmes, income generation programmes, etc.

### viii) Managerial Skills

Managerial skills for continuing education workers would include the following :

a) Maintenance of all continuing education centre material, such as furniture, equipments, books, broadsheets, newspapers and other material relating to continuing education activities.
b) Proper display of newspapers, broadsheets, magazines etc., at continuing education centre.
c) Managerial skills to organise variety of continuing education programmes.
d) Skill of involving the community in the activities.

### ix) Communication Skills

Communication skills for continuing education workers would include the following :

a) Continuing education worker should be able to communicate the objectives and significance of continuing education to the neo-literates and local community members.
b) Understanding of psychology of other people and to give a patient hearing to their views and opinions.
c) Logical and impressive way of presenting the thoughts and opinions, so that, other people could easily understand and adopt the same.

d) Competency to convince people to continue their learning in a right manner through variety of continuing education programmes.

**x) Skills to assess local needs and requirements**

These skills would include the following :

a) Assessment of the educational needs of the local people and other grass root requirements
b) Assessment of local situation and local requirements through discussion with people about their problems and requirements.
c) Survey skills to know different aspects relating to continuing education.

**xi) Skills for identification of local resources**

These skills would include the following :

a) Preparing a list of local agencies/bodies and persons who could provide technical support and expertise to continuing education programmes / activities.
b) Competency to orient the resource persons about the objectives and activities of continuing education centre.
c) Competency to utilise the services and expertise of local people / agencies in organization of continuing education programme.

**xii) Co-ordination skills for Convergence of Activities**

These skills would include the following :

a) To link the activities of continuing education centre with development programmes to improve the quality of life of the people.

b) To approach and contact the other agencies for obtaining information on developmental schemes and other programmes for the beneficiaries.

c) To establish a network between continuing education centre and other local bodies, like–Mahila Mandal, Youth Club, Primary Health Centre, Agriculture Extension Centre, Village Education Committee, Panchayat, Local Industrial Training

Institute, Anganwadi and Village Primary / Secondary Schools etc.

d) To co-ordinate the activities of continuing education centre with the programmes of other agencies to promote the quality of continuing education programmes.

**xiii) Evaluation Skills**

These skills would include the following:

a) Appraising the benefits of continuing education programmes and activities through observing its effects on the beneficiaries.
b) Assessing the improvement in the quality of life of the people by having a dialogue and discussion with the beneficiaries.
c) Collecting various types of information by using a questionnaire.
d) Using different types of tests to know how far acquisition of knowledge on different programmes of importance has taken place among the beneficiaries.
e) Observing the reaction and change in behaviour of those beneficiaries who have undergone the activities of continuing education centre.

**xiv) Record Keeping Skills**

These skills would include the following :

a) Maintenance of continuing education centre material, such as furniture, equipment, books, broadsheets, newspapers and all other material relating to continuing education centre activities.
b) Maintenance of registers that is – attendance register, stock register, issue register etc.
c) Recording the proceedings of the programmes conducted at continuing education centre.
d) Recording the effects of continuing education centre activities / programmes on beneficiaries.
e) Recording the reaction/change in behaviour or improvement in the quality of life of the people.
f) Recording the difficulties faced in conducting continuing education centre activities.

g) Recording of success stories, if any occurred through continuing education activities / programmes.
h) Recording the quality and type of co-operation received from other sources / agencies in conducting continuing education centre activities.

**xv) Report Writing Skills**

These skills would include the following:

a) Writing a report of the programme / activities conducted at continuing education centre. The report should be to the point and brief.
b) Writing an objective report.
c) Writing the brief proceedings of each and every programme and activity conducted during the month.
d) While writing the report, objectives of the programme and their afterward effects on the beneficiaries should be reported.
e) The difficulties, as well as, specific co-operation received from other agencies in conducting continuing education programmes / activities must be reported.
f) Submission of report on scheduled date and time.

Mastan (2005) concluded a study on 'influence of certain socio-psychological factors on the performance of continuing education workers organizing continuing education'. The investigator identified the following qualities to be possessed by the continuing education workers – time management, patience, sociability, moral values, knowledge in the subject matter, general knowledge and common sense, leadership qualities, knowledge about adult psychology, good nature, good physique, intelligence, emotional stability, discipline, dignity and self-respect, adaptability, affection, clarity in expression, creativity, curiosity, friendliness, impartiality, interest in social matters, sense of humor, sincerity, shrewdness, broadmindedness, co-operative nature and concern for others.

State Resource Centre for Adult Education, Hyderabad (2007) identified the managerial skills needed by continuing education workers. It was observed that continuing education workers need skills like initiation, time management, mind management, planning, knowledge skills, positive attitude, leadership qualities, decision making and inter-personal relations.

Charles J. Margerison (1996) in his discussion about conversation control mentioned that with practice we can control our conservation, and in time be able to influence others and encourage them to respond in a positive and relevant way. He expressed the need for conversation control skills for managers in the following areas .: (1) Summarising accurately what others say, (2) Asserting your rights, (3) Negotiating, (4) Dealing with differences of opinion, (5) Getting your message across in conflict situation, (6) Finding out what other people think, (7) Chairing a meeting, (8) Making proposals, (9) Giving criticism, (10) Providing information to others, (11) Contributing ideas to a meeting, (12) Avoiding interruption, (13) Making clear what you want others to do, (14) Giving recognition and praise to others, (15) Providing positive feedback to others, (16) Listening at the right time, (17) Knowing how to change the conversation, (18) Having the right word for the right occasion, (19) Knowing how to use the time available to cover the topics, (20) When to speak and when to listen, (21) How to move a conversation from the past to the present and to the future, (22) How to distinguish between parallel and sequential conversation, (23) How to raise energy levels in discussions, and (24) How to move between problem-centred conversation and solution-centred conversation. He observed that in modern conversation the first person to draw breath is declared as the listener. If one wants to improve conversation control skills, then he should start with listening. This is not, as is often assumed, a passive activity. It requires a great deal of action. It can indeed be quite tiring. The first thing to do is to listen and watch for the cues and clues. As indicated, these are the key words and phrases that people give during conversation which indicate points of interest or concern. In particular listen very hard when people use the words 'I', 'me', or 'my'. Concentrate especially when they follow this with an adjective which indicates a point of concern, showing that they are worried, annoyed, happy, dissatisfied, or whatever state they feel is of importance. In such situations do not change the topic of discussion. It is here that one can use reflective skills or open-ended enquiry questions, in particular refer to the key cue and clue words that have actually been used. Observe what is meant by the movement of the hands, the eyes or the head. Very often more is said in this way through signs and signals than by direct speech. Listening is a key skill in all matters especially when it involves decision-making. Those who are skilled in conversation control will know how to move from being problem-centred to solution-centred and vice versa. One should usually stay in the problem-centred area until people have sufficient understanding of the causes before moving off into suggesting solutions. While this is a general rule, it does not however always apply. Like everything else in life, time for conversation is limited. Most meetings have a fixed period of time. It is your job to ensure that you are able to get across your points and understand those made by others. Therefore do not let conversations get bogged down on just one dimension such as the past. Be sure you also deal with present and future issues. To do this you need to know how to link conversation between one time dimension and another. Too often conversations fail because people spend too much of their time discussing the past and never get to what is happening now or what should happen in the future.

**Take a personal interest in permissions**

All conversation requires certain permission in order for progress to be made. Be conscious of the permissions that other people are prepared to give you if you approach a conversation in the right way. Permission is a vital factor in conversation, and failure to get it can lead to serious problems.

**Seek the win *I* win option as the first priority**

Many conversations in the work environment will contain a large element of negotiation, and you will find people will be either moving against you, moving away from you or moving towards you. Where you want to establish a continuing relationship over a period of time, it is clearly important to set up the conversation so that, without compromising the best answer, there is a win/win element in it for both parties. Clearly this is not always possible, but use your first option for the win/win before looking for the win / lose option.

**Manage both the facts and the opinions**

All conversations are a mixture of facts and opinions. It is necessary to use both to resolve problems. However, we often allow one to dominate the other. Sometimes we have too many opinions with not enough facts and sometimes it is the other way round. Therefore where you have opinions, ask for facts and where you have a lot of facts, ask for opinions. Watch out for those who try to persuade you simply on the strength of their opinion. They may be right but it is best to take time and gather some facts before deciding.

**Convert the Verbals to the Visuals**

Wherever possible in the problem-solving process it is important to provide an opportunity for people to see as well as hear. One can speed up the conversational decision-making process by providing information in a visual form. This can be done by writing up key points in the discussion as it proceeds as well as the normal way of circulating papers before meetings and facilitating the exchange of views in a form that people can read. Therefore the more you can convert verbal discussion into a visual form, the more likely it is that there will be greater under-standing and the problem-solving process can be speeded up.

**Give accurate summaries – understand before you judge**

Conversation, like machinery, needs a lubricant to keep it moving smoothly. One of the best ways in which to facilitate smooth and effective conversation is to summarize regularly and accurately. In this way one can get agreement as one proceeds and people will recognize your skill in drawing the threads of complex debate together. Summarizing through recognizing, appreciating and understanding is an essential part of clarifying issues rather than agreeing them.

**Emphasize the positive**

If you analyse people's conversation, you will find a great deal of negative thinking. You will hear people saying 'We cannot do this' or 'That is not possible'. However, real achievements can make people think in a positive way. Therefore train yourself to think about the positive side and seek out ways in which things can be done. Relate to people in a positive way. If they are negative, ask for the facts on which they base their thinking. Reflect your concern at negative thinking. Try to get people thinking about 'how to' rather than 'how not to'.

Wallace and Masters (2006) referring to self-improvement as a component relevant of personality development have stated the following: (1) develop a realistic vision of future life; identifying specific and measurable objectives for each goal, prepare action plans and develop success identity. The long term plans should include career planning, social status and relationships, education and training, communication skills, physical well-being, learning and saving.

Vas Luis, S.R. (2007) emphasized on innovativeness, thinking skills, problem solving abilities, creativity, intuition, memory, learning ability, communication skills, health and fitness and time management as the essential skills for excellence in any field of human activity.

The review presented above clearly indicates that not many attempts were made to study the presence of life skills among continuing education workers. Hence, the present study was formulated.

# III

# Statement of the Problem

This chapter deals with the need for the study, statement of the problem, objectives, variables, hypotheses, scope and limitations of the study.

## NEED FOR THE STUDY

The success of continuing education programme depends upon the functionaries at the field level like Deputy Directors, Mandal Literacy Organizers, Nodal continuing education workers, continuing education worker, etc. continuing education worker means a motivator and the person appointed to carry out the activities of post-literacy and continuing education programmes under National Literacy Mission. Continuing education worker is a grass root level functionary in the programme and he is the actual 'doer' of the programme. He / she plays roles like planner, motivator, teacher of literacy, disseminator of functional information, librarian, co-ordinator, generator of awareness by organizing charcha mandal activities, recorder, organiser of the center, mobiliser of community resources, organiser of simple and short duration training programmes etc. He / she is also expected to organise and participate in all the development programmes meant for the well-being of the people on health, agriculture, animal husbandry, sanitation, dairy, individual interest promotion programmes, quality of life improvement programmes and income generation programmes. It may be noted that, improved physical facilities, teaching/learning materials, equipment etc., no doubt supplement the continuing education worker's efficiency, but they cannot be substituted for an effective continuing education worker. The importance of an effective continuing education worker for the successful organization of continuing education programmes is indeed indisputable. The continuing education worker has to disseminate the life skills to the neo-literates and others under equivalency programmes, individual interest promotion programmes, quality of life improvement programmes and under life enrichment education programmes of Jan Sikshan Sansthans. Continuing education worker requires communication skills, decision making skills, leadership skills, etc., to do justice to his functions. It is essential to understand to what extent the continuing education workers have these skills so that appropriate action may be taken up by the district administration and National Literacy Mission to inculcate them during the training programmes.

## STATEMENT OF THE PROBLEM

*"A Study on Life Skills among Continuing Education Workers"*.

## OBJECTIVES OF THE STUDY

1. To know the extent to which the continuing education workers are possessing the life skills;
2. To find out the differences in the response pattern of continuing education workers on life skills;
3. To know the differences in the life skills among continuing education workers due to personal variables; and
4. To suggest measures to enhance the life skills of continuing education workers.

## VARIABLES

### Independent Variable

Life skills on different aspects.

### Independent Variables

Gender, age, caste, locality, education, experience, marital status, occupation and income.

## HYPOTHESES

Based on the above objectives, the following hypotheses were formulated for testing.

1. Continuing education workers do not differ significantly in their response pattern for different items of life skills.
2. Gender does not significantly influence the life skills of continuing education workers.
3. Age does not significantly influence the life skills of continuing education workers.
4. Caste does not significantly influence the life skills of continuing education workers.
5. Education does not significantly influence the life skills of continuing education workers.
6. Experience does not significantly influence the life skills of continuing education workers.
7. Marital status does not significantly influence the life skills of continuing education workers.
8. Occupation does not significantly influence the life skills of continuing education workers.
9. Income does not significantly influence the life skills of continuing education workers.

## SCOPE OF THE STUDY

Government of India has launched continuing education programme with the objectives of organisation of evening classes, library, reading room, charcha mandal, simple and short duration training prgorammes, provision of information about development and communication aspects. The programmes are designed under post-literacy programmes, equivalency programme, quality of life improvement programme, income generating programmes and individual interest promotion programmes. The main motto is to improve the socio-economic standards of the people and encourage them to contribute their mite to the process of socio-economic development.

The continuing education workers have to provide different skills like communication skills, training skills, social skills, decision making, time management, creativity, stress management, planning skills, entrepreneurship skills, etc., to the neo-literates and others. Life skills through continuing education centres is an emerging issue in the context of lifelong learning and it is basically essential to know the extent to which the continuing education workers are possessing these skills. The study would be of immense help to know the extent of possession of life skills among the continuing education workers in Chittoor district and to design necessary strategies to promote life skills among them.

## LIMITATIONS OF THE STUDY

1. The study is limited to 200 continuing education workers of Chittoor District.
2. The study is limited to 5 mandals of Chittoor District.
3. Life skills among continuing education workers is assessed based on the self-ratings of continuing education workers.

## DEFINITION OF CERTAIN TERMS

**Prerak** : A motivator and an organiser of the activities of continuing education centre.

**Monitor** : A person who has organised post-literacy centre after literacy campaign in Chittoor District.

**Instructor** : A person who severed as a teacher of literacy, functionality and awareness and a post-literacy and continuing education worker under National Adult Education Programme..

**Nodal Prerak** : A person who is in-charge of 8-10 continuing education centres. Apart from organising his / her own continuing education centre, the nodal prerak assists and supervises the activities of the other continuing education centres.

**Volunteer** : A person who teaches literacy skills to illiterate adults under total literacy campaign / mopping up operation phase launched under National Literacy Mission.

**Assistant Prerak** : Assistant Prerak is a person who looks into the matters of literacy and reading room in the absence of the prerak and renders assistance to prerak wherever required.

**Corpus Fund**: It is the fund collected for the organisation of the activities of continuing education centre after the cessation of assistance from the government after five years. The fund has to be collected from the beneficiaries, philanthropists and others. A sum of Rs. 10,000/- is expected to be collected from the public and a matching grant of Rs. 10,000/- will be deposited by the government and the interest has to be used after five years for meeting the honorarium of the prerak, library books, newspapers and for the organisation of simple and short duration programmes by the continuing education centre.

**Membership Fee** : A sum of one rupee has to be contributed by every beneficiary of continuing education centre per month. It can also be paid at Rs.6/- for six months at a time or Rs. 10/- per annum at a time. By paying a nominal membership like this, the beneficiaries will have a right to question the prerak for facilities. About 500 beneficiaries of continuing education centre, if they pay membership, it becomes a huge amount and this will also add to the corpus fund. Corpus fund and membership fee are specific to Andhra Pradesh and this has not been outlined in the policy statement of National Literacy Mission on continuing education.

**Functional Literacy** : As specified in the National Literacy Mission document (1988) by Government of India, functional literacy implies achieving self-reliance in literacy and numeracy by the learners, becoming aware of the causes of their deprivation and moving towards amelioration of their condition through organisation and participation in the process of development, acquiring skills to improve the economic status and general well being, imbibing the values of national integration, conservation of the environment, women's equality, observance of small family norm etc.

**Equivalency Programmes** : These are one type of continuing education programmes which provide an opportunity to adults and out-of-school children who have acquired basic literacy skills or who have completed primary education and who are willing to continue their education beyond elementary literacy for acquisition of competencies equivalent to primary or secondary levels of formal education. Equivalency programmes are, therefore, designed as alternative education programmes equivalent to existing formal, general or vocational education.

**Income Generating Programmes** : Income generating programmes are those vocational and technical education programmes which help participants to acquire or upgrade vocational skills and enable them to conduct income generating activities. There can be a variety of income generating programmes delivered in a wide variety of contexts taking into account, the local needs and interests of learners.

**Quality of Life Improvement Programmes** : These are especially significant type of educational programmes designed to enhance the well being of citizens. These aim to equip learners and community with knowledge, skills, attitudes and values to enable them to improve quality of life as individuals and members of the community.

**Individual Interest Promotion Programmes** : These continuing education programmes aim to provide opportunity to individuals to participate and learn about their social, cultural, spiritual, health, physical and artistic interests. The focus of individual interest promotion programmes is on personal development by providing opportunities for promotion of specialized individual interests which may lead to improvement in the quality of human resource of the society.

## Continuing Education

Continuing education is one of the hallmarks of a learning society. It is based on the premise that all adults should be entitled to continued opportunities for education throughout their lives. It recognizes learning wherever it takes place – not only within the premises of organized institutions but also in the work place, home and other places. Even those who have had the most advanced education will be required to upgrade their knowledge. The broader concept of continuing education emphasizes the need of adult learners for lifelong opportunities for education and training. Continuing education which provides a second chance to those who missed formal education and is responsive to the needs of learners directly addresses structural inequalities in society. It is now emerging as one of the most important components of education as a whole and it includes all learning opportunities outside the basic literacy and primary education. It is in fact a continuum of basic literacy and post-literacy phase and visualized as an attempt to provide systematic, organized and well-co-ordinted mechanism to mobilise all the resources in support of literacy, post-literacy and continuing education in the perspective of lifelong education.

## Post-Literacy

The concept of post-literacy refers to those efforts carried out after literacy phase, the objectives of which are remedial (taking care of those persons who have not achieved adequate levels of literacy), continuation (which would enable the neo-literates transform from a guided learning situation to a self-learning situation, application of literacy skills to improve quality of life in the lives of neo-literates) and communitisation (where community participation and action for social development is initiated).

## Community Participation

A community is a primary group resulting from the social contacts, largely direct of those residing on a more or less definite but relatively small area as the people meet one another in an interplay of the various activities carried on by them. Participation is essentially a process of empowerment that initiates transition from the ignorant to informed, individual to collective, inactive to active, passive to partnership, dependent to self-reliant and decision receiver to decision-maker. Participation is understood as a process by which the people are enabled to organize themselves, able to share their own needs and share in the design, implementation and evaluation of the activity. Participation should not stop with information sharing or consultation but decision making and initiating it into action are important components of participation. Community participation in the context of the present study refers to the participation of community members (which includes all groups, sections, institutional members living in the locality) in planning and organizational aspects of the adult and continuing education programmes.

# IV

# Methodology

This chapter deals with the development of the tool, locale and sample of the study, collection of data and analysis of data.

## DEVELOPMENT OF THE TOOL

The aim of the investigation is to know the level of possession of life skills among continuing education workers. It can be studied through observation, checklist, interview, case study, questionnaire, rating scale, etc. For the purpose of the study, the investigator felt that rating scale would be appropriate to measure the life skills among continuing education workers.

## DESCRIPTION OF RATING SCALE

Rating scale is a tool which records judgements or opinions and indicates the degree or amount of opinion. It is a very useful tool in assessing the quality. It is a term applied to express opinion or judgement regarding some situation, object or character. Options are usually expressed on a scale of values. Rating techniques are devices by which such judgements can be quantified.

## TYPES OF RATING SCALES

The rating scales are classified into six categories. They are :

### a. Numerical Scale

Numerical values are assigned in this scale based on the trait I item. For different traits, the ratings can be assigned like outstanding (5), good (4), satisfying (3), unsatisfactory (2) and very unsatisfactory (1).

### b. Graphic Scale

Here the several levels or degrees of the trait are defined and placed at points along a horizontal line. The judge places a mark any where he I she chooses on the line between the two extremes. For example.

**Trait responsibility for competing work**

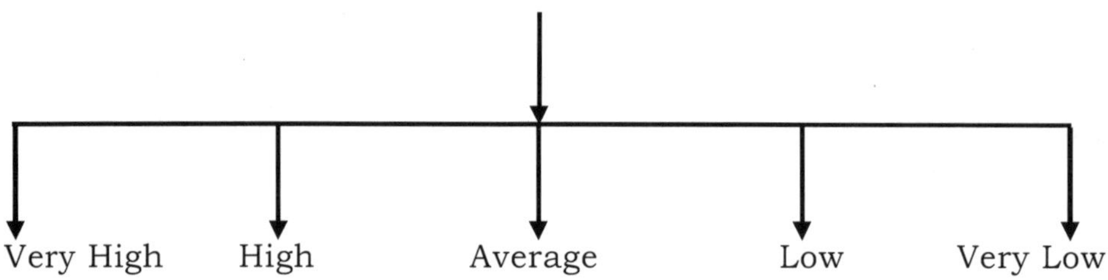


### c. Descriptive Scale

The rater selects a word or phrase and puts a tick mark in the blank for the given issue.

Ex. : Has the continuing education worker initiative?

(a) Shows marked originality (b) Willing to take initiative
(c) Quite inventive (d) On the whole enterprising
(e) Very dependent on others

### d. Cumulative Points Scale

Here ratings on the favourable (1) and unfavourable (0) items are counted based on the numerical values assigned.

### e. Standard Scale

A set of standards are represented to the ratings. Ratings through this scale become easier and meaningful. For example : Hand writing comparisons.

### f. Pooled Judgements

Pooled judgements increase the reliability of any rating sale. Several judges can be employed depending on the rating situation to obtain desirable reliability.

Out of the above types of rating scale, the numerical rating scale was developed for the present study.

## DEVELOPMENT OF SCALE ON LIFE SKILLS

For the purpose of the study, a tool that assesses the life skills of continuing education workers was desired. For this purpose, the investigator interacted with 50 continuing education workers, 5 mandal literacy organizers and 50 community members. Policy documents, publications of various agencies like State Resource Centres, Directorate of Adult Education, management books were referred. The items on life skills gathered from different sources were pooled together. The ambiguous and repetitive ones were deleted. The items were rewritten and the suggestions of 30 continuing education workers and 5 Mandal Literacy Organisers were taken. In all 30 items remained for the final form. It was felt that the rating should be as simple as possible to avoid unnecessary mental strain and confusion among the subjects while giving the responses. In the light of the above, the popular numerical rating scale consisting of 5 descriptive cues, namely very high, high, moderate, poor and very poor was chosen. The respondents were supposed to agree with anyone of the alternative cues to mark their level of possession of each of the skills. The numerical weights were given to each of the five categories of responses as indicated in the brackets - very high (5), high (4), moderate (3), poor (2) and very poor (1). It can be stated that the tool possessed content validity as the items were gathered from different sources like continuing education workers, community members, review of related literature, etc. The final form of the tool is appended. In addition, the personal data of the continuing education workers was gathered separately in order to study their influence on the life skills.

## LOCALE AND SAMPLE OF THE STUDY

Chittoor District consists of three revenue divisions, 66 mandals and 1143 continuing education centres. At the first stage one revenue division (Tirupati division) was randomly selected. At the second stage, out of the mandals of the division 5 mandals were randomly selected (Renigunta, Yerpedu, Srikalahasthi, Vadamalapet and Puttur). There are about 60 continuing education workers and Assistant Continuing education workers in each mandal. At the third stage, from each mandal 40 continuing education workers were randomly selected. Thus, the sample of the study consisted of 200 continuing education workers.

## COLLECTION OF DATA

The data was collected from the sample at the mandal level review meetings. The support of the Mandal Literacy Organisers was taken while collecting the data. Necessary permission was obtained from the Deputy Director, Zilla Saksharatha Samithi, Chittoor. The list of continuing education workers was obtained from the office of the ZSS, Chittoor. It took 30-40 minutes on an average to complete the tool.

## ANALYSIS OF DATA

The data collected was analysed by using relevant statistical techniques like percentages, chi-square, 't' test and 'F' test.

# V

# Results and Discussion

Keeping in view the objectives of the study, the results of the study are discussed in this chapter.

**TABLE 1 : Distribution of the Scores of Continuing Education Workers on Life Skills**

| Class Interval | Frequency | Mid Point | Cumulative Frequency |
|---|---|---|---|
| 20 – 30 | 4 | 25 | 4 |
| 30 – 40 | 8 | 35 | 12 |
| 40 – 50 | 16 | 45 | 28 |
| 50 – 60 | 27 | 55 | 55 |
| 60 – 70 | 60 | 65 | 115 |
| 70 – 80 | 55 | 75 | 170 |
| 80 – 90 | 22 | 85 | 192 |
| 90 – 100 | 5 | 95 | 197 |
| 100 – 110 | 3 | 105 | 200 |

The distribution of life scores of continuing education workers are as presented in Table 1. It can be observed from the table that the scores are more or less normally distributed. The mean, median and mode of the distribution are 66.25, 67.62 and 70.36. The range of the scores is 74, the lowest score and highest score being 28 and 102. The standard deviation and quartile deviation of the distribution are 15.10 and 9.30. The relation between quartile deviation and standard deviation 2/3 (standard deviation) = quartile deviation i.e., 2/3 (15.10) = 10.17 indicates that the distribution is slightly skewed. The distribution is negatively skewed since mode is maximum and the value of arithmetic mean is the least. The value of median is less than mode but greater than mean. The graphic representation of the scores is presented.

**TABLE 2 : Item-wise Response pattern of Continuing Education Workers on Life Skills**

| Sl. No. | Item | Very High | High | Mode rate | Poor | Very Poor | Total |
|---|---|---|---|---|---|---|---|
| 1. | Communication skills | 38 (19.00) | 69 (39.50) | 48 (24.00) | 20 (10.00) | 25 (12.50) | 200 (100.00) |
| 2. | Thinking skills | 36 (18.00) | 20 (100.00) | 102 (51.00) | 21 (10.50) | 21 (10.50) | 200 (100.00) |
| 3. | Planning skills | 59 (29.50) | 52 (26.00) | 37 (19.50) | 42 (21.00) | 10 (5.00) | 200 (100.00) |
| 4. | Goal setting | 46 (23.00) | 71 (35.50) | 20 (10.00) | 41 (20.50) | 22 (11.00) | 200 (100.00) |
| 5. | Decision-making skills | 13 (6.50) | 38 (19.00) | 37 (18.50) | 64 (32.00) | 48 (24.00) | 200 (100.00) |
| 6. | Negotiation skills | 66 (33.00) | 44 (22.00) | 38 (19.00) | 37 (18.50) | 15 (7.50) | 200 (100.00) |
| 7. | Time management | 26 (13.00) | 46 (23.00) | 28 (14.00) | 47 (23.50) | 53 (26.50) | 200 (100.00) |
| 8. | Creativity | 30 (15.00) | 45 (22.50) | 27 (13.50) | 49 (24.50) | 49 (24.50) | 200 (100.00) |
| 9. | Stress management | 39 (19.50) | 70 (35.00) | 21 (10.50) | 20 (10.00) | 20 (10.00) | 200 (100.00) |
| 10. | Entrepreneurship skills | 22 (11.00) | 28 (14.00) | 47 (23.50) | 65 (32.50) | 65 (32.50) | 200 (100.00) |
| 11. | General knowledge and commonsense | 61 (30.50) | 59 (29.50) | 22 (11.00) | 47 (23.50) | 47 (23.50) | 200 (100.00) |
| 12. | Reasoning abilities | 38 (19.00) | 37 (18.50) | 76 (38.00) | 28 (14.00) | 28 (14.00) | 200 (100.00) |
| 13. | Discipline | 30 (15.00) | 28 (14.00) | 89 (44.50) | 39 (19.50) | 39 (19.50) | 200 (100.00) |
| 14. | Tenacity | 55 (27.50) | 49 (24.50) | 38 (19.00) | 10 (5.00) | 10 (5.00) | 200 (100.00) |
| 15. | Interpersonal relations | 76 (38.00) | 66 (33.00) | 38 (19.00) | 5 (2.50) | 5 (2.50) | 200 (100.00) |
| 16. | Self-control | 48 (24.00) | 54 (27.00) | 56 (28.00) | 31 (15.50) | 11 (5.50) | 200 (100.00) |
| 17. | Result orientation | 32 (16.00) | 10 (5.00) | 41 (20.50) | 59 (29.50) | 58 (29.00) | 200 (100.00) |
| 18. | Emotional stability | 44 (22.00) | 31 (15.50) | 26 (13.00) | 51 (25.50) | 48 (24.00) | 200 (100.00) |
| 19. | Leadership skills | 74 (37.00) | 38 (19.00) | 51 (25.50) | 27 (13.50) | 10 (5.00) | 200 (100.00) |
| 20. | Managerial abilities | 66 (33.00) | 57 (27.50) | 32 (16.00) | 34 (17.00) | 11 (5.50) | 200 (100.00) |
| 21. | Problem solving skills | 43 (21.50) | 31 (15.50) | 28 (14.00) | 39 (19.50) | 59 (29.50) | 200 (100.00) |
| 22. | Training skills | 47 (13.50) | 22 (11.00) | 89 (49.50) | 32 (16.00) | 10 (5.00) | 200 (100.00) |
| 23. | Moral values | 22 (11.00) | 44 (22.00) | 86 (43.00) | 38 (19.00) | 10 (5.00) | 200 (100.00) |
| 24. | Co-ordination skills | 15 (7.50) | 37 (18.50) | 38 (19.00) | 54 (27.00) | 56 (28.00) | 200 (100.00) |
| 25. | Development orientation | 13 (6.50) | 57 (28.50) | 27 913.50) | 55 (27.50) | 48 (24.00) | 200 (100.00) |

| | | | | | | | |
|---|---|---|---|---|---|---|---|
| 26. | Report writing skills | 44 (22.00) | 58 (29.00) | 41 (20.50) | 40 (20.00) | 17 (8.50) | 200 (100.00) |
| 27. | Evaluation skills | 49 (24.50) | 42 (21.00) | 43 (21.50) | 48 (24.00) | 18 (9.00) | 200 (100.00) |
| 28. | Co-operative nature | 66 33.00) | 64 932.00) | 22 (11.00) | 28 (14.00) | 20 (10.00) | 200 (100.00) |
| 29. | Honesty and sincerity | 47 (23.50) | 41 (20.50) | 14 (7.00) | 76 (38.00) | 22 (11.00) | 200 (100.00) |
| 30. | Teaching skills | 38 (19.00) | 58 (29.00) | 68 (34.00) | 24 (12.00) | 12 (6.00) | 200 (100.00) |

The details relating to item-wise response pattern of continuing education workers is as shown in Table 2. The response pattern is presented under very high, high, moderate, poor and very poor levels. In order to have better understanding, the very high and high groups are categorized as high group and the poor and very poor groups are categorized under poor group. Detailed presentation of the items is as follows :

### 1. Communication Skills

Mere possession of knowledge about the programme aspects and developmental issues is not sufficient. The continuing education worker should be able to express it clearly and forcefully. Verbal expression should be made much more effective than the written expression. One must cultivate the habit of fluent speech and be able to put across ideas appropriately. It is clear from the table that the continuing education workers of the sample are possessing good communication skills as checked by majority (63.50%) of the sample.

### 2. Thinking Skills

Thinking skills involve critical listening and asking about the right questions. They can be developed among the continuing education workers through intelligence tests, projective tests, situational analysis, problem solving methods, role play, brain storming, discussion and methods of involving the community in development activities. Thinking skills for continuing education workers should be positive, analytical, constructive and comprehensive. It can be observed from the table that 51 % sample of the study are possessing moderate level of thinking skills.

### 3. Planning Skills

Planning is important to perform any task. If we want to achieve success in the task then there should be proper planning. Planning can be at individual level, group or organizational level. Planning involves proper framing of the work. Planning helps one to do the things systematically, reduces uncertainty, eliminates wasteful activities and resources, promotes co-ordination and finally focuses attention on achieving the objectives. Response pattern of the continuing education workers indicates that they have scored at a higher level on the planning skills.

### 4. Goal Setting

Goal setting is important for all aspects of life. It should be planned in a sequential manner like needs, comforts, luxuries as we observe in day to day life situations. Fixing the goal is not sufficient but the methods desired to accomplish the goal like investment of money, time and efforts need to be duly taken into consideration in goal getting. Response pattern of continuing education workers indicates that they have scored at a higher level on goal setting.

### 5. Decision Making Skills

Decision making forms an integral part of life. Some people depend on others for their own decisions so that the blame can be thrown on others if the decision is improper, some people take quick and fast decisions without weighing the strengths and weaknesses of the decisions. The continuing education workers should be trained to take appropriate decisions with regard to proper planning of their activities. Response pattern indicates that the continuing education workers are at a lower level on decision making skills.

### 6. Negotiating Skills

Negotiation means dealing with some matter or affair that requires ability for its successful handling. It is a process of reaching an agreement by contact. It also refers to transfer of rights in a negotiable instrument by endorsement and delivery. It involves preparation, discussion and closure of negotiation. Response pattern of continuing education workers reveals that they have scored at a higher level on negotiation skills.

### 7. Time Management

The ability to schedule time to complete the task is known as time management. If we analyse how we are spending our time, we can find the time wasted. If we implement some time saving methods, we will gain valuable time. One has to save time and put it to effective use. Response pattern of the continuing education workers reveals that they have scored at a lower level on time management.

### 8. Creativity

Creativity involves intuition and imagination. It requires the organization of ideas or experiences into new combinations or patterns in order to produce something which has not previously existed. A creative person is sensitive to his environment and he has the ability to see things in a novel manner. A creative person is able to adjust quickly to new and changed situations and abandon old assumptions in the light of new evidence. He has the ability, to break down into its components, to see relationships between the parts and at the same time, the ability to synthesize the components in a creative way to form a new whole. Response pattern of continuing education workers on the item reveals that majority of them have obtained lower level score.

### 9. Stress Management

Stress is experienced in the world of work. It is described as an emotional factor that causes bodily or mental tension. Stress is the feeling that one gets from prolonged emotions. If the emotions are pleasant and desirable like joy, elation, ecstasy, delight, one usually feels free to let them and they are not suppressed. Therefore, positive emotions do not cause stress. Negative emotions, on the other hand, are more held inside. They are hidden. Stress is caused due to anxiety, pressure, misery, strain, tension, anger, panic and dejection. The more one tries to hold emotions, the greater will be the building up of pressure. For most people, the body seems to adjust to stress. Atleast it does so in the short run. But sustained and increased stress may cause harmful physical and psychological problems including depression, anxiety, insomnia, irritability, stomach disorders, headaches, heart disease, etc. Response pattern of continuing education workers on stress management reveals that they have scored at higher level on the item.

## 10. Entrepreneurship Skills

Entrepreneurship is an attempt to create value through recognition of business opportunity. It requires communicative and managerial skills to mobilize financial, human and material resources. It is a process of giving birth to a new enterprise. It basically requires innovation, risk bearing and organizational abilities, apart from hard work, desire for high achievement and optimism. The continuing education workers should have an idea about the functions of entrepreneurship like idea generation, determination of business objectives, product analysis and market research, determination of the form of ownership, completion of promotional formalities, raising necessary funds, procuring machinery and materials, staff recruitment and understanding of business operations. The process of establishing an enterprise starts with project / product identification which is done through generation of ideas and these have to be subjected to SWOT (Strengths, Weaknesses, Opportunities and Threats) analysis before finalization. Visit to industries, case studies will be helpful in developing entrepreneurial skills among the continuing education workers. Response pattern of continuing education workers on the item reveals that they have obtained lower level scores which deserves attention of the administrators.

## 11. General Knowledge and Commonsense

Apart from knowledge about continuing education programme, the continuing education workers are expected to possess knowledge about agricultural aspects, old age pension schemes, self-help groups, marketing of agricultural and commercial products, formal and non-formal educational system, development programmes and mode of their operation, birth rate, death rate, communication facilities, environment, health aspects, etc. Common sense aspects like do's and don'ts in the public, spontaneity should be also present in the continuing education workers. Response pattern of continuing education workers reveals that they have scored at a higher level on general knowledge and commonsense.

## 12. Reasoning Abilities

Reasoning is related to understanding and perceiving the things.

It is an innate mental ability which grows and is influenced by the environment. It implies the capacity to learn different tasks and the ability to solve different problems. Individuals vary from one another in the amount and quality of their reasoning ability. In the present study, an attempt was made to assess the reasoning ability of the continuing education workers. It can be noticed from the table that a good majority of the continuing education workers have obtained a moderate level score on the item.

### 13. Discipline

Discipline is a basic requirement for any continuing education worker based upon which the success of his activities can be judged. Discipline means training to produce obedience to rules. It enables one to have an orderly behaviour and self-control. Discipline is what distinguishes man from animals. It is an essential factor in a democratic setup. Life without discipline is like a boat without a rudder. Only a regular way of life helps the proper development of one's character. Everyone should maintain punctuality. Everything has to be done at the right and scheduled time. We should not postpone the things to the eleventh hour and get worried. We enjoy a lot of freedom in a democracy and this freedom will be fruitful only when our life is disciplined. Discipline is the first step for self-development which leads to a better social order. Results relating to perceptions of continuing education workers reveals that they obtained a moderate score on the item.

### 14. Tenacity

Tenacity relates to the repeated or enduring nature of attempts to achieve a goal. Tenacity differs from independence, which can be expressed in the context, either of enduring behaviour or a single brief act. The continuing education worker has different types of problems related to context, inputs and organization. He should stick to the problem until it is resolved. He should be able to put forth efforts to achieve a goal despite encountering obstacles. He has to work for unusual hours in certain cases to accomplish a goal. Response pattern of the continuing education workers on the item reveals that they have scored at a higher level.

## 15. Interpersonal Relations

Interpersonal skills are concerned with the ability to relate to others in a socially meaningful way. They are a set of skills that enables one to get along with others. Though interpersonal skills are related to communication skills they are more specific about individual behaviours. They include co-operating, sharing and respecting others. Interpersonal skills enable continuing education workers to work well with others and to· seek their co-operation for effectively organizing various programmes. Results relating to the item indicate that the continuing education workers have obtained a higher level score on the item.

## 16. Self Control

It refers to performing effectively in stressful and difficult situations. This competency focusses management of pressure in stressful and difficult situations. The continuing education worker is supposed to keep things in perspective despite fatigue and frustration, maintain effectiveness in case of disappointments, work effectively under tight deadlines, and maintain objectivity, amidst disturbances. Results indicate that the continuing education workers have secured a higher level score on self-control.

## 17. Result Orientation

The continuing education worker has to perform his duties with a strong determination to accomplish the results. They should work on key objectives wanting an outcome. They should set specific goal for self and others. Adult education is a field oriented subject involving many people to attain the objectives. So, the continuing education workers should communicate clearly and concretely what others should do apart from his own continuous efforts. Results indicate that the continuing education workers have obtained a lower level score on result orientation.

## 18. Emotional Stability

Emotions play an important role in human life. If one wishes to influence another person's actions one can do so by exhibiting the appropriate emotions. Emotions give us the energy to carry out the activity. They provide change and colour to our life. Our lives would have been monotonous, drab and prosaic without them. Even the great works of art and literature have been influenced by emotional experiences of artists and literary men and women. Under ordinary circumstances, the psychological reactions during an emotion facilitate the adjustment of an individual. Generally, the physiological reactions do not have any harmful effects. Emotional reactions are related to fears, worries, anxieties, anger annoyance, irritability and resentment. In order to have control over emotions one should know about its causes, reactions involved and consequences. The more one knows about them, the greater is the power that one will have over them. One should cultivate hobbies, habits of good reading and making friendships, participating in dramatics, music or games. These activities will direct the attention from the emotion- provoking experiences. A desirable philosophy of life will enable one to avoid mental conflicts and emotional tensions. Response pattern of continuing education workers indicates that majority of them have scored at a lower level on emotional stability.

## 19. Leadership Skills

A leader is a person who influences number of people. The basic traits of a leader are initiative, courage, ambition, drive, vitality, tact, diligence, perseverance, self-confidence, thoughtfulness, trustworthiness, originality, common sense, humour, emotional stability, desire to accept, etc. A leader should develop team work, be able to manage the time and resources properly and strive for effectiveness. Response pattern of continuing education workers on leadership qualities indicates that they have scored at a higher level on the item.

## 20. Managerial Abilities

The role of management in any organization is of great importance. Management is a process. Those who perform this process are called as executives. Their main function is to make optimum utilization of scare resources of an organization for the benefit of the community. Management is the art of knowing exactly what you want men to do and then seeing that they do it in the best and cheapest manner. Management involves planning, organizing, staffing, directing, co-ordinating, reporting and budgeting. The continuing education worker should be able to maintain the continuing education centre materials, display the books, magazines, organize a variety of activities and involve the community members in the activities. Response pattern of continuing education workers on managerial skills reveals that they have scored at a higher level on the item.

## 21. Problem Solving Skills

The continuing education workers comes across a number of problems while implementing the continuing education programme. They are often related to motivation of learners, securing the support of the community in terms of physical facilities, procuring useful materials like books, pamphlets for the centre and identifying dedicated and committed volunteers for the literacy phase. He may face problems in organizing programmes related to equivalency, quality of life and individual interests. The continuing education worker is expected to possess problem-solving skills to run the centre on smooth lines. He should be able to identify the problem, causes for the problem, ability to analyse the problem, identify the various solutions to solve the problem and select the appropriate method of solving the problem in time with tact and diplomacy. Response pattern of the continuing education workers reveals that they have obtained a lower level score on problem solving skills.

## 22. Training Skills

In the context of adult education, the continuing education workers have to train the learners in vocational skills and improve their efficiency and productivity in their present occupations. Training the learners has to be .planned in a proper manner in consultation with resource organizations like State Resource Centres, Jan Sikshan Sansthans, Industrial Training Institutes, District level agencies. Response pattern of continuing education workers on the training skills revealed that they have obtained a moderate level score on the item.

## 23. Moral Values

Morality is concerned with how people actually live, how their behaviour affects others - a situation where man shows greatest care and responsibility with regard to others and himself. The continuing education worker is expected to conscientize the public about moral codes of conduct, inculcate and perpetuate the moral traits, attitudes and norms. The continuing education worker is expected to promote values like respect for others, respect for truth, honesty in dealings and relationships, consideration for others, responsibility for one's own actions, justice, courage and persistence in the face of difficulties, social responsibility, etc. Response pattern of continuing education workers about moral values indicates that they have obtained a moderate level score on the item.

### 24. Co-ordination Skills

Continuing education worker alone cannot perform all the activities of continuing education centre. Co-ordination skills are essential for him to link the activities of the centre with development programmes, establish network between continuing education centre and other local bodies like mahila mandals, youth clubs, primary health centre, village education committees, non-government organizations, etc. Response pattern of continuing education workers reveals that they have scored at a lower level on co-ordination skills.

### 25. Development Orientation

The continuing education workers are expected to possess the trait of development orientation if they have to inculcate such trait among the participants. Most success fearing people internalize society's mixed-up attitudes towards success. Those who succeed are admired for their competence, talent, courage and enterprise and other positive attributes. Individuals fail because they are incompetent or lazy. One has to translate the abstract and general aspects into specific and concrete ones, remember that all bright ideas are always not correct and must be tested, use a check list of categories and add new ones from time to time. Response pattern of the continuing education workers on development orientation reveals that they have scored at a lower level on the item.

### 26. Report Writing Skills

The continuing education worker should be able to write a report on the activities of the continuing education centre. The report should be to the point, brief and objective. The report should be written for every month. While writing the report, the objectives, the difficulties and impact on the beneficiaries should be duly considered. The report should be submitted to the higher authorities on scheduled date and time. Response pattern of continuing education workers reveals that they have obtained a higher level score on the report writing skills.

**27. Evaluation Skills**

Evaluation is a process of assessment or judgement. The continuing education worker is expected to assess the performance of neo-literates, assess the tangible and intangible benefits of literacy, observe the behaviour of learners and evaluate the performance of programmes like equivalency, income generation, individual interest and quality of life improvement programme. The purpose of evaluation is not limited to identifying the deficiencies but to suggest remedial measures to improve the overall performance of the programme. Response pattern of continuing education workers on the item reveals that they have scored at a higher level on the item.

**28. Co-operative Nature**

Continuing education activities are carried out at the community level and their success depends upon the co-operative nature of continuing education workers. The continuing education workers have to understand and work with the community members, various officials belonging to the development departments, members of self-help groups, NGOs and beneficiaries of the programmes. The co-operative nature of the continuing education workers with others will serve as a boon in securing the help of others and in discharging the duties in an effective manner. Response pattern of continuing education workers reveals that they have scored at a higher level on the item.

**29. Honesty and Sincerity**

Honesty and sincerity are necessary for continuing education workers based on which their performance can be enhanced. The regular opening of the continuing education centres, participation in training programmes, the mode of organizing different activities related to equivalency programmes, quality of life improvement programmes and income generating programmes, no doubt depend upon the honesty and sincerity of continuing education workers. Response pattern of continuing education workers reveals that they have obtained a lower level score on honesty and sincerity which deserves the attention of the administration.

## 30. Teaching Skills

The continuing education worker is expected to possess teaching skill. He is expected to teach the subject matter relating to literacy skills, awareness aspects in a systematic manner based on psychological principles like known to unknown, simple to complex, easy to difficult and concrete to abstract. He should utilize the low cost methods of teaching as well as audio-visual aids based on their necessity and availability. He should be well versed in different methods of teaching like lecture, discussion, demonstration, role play, project method, brainstorming, problem solving, etc. He should lay more emphasis on learning rather than teaching and make the teaching / learning process as interesting and effective. Results relating to the perceptions of continuing education workers reveals that they have scored at a moderate level on the teaching skills.

**TABLE 3 : Item-wise Response Pattern (Chi-square Values)**

| S. No. | Item | $x^2$ Value |
|---|---|---|
| 1. | Communication skills | 38.34 |
| 2. | Thinking skills | 124.54 |
| 3. | Planning skills | 35.44 |
| 4. | Goal setting | 43.05 |
| 5. | Decision-making skills | 34.55 |
| 6. | Negotiation skills | 33.25 |
| 7. | Time management | 14.86 |
| 8. | Creativity | 11.41 |
| 9. | Stress management | 44.04 |
| 10. | Entrepreneurship skills | 28.66 |
| 11. | General knowledge and commonsense | 50.40 |
| 13. | Discipline | 42.05 |
| 15. | Interpersonal relations | 99.65 |
| 18. | Emotional stability | 11.95 |
| 19. | Leadership skills | 54.53 |
| 20. | Managerial abilities | 47.66 |
| 21. | Problem solving skills | 14.89 |
| 22. | Training skills | 77.34 |

| | | |
|---|---|---|
| 23. | Moral values | 40.00 |
| 24. | Co-ordination skills | 27.25 |
| 25. | Development orientation | 30.89 |
| 26. | Report writing skills | 15.24 |
| 27. | Evaluation skills | 16.04 |
| 28. | Co-operative nature | 53.00 |
| 29. | Honesty and sincerity | 27.15 |
| 30. | Teaching skills | 53.80 |

**Note :** All the $x^2$ values are significant at 0.01 level.

Chi-squares were calculated to know whether there is an divergence in the response pattern of continuing education workers for different items of life skills. It is evident from the table that all the items are significant at 0.01 level and it is clear that there is divergence in the response pattern. Hence, the null hypothesis that 'Continuing education workers do not differ significantly in their response pattern for different items of life skills' is rejected.

## INFLUENCE OF PERSONAL VARIABLES ON LIFE SKILLS

The influence of personal variables on possession of life skills by the continuing education workers is as follows :

### Gender Vs. Life Skills

In the present study, an attempt was made to know the influence of gender on the possession of life skills by the continuing education workers. It can be observed from the table that continuing education workers belonging to men group have obtained a mean score of 69.11 with a standard deviation of 18.11. The continuing education workers belonging to women group have obtained a mean score of 63.39 with a standard deviation of 15.59. "t' test was employed to find out the significance of difference between the means and the calculated 't' value of 1.91 is found to be statistically not significant at 0.05 level. Hence, the null hypothesis that 'Gender does not significantly influence the life skills of continuing education workers' is rejected.

**TABLE 4 : Influence of Gender on Life Skills**

| Group | N | Mean | Standard Deviation | 't' Value |
|---|---|---|---|---|
| Men | 132 | 69.11 | 18.11 | 1.91[@] |
| Women | 68 | 63.39 | 15.59 | |

## Age Vs. Life Skills

Age is one of the biological factors. With age comes growth, intelligence and maturity. It is often observed that older age group people tend to perform better in social matters, economic dealings and decision-making in relation to lower age groups who can perform well in physical and motor skills. In a few cases, age may not exert any significant influence and it all depends upon the individuals. Keeping this in view, in the present study an attempt was made to know the influence of age on the life skills of continuing education workers, the details of which are as presented in Table 5. It can be observed from the table that the continuing education workers representing 20-30 years age group have secured a mean life skills score of 63.98 with a standard deviation of 14.68. Similarly, the mean scores and standard deviations obtained by 30-40 years and 40-50 years age groups are 65.74, 16.74 and 69.03 and 19.92. This clearly shows that higher the age level better is the possession of life skills among the continuing education workers. 'F' test was employed to find out the significance of difference among the means and the calculated 'F' value of 5.31 is found to be statistically significant at 0.01 level. Hence, the null hypothesis that 'Age does not significantly influence the life skills of continuing education workers' is rejected.

**TABLE 5 : Influence of Age on Life Skills**

| Group | N | Mean | Standard Deviation | 't' Value |
|---|---|---|---|---|
| 20 – 30 years | 56 | 63.98 | 14.68 | 5.31** |
| 30- 40 years | 98 | 65.74 | 16.74 | |
| 40 – 50 years | 46 | 69.03 | 19.92 | |

** Significant at 0.01 level

## Caste Vs. Life Skills

Caste is one of the social variables which is often considered in educational researchers. Different castes that exist in India can be grouped into forward castes, backward castes, scheduled castes and scheduled tribes. Forward castes are considered to be good educationally and economically whereas the other castes are considered to be at lower levels. It is likely that caste influences the life skills of continuing education workers. Keeping this in view in the present investigation it was proposed to study the influence of caste on the life skills of continuing education workers. The continuing education workers of the sample were categorized into four castes namely, forward, backward, scheduled castes and scheduled tribes. The details as presented in Table 6 reveal that the mean life skills score of continuing education workers representing forward castes is 72.92 whereas it is 65.18 in the case of backward castes. The mean scores of continuing education workers representing scheduled castes and scheduled tribes are 64.13 and 62.78 respectively. It can be noticed that the mean life skills scores of the forward castes is the highest duly followed by backward castes, scheduled castes and scheduled tribes. 'F' test was employed to find out the significance of difference among the means and the calculated 'F' value of 8.14 is found to be statistically significant at 0.01 level. Hence, the null hypothesis that 'Caste does not significantly influence the life skills of continuing education workers' is rejected.

**TABLE 6 : Influence of Caste on Life Skills**

| Group | N | Mean | Standard Deviation | 't' Value |
|---|---|---|---|---|
| Forward | 58 | 72.72 | 19.81 | 8.14** |
| Backward | 62 | 65.18 | 16.98 | |
| Scheduled Castes | 56 | 64.13 | 16.67 | |
| Scheduled Tribes | 24 | 62.78 | 14.86 | |

** Significant at 0.01 level

## Education Vs. Life Skills

Education enriches the quality of life of an individual in several dimensions (social, economic, political, etc.). Higher the level of education better will be the participation of person in general life situations. Keeping this in view, an attempt has been made in the present investigation to know the influence of education on the life skills of continuing education workers. By considering education as a criterion, the sample of the study were divided in three groups Le., degree and above, intermediate and SSC. From the Table 7, it could be seen that the mean life skills scores educational groups i.e., degree and above, intermediate and SSC are 72.75, 65.17 and 60.81 respectively. The trend of the mean scores indicates that degree and above qualified group have obtained better mean score in relation to the lower level educational groups i.e., Intermediate and SSC. Further, the mean score of Intermediate group is better than SSC group, which is still a lower level educational qualification. The 'F' value of 5.84 calculated to find out the mean differences among various levels of educational groups, is found to be statistically significant at 0.01 level. Hence, the null hypothesis that 'Education does not significantly influence the life skills of continuing education workers' is rejected.

**TABLE 7 : Influence of Education on Life Skills**

| Group | N | Mean | Standard Deviation | 't' Value |
|---|---|---|---|---|
| S.S.C. | 57 | 60.81 | 13.26 | 5.84** |
| Intermediate | 81 | 65.17 | 16.26 | |
| Degree and above | 62 | 72.75 | 18.88 | |

** Significant at 0.01 level

## Experience Vs. Life Skills

Experience in any profession contributes to better job performance, reduces time, energy and efforts and paves way to achieve quality. Through continuing education programme the continuing education workers over a period of time get managerial and organizational abilities. In the present study, it was intended to know the influence of experience on the possession of life skills by the continuing education workers. The continuing education workers were classified into 3 groups namely, those having below 2 years of experience, 2-4 years and 4 years and above experience and their respective scores were analysed. It is evident from Table 8 that the continuing education workers with less experience have obtained less mean score on life skills and the vice versa. This clearly demonstrates that higher the level of experience better will be the life skills among continuing education workers. 'F' test was employed to find out the significance of difference among the means and the calculated 'F' value of 5.11 was found to be statistically significant at 0.01 level. Hence, the null hypothesis that 'Experience does not significantly influence the life skills of continuing education workers' is rejected.

**TABLE 8 : Influence of Experience on Life Skills**

| Group | N | Mean | Standard Deviation | 't' Value |
|---|---|---|---|---|
| Below 2 years | 28 | 58.74 | 14.71 | 5.11** |
| 2 – 4 years | 77 | 66.39 | 16.98 | |
| 4 years and above | 95 | 73.62 | 19.91 | |

** Significant at 0.01 level

## Marital Status Vs. Life Skills

In the present study, an attempt was made to find out the influence of marital status on the life skills of continuing education workers. Out of 200 continuing education workers 139 are in the married group and the remaining 61 continuing education workers are in the unmarried group. The information pertaining to the influence of marital status on life skills is as shown in Table 9. It can be noticed from the table that the unmarried group of continuing education workers have secured a mean life skills score of 62.61 with a standard deviation of 14.38 whereas the continuing education workers belonging to the married group have secured a mean score of 69.89 with a standard deviation of 18.54. There is a difference of 7.28 points in the mean sores. 't' test was employed to find out the significance of difference between the means and the calculated 't' value of 3.02 is found to be statistically significant at 0.01 level. Hence, the null hypothesis that 'Marital status does not significantly influence the life skills of continuing education workers' is rejected.

**TABLE 9 : Influence of Marital Status on Life Skills**

| Group | N | Mean | Standard Deviation | 't' Value |
|---|---|---|---|---|
| Unmarried | 61 | 62.61 | 14.38 | 3.02** |
| Married | 139 | 69.89 | 18.54 | |

** Significant at 0.01 level

## Occupation Vs. Life Skills

The information pertaining to the influence of occupation on the life skills of continuing education workers is as presented in Table 10. The sample of the study were categorized into two groups i.e., agriculture and non-agriculture (tailoring, business, wood carving, etc.) based on their occupation. It is evident from the Table 10 that the continuing education workers representing agricultural occupation have secured a mean score of 63.11 whereas those representing the non-agricultural group have secured a mean score of 68.39. There is a difference of 5.28 points in the mean scores. The calculated 't' value of 1.91 denotes that the mean differences are not statistically significant at 0.05 level. Hence, the null hypothesis that 'Occupation does not significantly influence the life skills of continuing education workers' is accepted.

**TABLE 10 : Influence of Occupation on Life Skills**

| Group | N | Mean | Standard Deviation | 't' Value |
|---|---|---|---|---|
| Agriculture | 108 | 63.11 | 14.87 | 1.91@ |
| Non-agriculture | 92 | 68.69 | 16.52 | |

@ Not Significant

## Income Vs. Life Skills

It is income which decides the socio-economic status of the family. Income paves way to social mobility, acquaintance and helps one to excel in life. People with higher income are likely to possess better life skills in relation to lower income groups. Keeping this in view in the present investigation, an attempt was made to study the influence of income on the life skills of continuing education workers. The continuing education workers of the sample were categorized into two groups i.e., low group (possessing an annual income of less than Rs. 15,000/-) and high group (with Rs. 15,000/- and above per annum). Accordingly, there were 76 continuing education workers in the low income group and 124 continuing education workers in the higher income group. It can be observed from Table 11 that the continuing education workers representing low income have obtained a low mean life skills score (63.67) and the higher income group have obtained a higher mean life skills score (68.83). 't' test was employed to know whether the mean differences were significant or not. The calculated 't' value of 2.21 was found to be statistically significant at 0.05 level. Hence, the null hypothesis that 'Income does not significantly influence the life skills of continuing education workers' is rejected.

**TABLE 11 : Influence of Income on Life Skills**

| Group | N | Mean | Standard Deviation | 't' Value |
|---|---|---|---|---|
| Below Rs. 15,000/- per year | 76 | 63.67 | 15.16 | 2.21** |
| Rs. 15,000/- and above per year | 124 | 68.83 | 17.33 | |

** Significant at 0.05 level.

# VI

# Summary and Conclusions

## Introduction

Government of India has launched continuing education programme with the objectives of organisation of evening classes, library, reading room, charcha mandal, simple and short duration training programmes, provision of information about development and communication aspects. The programmes are designed under post--literacy programme, equivalency programme, quality of life improvement programme, income generating programmes and individual interest promotion programmes. The main motto is to improve the socio-economic standards of the neo-literates and others and encourage them to contribute their mite to the process of socio-economic development. The continuing education workers have to provide different skills like communication skills, training skills, social skills, decision making, time management, creativity, stress management, planning skills, entrepreneurship skills, etc., to the neo-literates and others. Life skills through continuing education centres is an emerging issue in the context of lifelong learning and it is basically essential to know the extent to which the continuing education workers are possessing these skills. The study would be of immense help to know the extent of possession of life skills among the continuing education workers and to design necessary strategies to promote life skills through different training programmes.

## STATEMENT OF THE PROBLEM

"A Study on Life Skills among Continuing Education Workers".

## OBJECTIVES OF THE STUDY

The following are the objectives of the study.

1. To know the extent to which the continuing education workers are possessing the life skills;
2. To find out the differences in the response pattern of continuing education workers on life skills;
3. To know the differences in the life skills among continuing education workers due to personal variables; and
4. To suggest measures to enhance the life skills of continuing education workers.

## HYPOTHESES

Based on the above objectives, the following hypotheses were formulated for testing.

1. Continuing education workers do not differ significantly in their response pattern for different items of life skills.
2. Gender does not significantly influence the life skills of continuing education workers.
3. Age does not significantly influence the life skills of continuing education workers.
4. Caste does not significantly influence the life skills of continuing education workers.
5. Education does not significantly influence the life skills of continuing education workers.
6. Experience does not significantly influence the life skills of continuing education workers.
7. Marital status does not significantly influence the life skills of continuing education workers.
8. Occupation does not significantly influence the life skills of continuing education workers.

9. Income does not significantly influence the life skills of continuing education workers.

## METHODOLOGY

For the purpose of the study, a five point rating scale on life skills of continuing education workers was developed by the investigator. The sample of the study consisted 200 continuing education workers (including Assistant continuing education workers) drawn randomly from 5 mandals of Chittoor District. The data was analysed by using relevant statistical techniques like percentages, chi-square, 't' test and 'F' test.

## FINDINGS

1. The distribution of life skills scores of continuing education workers revealed that the scores are more or less normally distributed. The mean, median and mode of the distribution are 66.25, 67.62 and 70.36. The range of the scores is 74. The lowest score and highest score being 28 and 102. The standard deviation and quartile deviation of the distribution are 15.10 and 9.30. The relation between quartile deviation and standard deviation 2/3 (standard deviation) = quartile deviation i.e., 2/3 (15.10) = 10.07 indicates that the distribution is slightly skewed. The distribution is negatively skewed since mode is maximum and the value of arithmetic mean is the least. The value of median is less than mode but greater than mean.

2. The details relating to item-wise response pattern of continuing education workers are presented under very high, high, moderate, poor and very poor levels. In order to have better understanding, the very high and high groups are categorized as high group and the poor and very poor groups are categorized under poor group. The response pattern denoted high scores on the following Items 1. Communication skills, 3. Planning skills, 4. Goal setting, 6. Negotiation skills, 9. Stress management, 11. General knowledge and common sense, 14. Tenacity, 15. Interpersonal relations, 16. Self control, 19. Leadership qualities, 20 Managerial abilities, 26. Report writing skills, 27. Evaluation skills and 28. Co-operative native. The items on which the scores are moderate include Item Nos. 2. Thinking skills, 12. Reasoning

abilities, 13. Discipline, 22. Training skills, 23. Moral values and 30. Teaching skills. The items on which the scores are poor are as follows : 5. Decision making skills, 7. Time management, 8. Creativity, 10. Entrepreneurship skills, 17. Result orientation, 18. Emotional stability, 21. Problem solving skills, 24. Co-ordination skills, 25. Development-orientation and 29. Honesty and sincerity.

3. Chi-squares were calculated to know whether there is an divergence in the response pattern of continuing education workers for different items of life skills. It was found that all the items were significant at 0.01 level and there is divergence of response for the items.

4. As far as the influence of personal variables is concerned variables namely age, caste, education, experience, marital status, income have significantly influenced the life skills of continuing education workers and variables namely, gender and occupation have not significantly influenced the life skills of continuing education workers.

5. The trend of the mean scores revealed that men have secured a better mean score on life skills than women. The higher the age better was the possession of life skills. Forward castes have secured a better mean score on life skills than backward castes, scheduled castes and scheduled tribes. Degree and above qualified continuing education workers exhibited a better mean score on life skills in relation to those possessing the lower level educational qualifications (Intermediate and SSC). The continuing education workers with 4 years and above experience had an edge over in the possession of life skills when compared with the lower level experience groups (2-4 years and below 2 years). The continuing education workers belonging to married group showed a better mean score on life skills in relation to the unmarried group. The continuing education workers belonging to non-agricultural occupations (tailoring, business, wood carving, etc.) obtained a good mean score on life skills in relation to those pursuing agricultural occupation. Further, it was found that the continuing education workers having higher income exhibited a better score of life skills in relation to the lower income groups.

## SUGGESTIONS

1. Steps should be taken by the district administration to organize training programmes to continuing education workers on life skills by involving subject experts.
2. In the context of lifelong learning it is essential to consider acquisition of life skills as a continuous process both from continuing education workers and learners point of view.
3. The Universities and State Resource Centres should design appropriate training materials on life skills in the local language.
4. During the course of training programmes on life skills the continuing education workers should be exposed to more demonstrations, brain storming sessions, group work presentations, problem solving methods, etc. The initiative to grow better on each aspect of life skills should emerge from within the continuing education workers. A self-motivated continuing education worker can do better in acquiring life skills and in disseminating the same to the neo-literates and others.
5. In the present study, it was found that the possession of life skills is at a lower level among the following groups of continuing education workers i.e., women, lower age, backward class, scheduled caste and scheduled tribes, continuing education workers having lower education, lower experience, and those pursuing agricultural occupation. Hence, more emphasis should be laid on these groups during training programmes.
6. Since the life skills of continuing education workers are moderate / low on the following areas more attention should be laid on them during the training / orientation programmes. The areas include thinking skills, training skills, moral values, teaching skills, decision making skills, time management, creativity, entrepreneurship skills, reasoning abilities, discipline, result orientation, emotional stability, problem solving skills, co-ordination skills, development orientation and honesty and sincerity.

### Suggestions for further research

1. A study on the impact of life skills on the performance continuing education workers may be undertaken.
2. A study on the effectiveness of training programmes for continuing

education workers on life skills may be carried out.
3. A study on the possession of life skills by neo-Iiterates may be attempted.
4. A study on the coverage of life skills by Jan Sikshan Sansthans may be taken up.

**REFERENCES**

1. Aikara and Henriques (1982). Functioning of the Adult Education Programmes in Maharashtra, Unit for Research in Sociology of Education, TISS, Bombay.
2. Aker, G.F. (1962). Identification of criteria for evaluating programmes in Adult Education, University of Wisconsin.
3. Cass, A.W. (1971). Matcrials and methods of Adult Literacy Programmes, Literacy Discussion, Vol. 11(3), 22-23.
4. Charles J. Margerison (1996). The art of effective communication, Excel Books, New Delhi.
5. Cobley, L.S. (1976). The qualities required for teachers of agriculture, Training for Agriculture and Rural Development, Paris, UNESCO, 54-59.
6. Grabowski, S.M. (1976). Training Teachers of Adults : Models and Innovative Programmes, Occasional Paper No. 46, Syracuse University.
7. Knox, A.B. (1971). In-service Education in Adult Basic Education, Tallahassee: Florida University
8. Kusum Vir (2000). The role of continuing education workers in continuing education programmes, Indian Journal of Adult Education, Vol. 63, No.3, July-Sept., 1,42-51.
9. Malakondaiah, C.C. (1980). Characteristics of an Effective Instructor, M.A. Dissertation, Department of Adult Education, S.V. University, Tirupati.
10. Mastan, V. (2005). Influence of certain Socio-Psychological factors on the performance of continuing education workers organizing Continuing Education Centres, Ph.D. Thesis, Department of Education, S.V. University, Tirupati.
11. Pearce (1966). Basic Education Teachers - Seven needed qualities, California, U.S. Department of Health Education and Welfare.
12. State Resource Centre for Adult Education (2007). Managerial Skills (Telugu Version), Literacy House, Andhra Mahila Sabha,

Hyderabad.

13. Tripathi, V. (1977). Training of Instructors for Non-Formal Education Programme, Literacy Work, 6(2), 35-50.
14. Van Luis, S.R. (2007). Skills for Excellence, Pusthak Mahal, New Delhi.
15. Wallance, H.R. and Masters, L.A. (2006). Personality Development, Learning India Private Limited, New Delhi.
16. White, T.J. (1950). Similarity of training interests among adult education leaders, Doctoral Dissertation, University of Chicago.
17. Yesanna (1986). A study of certain factors relating to instructor effectiveness in Adult Education Programme, M.A. Dissertation in Adult Education, S.V. University, Tirupati.

# 1. Lifelong Learning in the Global Knowledge Economy

*All agree that the single most important key to development and to poverty alleviation is education. This must start with universal primary education for girls and boys equally, as well as an open and competitive system of secondary and tertiary education...Adult education, literacy, and lifelong learning must be combined with the fundamental recognition that education of women and girls is central to the process of development.*

**...James D. Wolfensohn, President of the World Bank, 1999**

## Introduction

The emergence of the global knowledge economy has put a premium on learning throughout the world. Ideas and know-how as sources of economic growth and development, along with the application of new technologies, have important implications for how people learn and apply knowledge throughout their lives. Lifelong learning is becoming a necessity in many countries. It is more than just education and training beyond formal schooling. A lifelong learning framework encompasses learning throughout the lifecycle, from early childhood to retirement, and in different learning environments, formal, non-formal, and informal. Opportunities for learning throughout one's lifetime are becoming increasingly critical for countries to be competitive in the global knowledge economy.

**Lifelong learning**

Lifelong learning, also known as LLL, is the "lifelong, voluntary, and self-motivated" pursuit of knowledge for either personal or professional reasons. As such, it not only enhances social inclusion, active citizenship and personal development, but also competitiveness and employability.

Lifelong education/learning means education resulting from integration of formal, non-formal, and informal education so as to create ability for continuous lifelong development of quality of life. Learning is therefore part of life which takes place at all times and in all places. It is a continuous lifelong process, going on from birth to the end of our life, beginning with learning from families, communities, schools, religious institutions, workplaces, etc. Learning of the 6 – 24 age groups usually takes place in educational institutions, from primary and secondary to tertiary levels. The objective of learning in this period is the holistic development of learners in four aspects, namely: physical, intellectual, social capacity, emotional and mental development. Learning during the working life of the 25 – 60 age groups can learn informally through the use of instructional media, mostly from their occupations, work-places, colleagues, touring, mass media, information technologies, environment and nature. Adults learn from experiences and problems solving, they therefore need continuous development of intellect, capability and integrity. Learning in old age (over 60 years old) elderly people can learn a great deal from activities suitable to their age e.g. art, music, sports for the elderly, handicrafts and social work. They can also carry out voluntary work in community organizations, clubs and associations. Such work makes their lives meaningful as well as bringing benefits to society.

**Importance of Lifelong Learning in the Global Knowledge Economy**

A knowledge-based economy relies primarily on the use of ideas rather than physical abilities and on the application of technology rather than the transformation of raw materials or the exploitation of cheap labor. Knowledge is being developed and applied in new ways. Product cycles are shorter and the need for innovation greater.

Trade is expanding worldwide, increasing competitive demands on producers.

The global knowledge economy is transforming the demands of the labor market throughout the world. It is also placing new demands on citizens, who need more skills and knowledge to be able to function in their day-to-day lives.

Lifelong learning is crucial to preparing workers to compete in the global economy. But it is important for other reasons as well. By improving people's ability to function as members of their communities, education and training increase social cohesion, reduce crime, and improve income distribution.

Developing countries and countries with transition economies risk being further marginalized in a competitive global knowledge economy because their education and training systems are not equipping learners with the skills they need. To respond to the problem, policymakers need to make fundamental changes. They need to replace the information-based, teacher-directed rote learning provided within a formal education system governed by directives with a new type of learning that emphasizes creating, applying, analyzing, and synthesizing knowledge and engaging in collaborative learning throughout the lifespan.

## Characteristics of Traditional and Lifelong Learning Models

Being successful in the knowledge economy requires mastering a new set of knowledge and competencies. These include basic academic skills, such as literacy, foreign language, math, and science skills and the ability to use information and communication technology. Workers must be able to use these skills effectively, act autonomously and reflectively, and join and function in socially heterogeneous groups. In the globalized world, the methods of teaching and learning are changing. People prefer ICT based education. There are lot of difference between traditional learning and lifelong learning.

***Traditional learning***

- The teacher is the source of knowledge.
- Learners receive knowledge from the teacher.

- Learners work by themselves.
- Tests are given to prevent progress until students have completely mastered a set of skills

  and to ration access to further learning.
- All learners do the same thing.
- Teachers receive initial training plus ad hoc in-service training.
- "Good" learners are identified and permitted to continue their education.

***Lifelong learning***

- Educators are guides to sources of knowledge.
- People learn by doing.
- People learn in groups and from each other.
- Assessment is used to guide learning strategies and identify pathways for future learning.
- Educators develop individualized learning plans.
- Educators are lifelong learners. Initial training and ongoing professional development are linked.
- People have access to learning opportunities over a lifetime.

## Scope, Content, Delivery of Education and Training in Traditional and Lifelong

## Learning Models

| ***Dimension*** | ***Traditional model*** | ***Lifelong learning model*** |
|---|---|---|
| Scope | • Formal schooling from primary to higher education | • Learning throughout the Lifecycle in schools, on the job, after retirement |
| Content | • Acquisition and repetition of knowledge<br>• Curriculum driven | • Creation, acquisition, and application of knowledge<br>• Diverse sources of knowledge<br>• Empowerment of learners·<br>• Competency driven |
| Delivery | • Limited learning options and modalities<br>• Formal institutions | • Multitude of learning options, settings andmodalities. |

| | |
|---|---|
| • Uniform centralized Control | • New pedagogical approaches· |
| • Supply driven | • Technology -supposed deli-delivery<br>• Pluralistic, flexible decentralized system<br>• Learn driven |

## CONCLUSION

The impact of education is very much on the individuals of the society. Industrialization and Globalization brought enormous changes in the society. Importance of Science and Technology is also increasing day by day. Learning is a continuous process. In the global knowledge economy, education has a prominent in the process of national development. 'ICT' based teaching and learning is necessary not only in formal education but also in non-formal education. There is a need to engage national policymakers and stakeholders in a dialogue on lifelong learning, helping governments formulate visions and concrete action plans for establishing both lifelong learning and innovation frameworks appropriate to our country context.

## REFERENCES


1. Desforges, Charles (2001). "*Knowledge Base for Teaching and Learning*" ,Teaching and
   Learning Research Programme Newsletter 3: pp: 3–4.
2. Edwards, Karen (1997). "*Individual Development Accounts: Creative Savings for Families and Communities*", working paper, University of Washington, Center for Social Development, St. Louis.
3. Fiske, Edward (1996). "*Decentralization of Education: Politics and Consensus*", Washington, D.C., World Bank.
4. Gundlach, E. (2001). "*Education and Economic Development: An Empirical Perspective*", *Journal of Economic Development* 26 (1) pp: 37–60.

# 2. Importance of Lifelong Learning For Earning in the 21$^{st}$ Century

*For our people to benefit from new employment opportunities, we must ensure that every Indian is skilled and educated. Education alone is the foundation on which a prosperous and progressive society is built. I wish to see a revolution in education and skill development in the next five years. We will make India a nation of educated people, of skilled people, of creative people"....Manmohan Singh, Prime Minister of India, Red Fort, Aug 15$^{th}$, 2007*

*Anyone who stops learning is old, whether this happens at twenty or eighty. Anyone who keeps on learning not only remains young, but becomes constantly more valuable regardless of physical capacity. ...Harvey Ullman*

## Introduction

Lifelong learning and the learning society are not new issues. Some of the earliest ideas about lifelong learning can be traced back to the 17th century when Comenius wrote that "no age is too late to begin learning." Other references have been traced back to the 1940s and more recently in literature dating to the 1960s and 1970s. However, what was at one time a minority interest has exploded into world-wide significance in the late 1990s: lifelong learning has become an important focus for society. Factors such as the information society, the rapid expansion of new technologies, the rate of economic, industrial, commercial and cultural change and, in the West, increased competition from emerging economies in South and Central America and Asia, where labour is cheap, plentiful and increasingly skilled, have all contributed to a new political imperative.

The effect that rapid technological and organisational changes have had on lifestyles and attitudes to work is such that the traditional division of three stages of life: "education and learning - leading to work - lastly, to retirement" is diminishing and together with this has been the demise of the "job for life" culture. So `lifelong learning' is becoming much more than a passing political fad and instead describes a very real change in the lives of individuals and in the activities of societies.

**Lifelong learning**

*The illiterate of the 21st century will not be those who cannot read and write but those who cannot learn, unlearn and relearn."*

...**Alvin Toffler (Futurist)**

We are living through a transformation that will rearrange the politics and economics of the coming century. Each nation's primary assets will be its citizens' skills and insights. Each nation's primary political task will be to cope with the centrifugal forces of the global economy which tear up the ties binding citizens together - bestowing even greater wealth on the most skilled and insightful, while consigning the less skilled to a declining standard of living.

For people living in relatively isolated, rural communities, especially where the provision of public services is limited, engagement in locally based educational activity or distance learning can constitute an important dimension of sociability and connection with the rest of society. We know too that learning can play its part in social and economic regeneration, in building community capacity and in restoring a sense of self-worth and optimism to localities hit by sudden economic change, industrial collapse, restructuring and redundancy. Imaginative educational programmes can play a major part in regeneration partnerships between community-based initiatives, local business, local authorities and learning providers.

The Adult Education Committee of the British Ministry of Reconstruction concluded: "Adult education must not be regarded as a luxury for a few exceptional persons here and there, nor as a thing which concerns only a short span of early manhood, but that adult education is a permanent national necessity, an inseparable aspect of citizenship, and therefore should be both universal and lifelong.

The concept of lifelong learning as an educational strategy emerged some three decades ago, through the efforts of the OECD, UNESCO and the Council of Europe. It was a response to the anomaly that while individuals learn throughout life, the provision of education opportunities was limited largely to the early phase of life, dominated by formal education. There was a perceived need to provide a "second chance" to those who did not benefit from educational opportunities available during childhood and youth.

Lifelong learning is far broader than the provision of second-chance education and training for adults. It is based on the view that everyone should be able, motivated and actively encouraged to learn throughout life. This view of learning embraces individual and social development of all kinds and in all settings: formally, in schools, vocational, tertiary and adult education institutions; and non-formally, at home, at work and in the community.

**Four key factors determine people's participation in learning:**

- Individual disposition and attitudes towards learning
- Social environment
- Economic and financial context
- Institutional factors

The various aspirations and motivations of future learners vary according to their personal situations and may change over time. The decision to undertake some form of learning after school or to interrupt a period of employment is variously dependent on personal, social and economic circumstances.

### Importance of Life Long Learning for Earning

A number of important socio-economic forces are pushing for the lifelong learning approach. The increased pace of globalisation and technological change, the changing nature of work and the labour market and the ageing of populations are among the forces emphasizing the need for continuing upgrading of work and life skills throughout life. The demand is for a rising threshold of skills as well as for more frequent changes in the nature of the skills required. Firms' drive for greater flexibility has injected precariousness in jobs. There is a tendency towards shorter job tenures in the face of more volatile product markets and shorter product cycles.

Career jobs are diminishing and individuals are now experiencing more frequent changes in jobs over the working life. The large structural changes are threatening new polarisations between the knowledge-haves and knowledge have-nots; and this, in turn, can threaten the very basis of democracy. Opportunities for training later in life depend heavily on the qualifications with which one enters the labour force, and learning opportunities open to the unemployed, employees of small firms and the disadvantaged groups in society are far fewer than for the employees of the larger firms. The disparities are also reflected in the large earnings gaps between those with and without postsecondary education, which, furthermore, widen over the lifetime.

Investment in education and training in pursuit of lifelong learning strategies serves to address these social and economic objectives simultaneously by providing long-term benefits for the individual, the enterprise, the economy and society more generally. For the individual, lifelong learning emphasises creativity, initiative and responsiveness – attributes which contribute to self-fulfillment, higher earnings and employment, and to innovation and productivity. The skills and competence of the workforce are a major factor in economic performance and success at the enterprise level. For the economy, there is a positive relationship between educational attainment and economic growth.

## A Comprehensive Approach to Lifelong Learning

Lifelong learning encompasses general education and vocational education and training. These sectors provide the basis and the foundation (writing, reading, arithmetic, citizenship) as well as the preparation for working life. As part of lifelong learning, one can also find general education for adults, personal and career development as well as any form of learning taking place at work or in daily situations. Four "settings" can be distinguished as a frame for lifelong learning:

- General initial education
- Vocational education and training
- Professional development
- Personal development

**TABLE 1 : A comprehensive approach to lifelong learning**

| | Personal development | General initial education | Vocational education and training | Professional development |
|---|---|---|---|---|
| Funding | Non-profit based (learners and public funding) | Public | Public and private | Private |
| Objectives<br>What is done best? | - Promotion of democracy<br>- Equality<br>-Respect of plurality of values | - Basic and foundation education | - Vocational education and training;<br>- Transition to work | - Work specific training;<br>- Management<br>- Corporate universities |
| Focus of learning | - Democracy-Illiteracy (adults)<br>- Enlightenment (young and adults) | - Basic skills (read, write and count) for young;<br>- Little for adults (Prior learning assessment); | - Young adults;<br>- Training and retraining for unemployed<br>- Retraining of Under qualified employed | - Recognition of competences<br>-Human resource management<br>- Integration in Enterprise (young)<br>- Retraining of adults |
| Certification | Often nonexistent | -Formal general qualifications<br>- Credit towards a formal qualification | Formal vocational qualifications | - Attendance certificate<br>- Certificate of competences |
| | Non-formal | Formal | Formal | Non-formal |

## Benefits of Life Long Learning

We live in a society where diversity of background, culture, knowledge and skills should be valued and nurtured. We want a society where people actively engage in their communities, local and national, and learning can enable people to do that. Lifelong learning contributes to the development of society through the achievement of other social goals such as civic participation, sustainable development, improved health and wellbeing, reduced crime and greater social cohesion. *The availability of opportunities to learn* through*out* life *is crucial to the well being of any society, to strengthen its economy, enrich its culture and liberate its citizens. The following are the main benefits of lifelong learning:*

- Lifelong learning leads to an enriching life of self-fulfilment.
- Lifelong learning helps us make new friends and establish valuable relationships.
- Lifelong learning keeps us involved as active contributors to society.
- Lifelong learning helps us find meaning in our lives.
- Lifelong learning helps us adapt to change.
- Lifelong learning makes the world a better place.
- Lifelong learning increases our wisdom.
- Lifelong learning creates a curious, hungry mind.
- Lifelong learning opens the mind.
- Lifelong learning helps fully develop natural abilities.

## Conclusion

Everyone needs to know about the importance and benefits of lifelong learning that provides opportunities for intellectual, cultural exploration, and work place development (skill). This is accomplished through continuing education courses that provide opportunity for personal growth and social interaction in formal and informal academic settings. Continual learning benefits career success through developing additional work skills and self-satisfaction. The secrets to a lifelong learning are based on the fact that adults must realize is that early formal learning experiences no longer support them for a lifetime. Most people have multiple careers today. This one fact leads to the need to continually learn and prepare for wherever the future leads an adult. Lifelong learning helps more earnings of the individual.

## References

1. David R. Wetzel (2010). "*10 Secrets to Lifelong Learning for Everyone*".
2. Government of India, University Grants Commission, New Delhi.
3. OECD (1996). "*Lifelong Learning for All*", Organization for Economic
   Co-operation and Development, Paris.
4. UNESCO, Paris.

# 3. Adult Education – Way For Lifelong Learning and Earning

Development of human resources is essential that would like to be dynamic and growth oriented. Unlike other resources, human resources have unlimited potential and can be used only by creating a climate that can continuously identify, nurture and use these capabilities. For thus, there is an urgent need to provide learning opportunities throughout the lives of men which is known as lifelong learning. The term recognizes that learning is not confined to childhood or the class room, but takes place throughout life and in a range of situations. During the last fifty years, constant scientific and technological innovation and change has had a propound effect on learning needs and styles. Learning can no longer be divided into a place and time to acquire knowledge (school) and a place and time to apply the knowledge acquired (the work place). Instead, learning can be seen as something that takes place on an ongoing basis from our daily interactions with others and with the world around us. Lifelong learning is therefore acquiring and updating all kinds of abilities, interests, knowledge and qualifications from the pre-school years to post retirement. It promotes the development of knowledge and competences that will enable each citizen to adapt to the knowledge based society and actively participate in all spheres of social and economic life, taking more control of his or her future.

## Concept and Significance of Life Long Learning

"All learning activity undertaken throughout life- whether in formal, non-formal and informal settings- with the aim of improving knowledge, skills and competence within personal, civic, social and for employment related perspective"-Maria Torres, R.M.

Lifelong learning is the development of human potential through a continuously supportive process which stimulates and empowers the individual to acquire the knowledge, skills, and understanding they will require throughout their lifetime and to apply them with confidence, creativity and enjoyment in all roles, circumstances and environments.

Key purpose of lifelong learning is preparation for democratic citizenship which depends largely on effective development and growth of the disadvantaged sections of societies. The act of learning, lying as it does at the heart all educational activities, changes human beings from objects at the mercy of events to the subjects who created their own history (Declaration of Fourth UNESCO Conference on Adult Education, Paris, 1985). Lifelong learning has propounded implications for individuals throughout their lives as it aims to develop total personality of individuals. It disciplines the mind, broadens mental horizons, instills a sense of economic well being, helps one to understand the environment and provides a definite understandable view of the world with its values, beliefs, needs and growth patterns and opens doors to numerous sources of information.

The factors which necessitates the lifelong learning are

- Expanding educational needs.
- Explosion in knowledge and technology.
- Shift to an information society.
- Emergence of new occupations and careers.
- Financial stringencies

In order to provide lifelong learning opportunities to all sections of the society, six key aspects should be given prominence.

1. *Value learning*: Identification, assessment and recognition of non-formal and informal learning as per with the formal and to support valuing all forms of learning.
2. *Information, Guidance and Counseling*: Facilitating access to learning opportunities for all citizens through the availability of quality information and guidance services.

3. *Investment of time and money in learning*: Increased investment, targeted funding and transparency in the investment and decentralization.
4. *Bringing learning opportunities and learners closer together*: To encourage and support learning communities and to enable work places to become learning organizations.
5. *Basic skills*: To ensure that the foundations of lifelong learning are accessible to all and at all stages of life with a special attention to those with a lack of basic skills.
6. Innovative pedagogy: To take them from knowledge acquisition to competence development implies a new role of teachers and trainers' non-formal and informal learning are given prominence as priority of research and exchange of good practice.

As it is not possible to provide learning opportunities for all the sections of the society through formal learning alone it is the non-formal education through which we can facilitate the learning to the community. Adult education is a form of non-formal education which will meet the learning needs of the masses.

## Adult Education and Lifelong Learning

During the present decade, adult education has undergone substantial changes and experienced enormous growth in scope and scale. In the knowledge-based societies that are emerging around the world, adult and continuing education has become an imperative in the community and at the workplace. New demands from society and working life raise expectations requiring each and every individual to continue renewing knowledge and skills throughout the whole of his or her life. The objectives of adult education are to develop the autonomy and the sense of responsibility of people, to reinforce the capacity to deal with the transformations taking place in the economy in culture and in society as a whole, and to promote coexistence, tolerance and the informed and creative participation of citizens in their communities, in short to enable people and communities to take control of their destiny and society in order to face the challenges ahead.

Recognizing the importance of adult education as an essential tool for learning, communication, for acquisition and sharing of knowledge and information, the Government of India has been implementing the Adult Education Programmes continuously and National Literacy Mission was launched on 5th May 1988. The NLM had covered 597 districts under Total Literacy Campaign, 485 districts in post-literacy programme and to provide lifelong learning facilities to the community, Continuing Education Centers had been setup in 328 districts. Despite significant accomplishments of the mission, there exists the gender and regional disparities in literacy and it was low among females and north-eastern states. In recognition of the importance of the literacy and lifelong learning in developing human potential, Sakshar Bharat Mission was launched on September 8th, 2009 giving emphasis on the female literacy, to create the learning society and to meet the learning needs of different sections and different age groups.

In order to meet the needs of the community, an assortment of teaching, learning programmes like Literacy Programme, Basic Education, Skill Promotion Programme and Continuing Education Programme will be organized in the Lok Siksha Kendras (adult education centers). Library will be established in the centre and it will be venue for group discussions the centre will act as an information window and provide extension facility for other departments. .Jan sikshan sansthan and other vocational training centres will organize skill promotion programmes to promote employability. Adult education and lifelong learning take particular account of those groups of people who are most disadvantaged, in particular women, youth especially those in rural situations and the elderly.

**Women:**

Women constitute an important segment of any community and perform multiple roles as mothers, productive workers and wage earners. Despite significant improvements in the status of women, they are still at a disadvantage in gaining access to good-quality education, and to senior positions in politics, society and employment. Poor self image, deprivation of their rights, economic dependence is the reasons for their subordination. Recognizing the women's potentialities and weaknesses, the policymakers are in the processes of restructuring their national agenda and creating space for the women to enter into the economy by equipping them with the skills, abilities and knowledge so as to enable them to participate in the process of development on par with men.

Participation of women in today's knowledge society requires learning for both understanding and contribution to society. Learning in adult education centers opens the possibility of unlimited exposure to new information and more importantly new ways of thinking and new perspectives of existing information. Exposure to the short term thematic courses on health care, population education environment, consumer education and rural technologies and vocational training in the adult education centres can prevent skill depreciation among women and to obtain essential basic skills. Their participation in these programmes leads to sense of self worth, active participants in the process of development, employability and economic development.

**Youth:**

Youth the vital segment of the human resources can play a vital role in the development of the country with their vibrant ideas when properly motivated and sufficiently guided. The youth, who in their productive age group could be mould in as a productive force with the provision of knowledge, changing their attitudes and promoting skills. Giving them opportunities to plan, to decide and to work prepares them to face harsher realities in life. For this, India's youth need to be healthy, educated, forward looking, and skilled. Instead, the significant proportions of youth have little education; many are still illiterate and unemployed. In such a situation, youth development will increasingly become a prerequisite to meet the growing demands of knowledge based society and a condition for the development of society as a whole. Literacy promotion, basic education, access to information, awareness generation and skill promotion are the important aspects of adult and lifelong learning programme of the Sakshar Bhatrat Mission which leads to personal wellbeing, foster employability and economic productivity among the youth.

**Aged:**

Lifelong learning has special significance for the aged population. There are three potential areas for which the learning will help to meet the evolving economic and social needs of ageing population, for individual health, to strengthen community and family and for self-employment. Learning will help to reduce the human and financial burden of chronic health problem of the aged. Programmes of information and education can change the elders' knowledge, attitude and action to ensure a healthy and productive old age for themselves. Learning can mobilize the elderly as a resource to strengthen the community and family and to enhance social cohesion. The wisdom of the elderly with regard to child rearing, ethical behavior, and conflict resolution and in the political arena can be tapped to guide and benefit younger adults. The elders can choose vocational training programmes in the Adult Education Centres/ Loksiksha Kendras of Sakshara Bharat Mission as per their interest and capability. These will help to increase their earning capacity and for self-employment.

**Conclusion**

During the last fifty years, constant scientific and technological innovation and change has had a profound effect on learning needs. In order to meet the learning needs of the community, specified levels of educational preparation is required. Adult education such a type of education which provides lifelong learning opportunity and important input for human resource development, the programmes of Sakshar Bharat Mission will provide the opportunity to the community to the acquisition of literacy; enhance their communication skills, awareness and employability leading to self confidence and empowerment. The success of these efforts depends not only on the implementation but the active participation and utilization of the beneficiaries. The people should come forward and utilize the opportunity in an effective manner for their and the nation' development's.

# 4. Women Empowerment Through Lifelong Learning

## Introduction

Lifelong learning is widely regarded as playing a key role in enhancing the economic performance and prospects of individuals. The organizations such as the UN, the OECD and the EU have stressed the importance of lifelong learning in developing and regenerating the stock of human capital. In the modern, knowledge-driven economy, it has been argued; people must upgrade their skills in order to remain competitive and to prepare for frequent changes in jobs. Those who missed out on initial education require lifelong learning to acquire essential basic skills. Those out of the labour force should undertake lifelong learning to prevent skills depreciation. Adult learning, then, is seen as crucial for long-term employability. As well as these economic benefits, lifelong learning can also contribute to social inclusiveness and the reduction of inequality between men and women through its assumed effects on employment prospects.

Empowerment is now increasingly seen as a process by which the one's without power gain greater control over their lives. This means control over material assets, intellectual resources and ideology. It involves power to, power with and power within. Some define empowerment as a process of awareness and conscientization, of capacity building leading to greater participation, effective decision-making power and control leading to transformative action. This involves ability to get what one wants and to influence others on our concerns. With reference to women the power relation that has to be involved includes their lives at multiple levels, family, community, market and the state. Importantly it involves at the psychological level women's ability to assert them and this is constructed by the 'gender roles' assigned to her especially in a cultural which resists change like India.

**Women's Position in India**

There is no doubt that we are in the midst of a great revolution in the history of women. The evidence is everywhere; the voice of women is increasingly heard in Parliament, courts and in the streets. While women in the West had to fight for over a century to get some of their basic rights, like the right to vote, the Constitution of India gave women equal rights with men from the beginning. Unfortunately, women in this country are mostly unaware of their rights because of illiteracy and the oppressive tradition.

The literacy rate of women in 2009 is 54.50 per cent. Still, 245 million Indian women cannot read or write, comprising the world's largest number of unlettered women. National averages in literacy conceal wide disparities. For instance, while 95 per cent of women in Mizoram are literate, only 34 per cent of women in Bihar can read and write. The average Indian female has only 1.2 years of schooling, while the Indian male spends 3.5 years in school. More than 50 per cent girls drop out by the time they are in middle school. Similarly, life expectancy has increased for both the sexes; it has increased to 64.9 years for women and 63 years for men according to UN Statistic Division (2000). The Working women population has risen from 13% in 1987 to 25% in 2001.

However the UNFPA State of World Population 2005 states that about 70% of graduate Indian women are unemployed. Women constitute 90 per cent of the total marginal workers of the country. Rural women engaged in agriculture form 78 per cent of all women in regular work. They are a third of all workers on the land. The traditional gender division of labour ensures that these women get on average 30 per cent lower wages than men. The total employment of women in organized sector is only 4 per cent. Although industrial production increased in the 1980s; jobs in factories and establishments — or non-household jobs — stagnated at eight per cent of the workforce. Increasingly, companies tend to rely on outsourcing, using cheap labour. It is well known that women and children work in huge numbers in bidi-rolling, agarbatti-rolling, bangle making, weaving, brassware, leather, crafts and other industries. Yet, only 3 per cent of these women are recorded as laborers. They are forced to work for pitiable wages and are denied all social security benefits. A study by SEWA of 14 trades found that 85 per cent of women earned only 50 per cent of the official poverty level income.

The sociological research on the status of women has generally suggested that the Indian women enjoy a low status in their households because family decisions relating to finances, kinship relations, selection of life partner are made by the male members and women are rarely consulted. Although there has been an expansion in health facilities maternal mortality rate continue to be high at 407 per 1, 00,000 live births (1998).WHO estimates show that out of the 529,000 maternal deaths globally each year ,136,000 (25.7%) are contributed by India. A factor that contributes to India's high maternal mortality rate is the reluctance to seek medical care for pregnancy - it is viewed as a temporary condition that will disappear. The estimates nationwide are that only 40-50 per cent of women receive any antenatal care. Evidence from the states of Bihar, Rajasthan, Orissa, Uttar Pradesh, Maharashtra and Gujarat find registration for maternal and child health services to be as low as 5-22 per cent in rural areas and 21-51 per cent in urban areas. Even a woman who has had difficulties with previous pregnancies is usually treated with home remedies only for three reasons: the decision that pregnant women seek help rests with the mother-in-law and husband; financial considerations; and fear that the treatment may be more harmful than the malady.

## Why is Lifelong Learning Needed?

It is generally agreed that education has become one of the most significant vehicles in the development of human life in general and woman life in particular. Education can contribute toward personal well-being and happiness. To lead a happy life in society, one should be involved in education throughout life. Education is a tool for human beings to use for solving daily problems, or adjusting to the environment: in other words, "education for life and life for education." In this regard, education does not only mean learning through the formal school system or "formal education." The concept of "education" includes formal education, non-formal education and informal education, and the combination of all three is referred to as "lifelong education."

At present, the educational system that serves the majority of people all over the world emphasizes formal education, which is basically a classification system of formal performance, involving rigid curricula. The formal school system is usually classified into the primary or elementary, the secondary, high school and university levels. The second type of educational system is known as non-formal education, which educational planners are using as a substitute to the formal system for out-of-school youth and adults. Non-formal education is less formal in terms of its performance criteria and is more concerned with daily life problems. This includes adult school programs and other short-training courses. The last type of educational system is informal education, which is truly a lifelong process where every individual acquires attitudes, values, skills and knowledge from daily experience. It includes any kind of education besides formal and non-formal and any method of learning using various sources of knowledge. For example, knowledge may be acquired during conversation and travelling; attending shows or movies; reading books and newspapers; listening to the radio or watching television. It indicates that lifelong learning takes place in every life of human beings.

Considering the potential reach and the effectiveness of these three types of educational systems (formal, non-formal and informal), it is apparent that informal education is the most efficient and effective means to reach the rural adult population. Most rural people have little time for formal schooling due to the exigencies of meeting their personal, familial, occupational and societal needs. Each individual and society is unique in terms of its educational needs. It has been demonstrated that formal education is unable to serve individual needs since its curriculum is directed to respond to the needs of the majority target group. Moreover, the present formal school curriculum stresses general knowledge, while skills and experiences for living are left to the learners to acquire by themselves outside the school system. Through lifelong learning it is possible to acquire up to date knowledge and skills in the globalized world.

In the sociological aspect majority of married women are house wives. They are depending on theirs' husbands. Even though they have good educational qualifications and skills, they are wasting theirs' time with chit-chat. They have good capacity to do any work. They want only proper guidance and training. Lifelong learning is the correct platform for the empowerment of women in the society.

## Women Empowerment through Lifelong Learning

"Education is the most critical element in empowering women with skills and knowledge and giving them access to productive employment in the future. The 11th Plan should pay special attention to this area. An ideal we should strive for is that all girls should be able to get as much education as they are capable of getting, irrespective of their parents' ability to pay".

Lifelong learning is not just a matter of transferring skills but also of enabling women to use their skills to negotiate more effectively and to deal with structures of power. The training of women as hand pump mechanics, for example, has led to building confidence and mobility and breaking stereotypes. It has enhanced competencies in:

- Dealing with structures of power
- Lobbying government for change
- Demanding basic necessities from the power structures
- Demanding information

The lifelong learning helps to inculcate the following Empowerment capabilities in the women. These capabilities are more helpful for individual development of women.

- The ability to make decisions about personal/collective circumstances.
- The ability to access information and resources for decision-making.
- Ability to consider a range of options from which to choose.
- Ability to exercise assertiveness in collective decision making.
- Having positive-thinking about the ability to make change.

- Ability to learn and access skills for improving personal/collective circumstance.
- Ability to inform others' perceptions though exchange, education and engagement.
- Involving in the growth process and changes that is never ending and self-initiated.
- Increasing one's positive self-image and overcoming stigma.
- Increasing one's ability in discreet thinking to sort out right and wrong.

The Chinese say, "Continue to learn in the journey of life". According to the European Lifelong Learning Initiative and the American Council on Education, "lifelong learning is the development of human potential through a continuously supportive process which stimulates and empowers individuals to acquire all the knowledge, values, skills, and understanding they will require throughout their lifetimes and to apply them with confidence, creativity and enjoyment in all roles, circumstances, and environments". The above statement indicates that women empowerment is possible through lifelong learning.

## Powerful benefits

### *Lifelong Learning Sharpens Women Mind*

Continuous learning helps to keep women mind sharp and improve their memory, especially as they grow older. It is a known fact that learning in general has beneficial effects on the brain. Research has shown that people with more education are less likely to have dementia in old age. Just like our body requires exercise to stay fit, our brain requires exercise to remain healthy. The best way to improve our reasoning and cognitive skills is to continually learn something new.

### *Lifelong Learning Sharpens Women Confidence*

Sometimes, when someone has not stepped out of their routine for a while, they haven't taken on a new challenge or really applied themselves to learning something new, they may find the experience a bit daunting. With lifelong learning this fear is more easily overcome.

Women gain confidence in their ability to learn and to share the information with others.

### *Lifelong Learning Sharpens Women Interpersonal Skills*

While lifelong learning can take place in the quiet of a library reading a book, much of women learning will likely take place where they meet other people who share their same interest. The opportunity to socialize can help to greatly improve their interpersonal skills. When women are learning, they are engaged in life; they are engaged in those around them. And when they share what they know, they help others learn and further enhance their relationships.

### *Lifelong Learning Sharpens Women Career Opportunities*

For anyone who has aspirations of moving their career to the next level, lifelong learning will very much need to be part of the package. Not only can learning enhance the skills women already have, it provides women with the opportunity to learn a new skill or trade and improve their chances of career growth. The more they know about their company, the industry, and current events, the more relevant their skills are to their organization.

### *Lifelong Learning Sharpens Women Ability to Communicate*

When women learn, they generally employ the skills of reading, listening and writing; skills essential to their ability to communicate. Because human communication is such a large part of our daily work lives, it is a skill that most employers seek in their new hires. By enhancing these skills, women improve their ability to write a business letter, compile a marketing report, give a department presentation or even speak one-on-one to the company president.

## Conclusion

Nothing in the world gives more energy, power, courage and confidence to women than education. Learning is a lifelong process. That's why lifelong learning is important and necessary for all people in general and women in particular. In the scientific, technological and globalized world, the way of life style is changing from moment to moment. Mother is the first teacher to their children. Mother spends more time with their children than father. If woman is educated entire family is educated. Some more concentration is necessary on strategies for lifelong learning research area. I would like to give only one suggestion for women empowerment through lifelong learning; it is important to establish learning, training and employment centers at a single platform. This type of institution gives more strength and confidence to women to learn more and more things. None in the world is ready to learn new things without benefit. At the same time it is also true that nothing is useless in the universe. So, learn to live and live with learning for better survive.

## References

1. Government of India, University Grants Commission, New Delhi.
2. Government of India, Ministry of Women and Child Development, New Delhi.
3. OECD (1996). "*Lifelong Learning for All*", Organization for Economic Co-operation and Development, Paris.
4. Report of International Conference on "*Lifelong Learning for Social Development*", Dept. of Adult & Continuing Education, University of Kerala, August 13-15, 2002.
5. UNESCO, Paris.
6. UNFPA State of World Population Report-2005.
7. UN Statistic Division, 2000.

# 7. Employability Skills For Youth Through Lifelong Learning

## Introduction

The report ILO Global Employment Trends for Youth 2010 says that of some 620 million economically active youth aged 15 to 24 years, 81 million were unemployed at the end of 2009 — the highest number ever. This is 7.8 million more than the global number in 2007. The youth unemployment rate increased from 11.9 percent in 2007 to 13.0 percent in 2009.World Economic Forum report-2010 said that India will face huge skills gaps in some job categories due to low employability over the next 20 years and also warned of a looming global labour crisis. The report said that increasing mobility among countries will be a key part of the solution.

Every year lakhs of graduates (6 lakhs in engineering) are completing their degree. Among them majority of students have no employability skills. Unemployability is today a greater issue than unemployment. As APJ Abdul Kalam, Former President of India said, "*It is not unemployment that is the major problem; it is the question of unemployability that is the major crisis in this competitive arena...*"

Employability skills are those basic skills necessary for getting, keeping, and doing well on a job. These are the skills, attitudes and actions that enable workers to get along with their fellow workers and supervisors and to make sound, critical decisions. Unlike occupational or technical skills, employability skills are generic in nature rather than job specific and cut across all industry types, business, and job levels from the entry-level worker to the senior-most position. Lifelong learning helps to improve employability skills in the individual.

## Youth in India

Young people (aged 10–24) constituted almost 315 million and represented 31% of the Indian population in 2001. Not only does this cohort represent India's future in the socio-economic and political realms, but its experiences will largely determine India's achievement of its goal of population stabilization and the extent to which the nation will be able to harness its demographic dividend. While today's youth are healthier, more urbanized and better educated than earlier generations, social and economic vulnerabilities persist. In the course of the transition to adulthood, moreover, young people face significant risks related to sexual and reproductive health, and many lack the knowledge and power to make informed sexual and reproductive choices.

According to UN definition; persons between the ages of 15 years and 24 years are youth. The youth population in total population of India was 41.05 per cent in 2001. Between the years 2010-2030, India will add 241 Million people in working-age population. According to UNESCO-2002 the youth literacy rate of India was 73.3 per cent; where as China's youth literacy was 98.9 per cent. United Nations Statistic Division (2005) says that the youth unemployment of India was 10.5per cent. Through youth empowerment only the development of India is possible.

### *Many Youth are Illiterate or Have Very Low Educational Attainment*

- Thirty-one per cent of young women and 14 per cent of young men are illiterate. However, literacy is much higher among the youngest youth age 15 years (77% among women and 92% per cent among men) than among youth only a decade older (63% among women and 84% among men).
- Despite improvements over time, educational attainment remains very low even among youth: only 29 per cent of young women and 38 per cent of young men have completed 10 or more years of education.

- Urban-rural differentials are much wider for women than men in literacy and educational attainment and the gender gap is also much greater in rural than in urban areas.
- Only 41 per cent of adolescents age 15-17 were attending school in the school year 2005-06, suggesting a very high school dropout rate. School attendance rates for youth age 15-17 years increase sharply with household wealth. The gender gap is also much narrower in wealthier households than in poorer households.

## Youth –Employment/Unemployment

According to National Family Health Survery-3 (2005-06):

- Thirty-four per cent of women and 67 per cent of men age 15-24 were employed at any time in the 12 months preceding the survey, with the vast majority being currently employed.
- Among men, the proportion employed increases sharply with age from 33 per cent among those age 15 to 92 per cent among those age 24; among women, by contrast, employment varies little with age.
- Employment is higher among rural than among urban youth and is much lower among youth with 10 or more years of education than among those with no education. Almost all men with no education are employed.
- The majority of employed women are agricultural workers; however, there is greater diversity in male employment.
- Less than two-thirds of employed women (64%) earn cash for their work, compared with 88 per cent of employed men.

**Youth Unemployment Rate (aged 15-24)**

| S.No. | Year | Male | Female | Total |
|---|---|---|---|---|
| 1 | 1994 | 8.4 | 8 | 8.3 |
| 2 | 2000 | 10.1 | 10.2 | 10.1 |
| 3 | 2004 | 10.4 | 10.8 | 10.5 |

**Source:** *United Nations Statistics Division*

The unemployment rate of youth is increasing gradually. In the year 1994, the unemployment rate of female youth was better than male youth, but in the year 2004, the unemployment rate of female youth was more than male youth. Overall, the unemployment rate of youth was increased from 8.3 per cent in the year 1994 to 10.5 per cent in the year 2004.

**Employability**

Employability refers to a person's capability of gaining employment. On the one hand a person's employability depends on the knowledge, skills and attitudes of this person. On the other hand labour market rules and institutions have significant impact on the ability of an individual to gain employment. Hence, a person with the same knowledge and skills characteristics might fare very differently in different national or regional labour markets.

While there is no singular definition of employability, a review of the literature suggests that employability is about work and the ability to be employed, such as:

- The Ability To Gain Initial Employment; Hence The Interest In Ensuring That 'Key Skills', Careers Advice And An Understanding About The World Of Work Are Embedded In The Education System.
- The Ability To Maintain Employment And Make 'Transitions' Between Jobs And Roles Within The Same Organization To Meet New Job Requirements, And
- The Ability To Obtain New Employment If Required, I.e. To Be Independent In The Labour Market By Being Willing And Able To Manage Their Own Employment Transitions Between And Within Organizations.
- It Is Also, Ideally, About:
- The Quality Of Such Work Or Employment. People May Be Able To Obtain Work But It May Be Below Their Level Of Skill, Or In Low Paid, Undesirable Or Unsustainable Jobs, And So Forth.
- The Capacity And Capability Of Gaining And Maintaining Productive Work Over The Period Of One's Working Life.

Employability was one of the four 'pillars' of the European Employment Strategy until its reformulation in 2000, along with entrepreneurship, adaptability and equal opportunities. It has thus also been a key theme of the EQUAL Community Initiative.

***For individuals, employability depends on:***

- Their Assets In Terms Of The Knowledge, Skills And Attitudes They Possess
- The Way They Use And Deploy Those Assets
- The Way They Present Them To Employers
- Crucially, The Context (E.g. Personal Circumstances And Labour Market Environment) Within Which They Seek Work.

The balance of importance between and within each element will vary for groups of individuals, depending on their relationship to the labour market.

## Employability Skills

Employability skills are technical and non-technical skills and competencies which have always been an important part of an individual's effective and successful participation in the workplace. Their explicit inclusion in Training Packages represents the progression of competency based training into a system which develops the full range of transferable skills, attitudes and behaviour required for successful participation in the workplace.

Employability skills have been developed from a business and industry need for a broader range of skills beyond the Mayer Key Competencies that were developed in 1992. The 2002 report, *Employability Skills for the Future*, published by the Business Council of Australia and the Australian Chamber of Commerce and Industry, outlined an 'Employability Skills Framework' which identifies eight employability skills. They are:

1) Communication
2) Teamwork
3) Problem solving
4) Initiative and Enterprise
5) Planning and Organizing
6) Self-management
7) Learning
8) Technology

## Top Ten Skills That Employers Want

Based on a number of surveys on the skills required by graduates undertaken by Microsoft, Target Jobs, the BBC, Prospects, NACE and AGR and other organisations, here is summary of the skills which were most often deemed important.

| S.No. | SKILL | |
|---|---|---|
| 1 | Verbal Communication | Able to express your ideas clearly and confidently in speech |
| 2 | Teamwork | Work confidently within a group |
| 3 | Commercial Awareness | Understand the commercial realities affecting the organisation. |
| 4 | Analysing & Investigating | Gather information systematically to establish facts & principles. Problem solving. |
| 5 | Initiative/Self Motivation | Able to act on initiative, identify opportunities & proactive in putting forward ideas & solutions |
| 6 | Drive | Determination to get things done. Make things happen & constantly looking for better ways of doing things. |
| 7 | Written Communication | Able to express yourself clearly in writing |
| 8 | Planning & Organising | Able to plan activities & carry them through effectively |
| 9 | Flexibility | Adapt successfully to changing situations & environments |
| 10 | Time Management | Manage time effectively, prioritising tasks and able to work to deadlines. |

### *Other Important Skills*

| S.No. | SKILL | |
|---|---|---|
| 1 | **Global Skills** | Able to speak and understand other languages. Appreciation of other cultures. See<br>· Study and work placements outside the UK<br>· Working Abroad |
| 2 | **Negotiating & Persuading** | Able to influence and convince others, to discuss and reach agreement. |
| 3 | **Leadership** | Able to motivate and direct others |
| 4 | **Numeracy** | Multiply & divide accurately, calculate percentages, use statistics & a calculator, interpret graphs & tables. |
| 5 | **Computing Skills** | Word-processing, using databases, spreadsheets, the Internet & email, designing web pages etc. |
| 6 | **Self Awareness** | Awareness of achievements, abilities, values & weaknesses & what you want out of life. |

| 7 | **Personal Impact/ Confidence** | Presents a strong, professional, positive image to others which inspires confidence & commands respect. |
|---|---|---|
| 8 | **Lifelong Learning** | Continues to learn throughout life. Develops the competencies needed for current & future roles |
| 9 | **Stress Tolerance** | Maintains effective performance under pressure |
| 10 | **Integrity** | Adheres to standards & procedures, maintains confidentiality and questions inappropriate behaviour. Graduate youth come |
| 11 | **Independence** | Accepts responsibility for views & actions and able to work under their own direction & initiative. |
| 12 | **Developing Professionalism** | Pays care & attention to quality in all their work. Supports & empowers others. |
| 13 | **Action Planning** | Able to decide what steps are needed to achieve particular goals and then implement these. |
| 14 | **Decision-Making** | Determines the best course of action. Evaluates options based on logic & fact & presents solutions |
| 15 | **Interpersonal Sensitivity** | Recognises & respects different perspectives. Open to the ideas & views of others |
| 16 | **Creativity** | Generates & applying new ideas & solutions |

## Need of Employability Skills

Graduate youth come out of college, polished in academic skills. But as we all know working for a Corporate is a different ball game altogether. While their academic skills definitely count, various other skills such as spoken and written English, interpersonal skills, the art of communication, situational behavior, and so on play a pivotal role in helping the student or candidate fit into the workplace. Lack of these skills may hamper the candidate's prospects at the interview stage itself. So a powerful program that aims to impart these skills in a candidate, implemented while the student is pursuing his graduation should make him/her completely employable by the time he is out of college and into the job hunt.

## Programme for Indian Youth

Skill Bridge is a program that aims at making Indian youth employable. The skills imparted through Skill Bridge will make them confident, and help them face the corporate with more than just an academic degree. The Skill Bridge curriculum covers written and spoken English, business communication, resume writing and

| Communication | Teamwork | Problem Solving | Initiative and Enterprise | Planning and Organising | Self-management | learning | Technology |
|---|---|---|---|---|---|---|---|
| Listening and understanding<br>Speaking clearly and directly<br>Reading and interpreting documentation<br>Using numeracy effectively<br>Sharing information<br>Being assertive<br>Writing to the needs of the audience<br>Empathizing<br>Negotiating responsively<br>Persuading effectively<br>Establishing and using networks | Working an individual and team member<br>Applying teamwork to a range of situations<br>Working with people of different ages, genders, races, religions or political persuasions<br>Coaching, mentoring and giving feedback<br>Knowing how to define a role as part of a team<br>Identifying the strengths of team members | Developing apractical situations<br>Solving problem in teams<br>Showing independence and initiative in identifying problems and solving them<br>Resolving customer concerns in relation to complex project issues<br>Using mathematics, including budgeting and financial management, to solve problems<br>Testing assumptions, taking the context of data and circumstances into account | Adapting to new situations – including changing work conditions<br>Identifying opportunities not obvious to others<br>Being creative<br>Generating a range of options<br>Translating ideas into action | Managing time and priorities<br>Collecting, analyzing and organizing information<br>Identifying contingency situations<br>Implementing contingency plans<br>Being resourceful<br>Allocating resource allocations to cope with contingencies<br>Adapting resource allocations to cope with contingencies<br>Participating in continuous improvement and planning processes<br>Planning the use of resources including time management<br>Developing a vision and a proactive plan to accompany it | Evaluating and monitoring own performance<br>Taking responsibility<br>Having knowledge and confidence in own vision and goals<br>Articulating own ideas and vision | Using range of mediums to learn<br>Applying learning to technical issues and operations<br>Being open to new ideas and change<br>Contributing to the learning community at the workplace | Having a range of basic IT skills<br>Having the OHS knowledge to apply technology<br>Having appropriate physical capacity<br>Operating equipment<br>Using IT to organize data<br>Applying IT as a management tool |

interview skills, pronunciation, etiquette, leadership skills and more, making it a comprehensive training on employable skills.

## Employability Skills through Lifelong Learning

The job market is getting competitive, especially since there is a decline in jobs. The small percentages of jobs that are available are given to anyone who shows exceptional employability skills. You, too, can be a part of that small percentage. There are many resources available to anyone who would like to increase their chances of being employed. Lifelong learning is important to develop employability skills.

- Enroll in a career center that offers skills to improve employability. Career centers offer career advice and classes that teach skills that are needed to be successful in the job market. The skills will also help to lead each individual down the right career path.
- Search the Internet for useful information and tips to help improve employability skills. There are many great resources online for free. Online courses are also available.
- Go to the library and choose books that cover the different types of marketable skills. Reading as much information as possible will help to improve the skills that are needed for employment success.
- Read business literature with the most updated information of the types of skills that employers are looking for. The more skills a person has, the greater possibility of his being hired.
- Search for popular interview questions. Go in front of a mirror and practice the questions and answers until you feel confident. The other option is to have someone pretend to be the interviewer.
- Take a typing course to improve your typing speed. Many jobs require some typing skills. Improving typing skills can increase productivity on the job.

## Conclusions

We are living in the high-tech, modernized and globalized world. Science and technology has made tremendous changes in the society. Nothing is impossible for people in general and youth in particular.

According to Swami Vivekananda... "*All powers with in you. You can do anything and everything. Believe in that*". *Atma-nirmana, Atma-vikasa* and *Atma-sakshatkara* are more important according to him. Youth is a main source for development. In India we have more than 40 per cent of youth. *Education for All Programme, Universalization of Primary Education, National Literacy Mission, Sakshara Bharat*....etc. programme were formulated to provide education for all without considering caste, religion, colour and region. It is the time to change our curriculum. Job oriented curriculum is more important. Employability skills oriented education is necessary for students in general and youth in particular. Without elimination of social evils, poverty and illiteracy overall development of India is not possible. It is the duty of the government, NGOs and community to take part in the mega event "*Education and Employment for All*". Lifelong learning is the main strength for success in the globalized world.

**References**

1. "*A Profile of Youth in India*", National Family Health Survey (NFHS-3) 2005-06, Ministry of Health and Family Welfare, Government of India, New Delhi.
2. "*Education and Youth Welfare*", Working paper, Government of India, New Delhi.
3. "*Employability Skills – From Framework to Practice*", Commonwealth of Australia-2006.
4. "*Empowering Youth through National Policies*", UNESCO.
5. "*India's New Opportunity-2020*", Confederation of Indian Industry, All India Management Association, India.
6. "*Youth in India: Situation and Needs 2006-07",* Ministry of Health and Family Welfare, Government of India, New Delhi.
7. Anil Bordia (2009): "*Education of Youth and Adolescents in India*", NCERT, New Delhi.
8. EMPLOYABILIT UNIVERSE.COM, 24X7 Learning.
9. Pravin Visaria (1998): "*Unemployment among Youth in India: Level, Nature and Policy Implications*", Employment and Training Department, International Labour Office, Geneva.
10. Report of UNDP-2003, United Nations, New York.
11. Reports of RGNIYD, Sriperumbudur, Tamil Nadu.

# 8. Higher Education For Sustainable Development

## Introduction

Education is an essential tool for achieving sustainability. People around the world recognize that current economic development trends are not sustainable and the key to moving society toward sustainability are public awareness, education, and training. People argue about the meaning of sustainable development and whether it is attainable or not. They have different visions of what sustainable societies will look like and how they will function. These same people wonder why educators have not moved more quickly to develop Education for Sustainability (ES) programs.

It is curious to note that while we have difficulty envisioning a sustainable world, we have no difficulty identifying what is unsustainable in our societies. We can rapidly create a laundry list of problems - inefficient use of energy, lack of water conservation, increased pollution, abuses of human rights, overuse of personal transportation, consumerism, etc. An important distinction is the difference between education *about* sustainable development and education *for* sustainable development. The first is an awareness lesson or theoretical discussion. The second is the use of education as a tool to achieve sustainability. Education for Sustainable Development (ESD) promises to make the world more livable for this and future generations. Of course, a few will abuse or distort ESD and turn it into indoctrination. This would be antithetical to the nature of ESD, which, in fact, calls for giving people knowledge and skills for lifelong learning to help them find new solutions to their environmental, economic, and social issues.

Higher education institutions play a major role in improving the environment, preserving natural resources and making an economic and social impact. Graduates are entering a volatile world and higher education needs to respond to challenging, rapidly changing socio-economic and environmental conditions. Through their roles as educators and researchers, institutions can contribute to securing a safer and more sustainable future against recognised threats such as climate change and global poverty.

Our choices now will influence whether current and future generations will live with a changed climate, depleted resources and without the open space and biodiversity, adversely affecting standard of living and quality of life. Higher education can help to promote new and sustainable ways of living, working, producing and travelling that will help achieve wider benefits to human health and wellbeing.

**Sustainable Development**

*"Our biggest challenge in this new century is to take an idea that seems abstract — sustainable development — and turn it ... into a daily reality for all the world's people."*

**Kofi Annan, United Nations Secretary-General, 2001**

*"Development must be sustainable not only ecologically, but socially and economically, too ... Governments, corporations, and individuals need to understand the links between these different kinds of sustainability."*

**Kofi Annan, United Nations Secretary-General, 2004**

Sustainable development is a difficult concept to define; it is also continually evolving, which makes it doubly difficult to define. One of the original descriptions of sustainable development is credited to the Brundtland Commission: "Sustainable development is development that meets the needs of the present without compromising the ability of future generations to meet their own needs" (World Commission on Environment and Development, 1987, p 43). Sustainable development is generally thought to have three components:

environment, society, and economy. The well-being of these three areas is intertwined and not separate. For example, a healthy, prosperous society relies on a healthy environment to provide food and resources, safe drinking water, and clean air for its citizens. Sustainable development may be also defined as "A vision of development that encompasses populations, animal and plant species, ecosystems, natural resources – water, air, energy – and that integrates concerns such as the fight against poverty, gender equality, human rights, education for all, health, human security, intercultural dialogue, etc". The sustainability paradigm rejects the contention that casualties in the environmental and social realms are inevitable and acceptable consequences of economic development. Thus, the authors/researchers consider sustainability to be a paradigm for thinking about a future in which environmental, societal, and economic considerations are balanced in the pursuit of development and improved quality of life.

## Principles of Sustainable Development

Many governments and individuals have pondered what sustainable development means beyond a simple one-sentence definition. The *Rio Declaration on Environment and Development* fleshes out the definition by listing 18 principles of sustainability.

- People are entitled to a healthy and productive life in harmony with nature.
- Development today must not undermine the development and environment needs of present and future generations.
- Nations have the sovereign right to exploit their own resources, but without causing environmental damage beyond their borders.
- Nations shall develop international laws to provide compensation for damage that activities under their control cause to areas beyond their borders.
- Nations shall use the precautionary approach to protect the environment. Where there are threats of serious or irreversible damage, scientific uncertainty shall not be used to postpone cost-effective measures to prevent environmental degradation.
- In order to achieve sustainable development, environmental protection shall constitute an integral part of the development

process, and cannot be considered in isolation from it. Eradicating poverty and reducing disparities in living standards in different parts of the world are essential to achieve sustainable development and meet the needs of the majority of people.

- Nations shall cooperate to conserve, protect and restore the health and integrity of the Earth's ecosystem. The developed countries need to acknowledge the responsibility that they bear in the international pursuit of sustainable development in view of the pressures their societies place on the global environment and of the technologies and financial resources they command.
- Nations should reduce and eliminate unsustainable patterns of production and consumption, and promote appropriate demographic policies.
- Environmental issues can best handled with the participation of all concerned citizens. Nations shall facilitate and encourage public awareness and participation by making environmental information widely available.
- Nations shall enact effective environmental laws, and develop national law regarding liability for the victims of pollution and other environmental damage. Where they have authority, nations shall assess the environmental impact of proposed activities that are likely to have a significant adverse impact.
- Nations should cooperate to promote an open international economic system that will lead to economic growth and sustainable development in all countries. Environmental policies should not be used as an unjustifiable means of restricting international trade.
- The polluter should, in principle must bear the cost of pollution.
- Nations shall warn one another of natural disasters or activities that may have harmful trans-boundary impacts.
- Sustainable development requires better scientific understanding of the problems. Nations should share knowledge and innovative technologies to achieve the goal of sustainability.
- The full participation of women is essential to achieve sustainable development. The creativity, ideals and courage

of youth and the knowledge of indigenous people are needed too. Nations should recognize and support the identity, culture and interests of indigenous people.

- Warfare is inherently destructive of sustainable development, and Nations shall respect international laws protecting the environment in times of armed conflict, and shall cooperate in their further establishment.
- Peace, development and environmental protection are interdependent and indivisible.

## Higher Education for Sustainable Development

More than three decades ago and in his assessment of the roles of higher education, the French professor of philosophy and the sixth Director-General of UNESCO, Rene Maheu (1974), lamented that the problem with higher education institutions is that they were not responding quickly enough and are not proactive to the changing context of the society and the globe. He suggested that it is necessary to regenerate higher education to cope with the changes affecting the society, and to do this, we have to transform higher education to the new needs of the community and the individuals economically, socially and culturally. His view was similarly echoed later by the President of the Club of Rome, Richard Diez-Hogcheitner (1996) who said that "Education must not only be adapted to the needs of our age, it must also make real effort to look ahead some twenty-five years".

From the time sustainable development was first endorsed at the UN General Assembly in 1987, the parallel concept of education to support sustainable development has also been explored. From 1987 to 1992, the concept of sustainable development matured as committees discussed, negotiated, and wrote the 40 chapters of *Agenda 21*. Initial thoughts concerning ESD were captured in Chapter 36 of *Agenda 21*, "Promoting Education, Public Awareness, and Training."

Unlike most education movements, ESD was initiated by people outside of the education community. In fact, one major push for ESD came from international political and economic forums (e.g., United Nations, Organization for Economic Co-operation and Development, Organization of American States). As the concept of sustainable development was discussed and formulated, it became apparent that education is a key to sustainability. In many countries, ESD is still being shaped by those outside the education community. The concepts and content of ESD in these cases are developed by ministries, such as those of environment and health, and then given to educators to deliver. Conceptual development independent of educator input is a problem recognized by international bodies as well as educators.

"Higher education institutions play a strategic role in finding solutions to today's leading challenges in the fields of health, science, education, renewable energies, water management, food security and the environment," said UNESCO's Director-General Koichiro Matsuura. Speakers at the opening ceremony of UNESCO World Conference on Higher Education-2009 highlighted the importance of education as a response to the global economic crisis and stressed equity, quality and international cooperation as critical challenges for all governments.

"President Obama sees higher education as critical to the administration's plans to revitalize the American economy and he has moved quickly to support students and their families," said Jill Biden, wife of US Vice-President Joe Biden and a community college teacher. President Danilo Turk of Slovenia urged that higher education be fully engaged in achieving the Millennium Development Goals, "the most ambitious objectives of our time" and fostering dialogue among civilizations. Prime Minister Nahas Angula of Namibia stressed that higher education should "put new techniques to work for the public good" and "develop new leaders who are guided in their decision-making by a moral compass rather than short-term gains."

Higher education is going through a 'veritable revolution,' said UNESCO's Director-General, outlining four dynamics that are transforming higher education. The first is accelerating demand, with an additional 51 million new students enrolled in tertiary education worldwide since 2000. The second is the diversification of providers, with private higher education now accounting for more than 30 per cent of enrolments worldwide. The third is the impact of information and communication technologies; the fourth is globalization that is "manifest in how we teach, learn, study, research and communicate."

In this context, he said, "we must strike a balance between cooperation and competition with a view to promoting excellence for the largest numbers."

## A Decade for Change (2005-2014)

United Nations General Assembly in 2002 declared 2005-2014 as the "Decade of Education for Sustainable Development" (DESD). UNESCO has the task of promoting the Decade, which aims to promote sustainable skills and behaviour, inspired by creative and critical ways of thinking, in order to encourage the resolution and management of problems that stand in the way of sustainable development.

**The four priority areas of action for the Decade of Education for Sustainable Development aim to:**

- **Promote basic education:** It will not be enough to reinforce literacy and numeracy to make significant progress in sustainable development. Efforts must also have impact on the content and methods of education and its adaptation to the cultural context. Basic education must also encourage and support people's involvement in community life and decision-making.
- **Reorient and revise education programs:** Programmes must be restructured from nursery school to university to include explicitly the study and comprehension of problems linked to the social, economic, environmental and cultural sustainability of our planet, emphasizing interdisciplinary approaches.
- **Develop public understanding and awareness**: While the concept of sustainable development is now familiar in institutional, academic and specialized milieus, it still needs to be spread at the grass-roots level. All sectors of society must be targeted, from business people to children in the most remote areas.
- **Provide practical training:** All trained, informed people can play an active role: this is a basic precept of sustainable development. Specific training must be provided not only through scientific and technological education, but also with

the help of partners in the world of work, particularly in business and industry.

**Strategic Perspectives to Inform Education and Learning for Sustainable Development**

| Socio-cultural perspectives | Environmental perspectives | Economic perspectives |
|---|---|---|
| o Human rights<br>o Peace and human security<br>o Gender equality<br>o Cultural diversity and intercultural understanding<br>o Health<br>o HIV/AID<br>o Governance | o Natural resources (water nergy, agriculture, biodiversity)<br>o Climate change<br>o Rural development<br>o Sustainable urbanization<br>o Disaster prevention and mitigation | o Poverty Reductiono<br>o Corporate responsibility & accountability<br>o Market economy |

To promote a more sustainable future, we need to change the system of our society. People must work together regardless of status and hierarchy to make their environment more sustainable by integrating sustainable operations, policy and practices. The starting point is to integrate sustainable development into the educational system so that future generations can be nurtured and imbued with the need to embrace ecological protection, conservation of resources and human development.

The emphasis here should be to recognise that the many crises facing the planet are interrelated and are elements of a single crisis of the whole. Therefore, it is important that all sectors of the society consult and actively participate in decisions relating to sustainable development. Looking back at the progress of the Rio Summit which was held more than one and half decade ago, or rather its failure to set in motion processes that would lead to genuine sustainable development, it is incumbent now for the education system, higher education in particular, to be actively involved and to take steps in the promotion and acculturation of sustainable development. Since education is a major vehicle for, and contributor to, national and global development as well as the well-being of the community, it is strategic and appropriate for it to become the conduit for this promotion and nurturing.

It has been argued that education enables people to develop the knowledge, values and skills to participate in decisions about the way we do things, individually and collectively, locally and globally, that will improve the quality of life now without damaging the planet of the future.

The Organisation for Economic Cooperation and Development (OECD, 2007:173-174) suggested that institutions of higher learning can contribute to sustainable development in the following ways:

- Generating human capital in the region through their learning and further education programmes in areas of sustainable development;
- Acting as a source of expertise through research, consultancy and demonstration;
- Playing a brokerage role in bringing together diverse regional actors and elements of capacity to the sustainability process;
- Demonstrating good practice through on-campus management and development activities, strategic planning, building design, waste minimisation and water and energy efficiency practice, responsible purchasing programmes and pursuing good citizen type initiatives like the "green campus" concept; and
- Offering recognition and reward incentive for staff to be involved in sustainable development leadership groups in the regional community.

This suggestion implies that one has to transform higher education according to the new needs of the community and the individuals both economically, socially and culturally. This transformation requires a re-examination on how we approach and plan education, especially at the tertiary level. We need to strategise higher education for the promotion of sustainable development and growth. To do that, we need to position higher education toward sustainability.

## Conclusion

Education is a major factor in developing the human capital to enable countries to compete successfully in the global economy. Higher education is of paramount importance for social and economic development. Institutions of higher education have the main responsibility for equipping individuals with advanced knowledge and skills required for positions of responsibility. They play a major role in improving the environment, preserving natural resources and making an economic and social impact. The recent economic crisis has highlighted societal commitment to education, underscored by the decision of some of the leading economic powers to spend massively on education as a sound investment for economic recovery and growth. It is the right time to think about quality and quantity of higher education. Eco-friendly ways of life style is good for healthy environment. It is necessary to inculcate eco-friendly mindset among students through education in general and higher education in particular. Education for sustainable development (ESD) is an approach to the whole curriculum and management of an institution viz., school, college, universities, organizations etc. It has its roots in environmental education and development education and it is not a new subject. Therefore, many of the building blocks of education for sustainable development are already present in most institutions. ESD is also helping pupils to develop knowledge, understanding, values and skills. It is necessary to give importance for skilled persons at the time of appointments at university level. Education can be a vital factor to bring radical changes for the wellbeing of human society.

**References**

1. Abhay Pethe, "*Some Essays on Higher Education in India*".
2. Government of India, University Grants Commission, New Delhi.
3. The Hindu, "*Higher Education in India*", 12th April, 2005.
4. Report of "*Organization for Economic Cooperation and Development*".
5. *UNESCO,* Education for Sustainability—from Rio to Johannesburg: Lessons Learnt from a Decade of Commitment, *2002.*
6. UNESCO World Conference on Higher Education-2009.
7. United Nationas, "*Rio Declaration on Environment and Development*", Rio de Janeiro, 3 to 14 June 1992,

# 9. Lifelong Learning For Sustainable Development

*"Study without thought is labour lost; thought without study is dangerous."*

**...Confucius (551 – 479 BC)**

*"Where the mind is without fear*
*And the head is held high*
*Where knowledge is free;*
*Where the world has not been broken up into fragments by narrow domestic walls;*
*Where words come out from the depth of truth;*
*Where tireless striving stretches its arms toward perfection;*
*Where the mind is led forward by Thee into ever widening thought and action;*
*Into that heaven of freedom*
*My Father let my country awake."*

**...Rabindranath Tagore (1861–1941)**

## Introduction

Globalization should lead to the promotion of shared understanding, values and cooperative actions on a transnational and trans-societal level. It would be a movement that recognizes and respects the diversity, variety and richness of local discourses, codes and practices, while developing viewpoints and the understanding that facilitates cooperation and coordination at a global and totally inclusive level. Learning for sustainable development is a process that continues lifelong and therefore takes place in a whole range of learning environments that may be formal, non-formal and informal in nature; the ultimate objective is 'a better future for all'. One of the challenges of lifelong learning for sustainable development is how to put global solidarity, rather than international competitiveness at the heart of learning. There have been a number of recent initiatives designed to foster dialogue between those working in the fields of lifelong learning and education for sustainable development.

## Lifelong learning

Literacy as a qualitative attribute of the population is one of the most important indicators of the socioeconomic and political development of a society. It is a major component of human resource development and is thus basic to any programme of social and economic progress.

Lifelong learning offers a more holistic perspective on the role of education in the life-cycle of an individual and affirms that learning is continuous and plays a critical role in enabling individuals to adapt to and deal with new challenges and changes in their lives and their surrounding environment. Lifelong learning, embracing all forms of educational and learning experiences, can help prepare individuals to engage in purposeful interaction with their own environment by developing their knowledge, skills and their critical thinking abilities. Implicit in the idea of lifelong learning is life-wide learning. While the former emphasizes the continuity of learning through the human life-cycle, the latter recognizes that people find it necessary to engage in multiple learning activities simultaneously through different modalities of learning and in varying settings. Lifelong learning is intended to develop individuals as active social agents – people who are able to act, reflect and respond appropriately to cultural, social and development challenges they face. Its connotations are thus contextually determined.

## Sustainable development

"Sustainable development is development that meets the needs of the present without compromising the ability of future generations to meet their own needs." Among higher education institutions, lifelong learning institutions are also plays a strategic role in finding solutions to today's leading challenges in the fields of health, science, education, renewable energies, water management, food security and the environment.

Sustainable development is a vision of development that encompasses populations, animal and plant species, ecosystems, natural resources and that integrates concerns such as the fight against poverty, gender equality, human rights, education for all, health, human security, intercultural dialogue, etc.

## Current Global Issues – Sustainable Development

At the turn of the new millennium, global issues have spurred most countries and governments to take stock of their human resources and infrastructure in order to respond to those issues. At the top of the list is the issue of climate change and its corollary impact on bio-capacity and environmental challenges, the breach on the global ecological footprint and the widening gap between developed and developing societies.

With regard to climate change, the concern is over global warming, the depletion of fish stocks and fossil fuel reserves and the irreversible loss of biodiversity. These were brought about by the depletion of the ozone layer in the atmosphere. It is said that climate change is due to the variation within the earth's climate which has impacted on glaciations, ocean variability and the climate as a whole. Climate change has also been affected by non-climate factors, such as greenhouse effects, plate tectonics, solar variations, orbital variations and volcanism. Human activities have also played a major role in climate change, including the high usage of fossil fuels and aerosols. This is compounded by poor planning and resource utilization in land use and livestock rearing. Through lifelong learning, it is possible to solve or minimize the global issues. Lifelong learning is a correct weapon to change the society towards human well-being.

## Lifelong Learning for Sustainable Development

Education for sustainable development aims to help people to develop the attitudes, skills and knowledge to make informed decisions for the benefit of themselves and others, now and in the future, and to act upon these decisions.

In December 2002, the General Assembly of the United Nations adopted the Decade of Education for Sustainable Development (2005-2014). UNESCO was designated as the lead agency for the promotion and coordination of the Decade. The overall goal of the DESD is to integrate the principles, values, and practices of sustainable development into all aspects of education and learning in order to encourage changes in behaviour that will create a more sustainable future in terms of environmental integrity, economic viability, and a just society for present and future generations.

Educators from South East Asia recently convened at the Legend Villas Hotel on 9th March, 2009 in Mandaluyong City of Manila for the 1st Regional Workshop for Lifelong Learning for Sustainable Development which aims to promote linkages and develop policies for lifelong learning and sustainable development. The event was organized by UNESCO Philippines, is in support of the United Nations declaration that the Year 2005-2014 is the Decade of Education for Sustainable Development (DESD).

## Statements of Lifelong Learning for Sustainable Development

- Lifelong learning for sustainable development should develop those competences that people require to develop appropriate technologies and sustainable livelihoods within the informal economy.
- Lifelong learning for sustainable development should develop those competencies that would improve the labour market for environmentally friendly technologies, and thus lifelong learning for sustainable developments relevance for employment.
- Lifelong learning for sustainable development should not develop pre-determined competences. Those that people require will only emerge as they address issues facing their community and learn alongside others.

- Lifelong learning for sustainable development should develop those competences that people require to resist the further dispossession and privatization of environmental knowledge and resources and work with others to realize environmental justice.
- Lifelong learning for sustainable development should develop those competences that people require to understand their relations with one another and the rest of nature and realize forms of citizenship that enable the continued co-evolution of human and non-human nature.

## Conclusion

Sustainable development stresses the need for action which recognizes that, global as well as local and national contexts impact upon our daily lives and are fundamentally inter-related. Risk, complexity and uncertainty are central challenges for individuals and communities in this globalised context. Lifelong learning has an important role to play in the development of the 'global skills' that will strengthen people's capacity to deal individually and collectively with the opportunities and challenges that are presented by globalization. Critical thinking skills and the capacity to evaluate and interpret political, scientific and media messages are particularly desirable. Global skills are not only practical, but also address questions of culture and values. While evidence points to growing awareness of issues associated with sustainable development, such as climate change. Lifelong learning has the potential to open up creative spaces in which people can explore their own values, behaviours and attitudes towards risk, uncertainty and change. At key transition points in the life course, such learning interventions may prove to be particularly powerful. However, behaviour change is needed not only at the individual but also at the societal level for all human well-being in the society. Lifelong learning is important for sustainable development in the present globalized world.

## References


1. Douglas Bourn. "*Global Perspectives and Education for Sustainable Development for Lifelong Learning*".
2. Kelly, K. "*New rules for the new economy*", Wired Magazine, September 1997.
3. Report of Expert Seminar on "*Sustainable Development*", United Kingdom, 31st July 2008.
4. Report of Regional Workshop for "*Lifelong Learning for Sustainable Development*", Manila, 9th March, 2008.
5. Report of United Nations on "*Education for Sustainable Development*".

# 10. Life Skills

## INTRODUCTION

In order to make a successful return to family, community, and workplace, individuals who leave correctional facilities need an array of skills. Most important, of course, are the basic skills-reading, writing and arithmetic-which are usually offered in adult education programs in correctional facilities. However, being literate alone does not ensure a successful transition to independent living and a job.

To get a job, a person must know how to write an application letter and resume, and how to prepare for and participate in a job interview. He or she must have job skills to offer. To keep a job, the person needs a number of social skills: he or she must know how to get along with peers, deal with supervisors and other authority figures, and provide timely, responsible, and consistent work performance. Additionally, providing for a family requires knowledge about budgeting, leases, credit, insurance, taxes, and other daily living areas, all of which used to be called survival skills. Personal relationships, parenting, health, and nutrition are a few examples of other types of skills required for the person to be an effective spouse, parent and officer etc. The other types of skills are called as life skills.

## DEFINITION OF LIFE SKILLS

Life skills are abilities for adaptive and positive behaviour, which enable individuals to deal effectively with the demands and challenges of everyday life. Described in this way, skills that can be said to be life skills are innumerable, and the nature and definition of life skills are likely to differ across cultures and settings. However, analysis of the life skills field suggests that there is a core set of skills that are at the heart of skills-based initiatives for the promotion of the health and well-being of children and adolescents.

UNICEF defines life skills as "a behaviour change or behaviour development approach designed to address a balance of three areas: knowledge, attitude and skills".

Life skills are essentially those abilities that help promote mental well-being and competence in young people as they face the realities of life. Most development professionals agrcc that life skills are generally applied in the context of health and social events. They can be utilized in many content areas: prevention of drug use, sexual violence, teenage pregnancy, HIV/AIDS prevention and suicide prevention. The definition extends into consumer education, environmental education, peace education or education for development, livelihood and income generation, among others. In short, life skills empower young people to take positive action to protect them and promote health and positive social relationships.

## TYPES OF LIFE SKILLS

There are different types of life skills in general. The most important top 10 life skills are given below:

1. **Decision making:** Decision making helps us to deal constructively with decisions about our lives. This can have consequences for health if young people actively make decisions about their actions in relation to health by assessing the different options, and what effects different decisions may have.
2. **Problem solving:** Problem solving enables us to deal constructively with problems in our lives. Significant problems that are left unresolved can cause mental stress and give rise to accompanying physical strain.
3. **Creative thinking:** Creative thinking contributes to both decision making and problem solving by enabling us to explore the available alternatives and various consequences of our

actions or non-action. It helps us to look beyond our direct experience, and even if no problem is identified, or no decision is to be made, creative thinking can help us to respond adaptively and with flexibility to the situations of our daily lives.

4. **Critical thinking:** Critical thinking is an ability to analyze information and experiences in an objective manner. Critical thinking can contribute to health by helping us to recognize and assess the factors that influence attitudes and behaviour, such as values, peer pressure, and the media.
5. **Effective communication:** Effective communication means that we are able to express ourselves, both verbally and non-verbally, in ways that are appropriate to our cultures and situations. This means being able to express opinions and desires, but also needs and fears. And it may mean being able to ask for advice and help in a time of need.
6. **Interpersonal relationship skills:** Interpersonal relationship skills help us to relate in positive ways with the people we interact with. This may mean being able to make and keep friendly relationships, which can be of great importance to our mental and social well-being. It may mean keeping good relations with family members, which are an important source of social support. It may also mean being able to end relationships constructively.
7. **Self-awareness:** Self-awareness includes our recognition of ourselves, of our character, of our strengths and weaknesses, desires and dislikes. Developing self-awareness can help us to recognize when we are stressed or feel under pressure. It is also often a prerequisite for effective communication and interpersonal relations, as well as for developing empathy for others.
8. **Empathy:** Empathy is the ability to imagine what life is like for another person, even in a situation that we may not be familiar with. Empathy can help us to understand and accept others who may be very different from ourselves, which can improve social interactions, for example, in situations of ethnic or cultural diversity. Empathy can also help to encourage nurturing behaviour towards people in need of care and

assistance, or tolerance, as is the case with AIDS sufferers, or people with mental disorders, who may be stigmatized and ostracized by the very people they depend upon for support.

9. **Coping with emotions:** Coping with emotions involves recognizing emotions in us and others, being aware of how emotions influence behaviour, and being able to respond to emotions appropriately. Intense emotions, like anger or sorrow can have negative effects on our health if we do not react appropriately.
10. **Coping with stress:** Coping with stress is about recognizing the sources of stress in our lives, recognizing how this affects us, and acting in ways that help to control our levels of stress. This may mean that we take action to reduce the sources of stress, for example, by making changes to our physical environment or lifestyle. Or it may mean learning how to relax, so that tensions created by unavoidable stress do not give rise to health problems.

## MAIN COMPONENTS OF LIFE SKILLS

World Health Organization (WHO) categorizes life skills into the following three components:

1. Critical thinking skills/Decision-making skills
2. Interpersonal communication skills
3. Coping and self-management skills

## IMPORTANCE OF LIFE SKILLS

Life skills are more important for all human beings. With life skills, one is able to explore alternatives, weigh pros and cons and make rational decisions in solving each problem or issue as it arises. It also entails being able to establish productive interpersonal relationships with others. Life skills enable effective communication, for example, being able to differentiate between hearing and listening and ensuring that messages are transmitted accurately to avoid miscommunication and misinterpretations.

## LIFE SKILLS & LIFELONG PLEDGE

The following life skills are important for all human being for healthy and wealthy life. It is our duty to follow these skills for happy life.

| S. No. | Type of Skill | General Meaning |
|---|---|---|
| 1 | Integrity | To be honest and sincere and do the right thing |
| 2 | Initiative | To do something because it needs to be done |
| 3 | Flexibility | The ability to alter plans when necessary |
| 4 | Perseverance | To stay with something until it is complete |
| 5 | Organized | To plan, arrange, keep things together |
| 6 | Caring | To feel concern for others |
| 7 | Friendship | To make and keep a friend |
| 8 | Common Sense | To use good judgment |
| 9 | Problem Solving | To seek solutions in difficult situations |
| 10 | Responsibility | To be accountable for your actions |
| 11 | Patience | To wait calmly for someone or something |
| 12 | Effort | To try your hardest |
| 13 | Curiosity | A desire to learn or know about things |
| 14 | Cooperation | To work together toward a common goal |
| 15 | Sense of Humor | To laugh and be playful without hurting others |
| 16 | Courage | To act according to one's beliefs |
| 17 | Pride | To be proud of oneself and what you can do |

## CONCLUSIONS

Life skills are problem solving behaviors used appropriately and responsibly in the management of personal affairs. They are a set of human skills acquired via teaching or direct experience that are used to handle problems and questions commonly encountered in daily human life. The subject varies greatly depending on societal norms and community expectations. So, it is the duty of teachers and parents to inculcate life skills in the students and children for their better life. Life skills are important for all types of persons in the society for their all-round development in the technological world.

## REFERENCES

1. Padmini Nagesh Pai (2006). 'life Skills Education for School Effectiveness and Improvement', Round Table Presentation at International Congress for School Effectiveness and Improvement(3rd to 6th January 2006), Fort Lauderdale- Florida – U.S.A
2. Peace Corps (2001).'Life Skills Manual', Information Collection and Exchange Publication No. M0063.

# 11. Soft Skills

## INTRODUCTION

Soft skills is a sociological term relating to a person's "EQ" (Emotional Intelligence Quotient), the cluster of personality traits, social graces, communication, language, personal habits, friendliness, and optimism that characterize relationships with other people. Soft skills complement hard skills (part of a person's IQ), which are the occupational requirements of a job and many other activities.

A person's soft skill EQ is an important part of their individual contribution to the success of an organization. Particularly those organizations dealing with customers face-to-face are generally more successful, if they train their staff to use these skills. Screening or training for personal habits or traits such as dependability and conscientiousness can yield significant return on investment for an organization. For this reason, soft skills are increasingly sought out by employers in addition to standard qualifications.

It has been suggested that in a number of professions soft skills may be more important over the long term than occupational skills. The legal profession is one example where the ability to deal with people effectively and politely, more than their mere occupational skills, can determine the professional success of a lawyer.

Increasingly, over the last two decades, it has been recognized that when IT Professionals acquire soft skills, better relationships are built between IT and the other business units within the enterprise, fostering *alignment*. A key element of IT Professionals building these relationships is their ability to communicate, it has been suggested that communication is a measurable and improvable type of intelligence, "CQ" (Communication Quotient).

Soft Skills are *behavioral* competencies. Also known as *Interpersonal Skills,* or *people skills,* they include proficiencies such as communication skills, conflict resolution and negotiation, personal effectiveness, creative problem solving, strategic thinking, team building, influencing skills and selling skills, to name a few.

## DEFINITION OF SOFT SKILLS

- Soft Skills – Personality attributes that enhance a person's job performance (Oxford English Dictionary).
- Set of skills that influence how we interact with each other. It includes such abilities as effective communication, creativity analytical thinking, diplomacy flexibility change readiness and problem solving, leadership, team building and listening skills. The goal of soft skill training is to give the personnel an opportunity to learn and practice new patterns of behavior and in doing so to enhance human relations.
- The skills, traits, work habits, and attitudes that all workers across all occupations must have in order to obtain, maintain, and progress in employment. These include being dependable, responsible, punctual, adaptable, hones, honorable, well-mannered, positive toward work, and appropriately dressed/groomed. Soft skills also refer to such attributes as ability to get along with others, work in teams, attend to tasks, work independently, and provide excellent customer service, both within the company and externally.
- Non-technical skills, such as the ability to communicate, problem-solve, empathize, be courteous, etc. Long assumed that these employee skills are naturally occurring, businesses are only now coming to the realization that their employees lack the soft skills to deal with others.
- Skills needed to perform jobs where job requirements are defined in terms of expected outcomes, but the process to achieve the outcomes may vary widely. Usually, an area of performance that

does not have a definite beginning and end (i.e., counseling, supervising, and managing).

- Communication and interpersonal skills those are behavioral and abstract in nature, but nevertheless essential to performing most jobs.
- Business term for non-technical/non-IT related business skills such as communication, negotiation, time management, team building etc.

## IMPORTANCE OF SOFT SKILLS

Soft skills play a vital role for professional success; they help one to excel in the workplace and their importance cannot be denied in this age of information and knowledge. Good soft skills — which are in fact scarce — in the highly competitive corporate world, will help you stand out in a milieu of routine job seekers with mediocre skills and talent.

Positive thinking brings inner peace, success, improved relationships, better health, happiness and satisfaction. It also helps the daily affairs of life move more smoothly, and makes life look bright and promising.

In order to make positive thinking yield results, you need to develop a positive attitude toward life, expect a successful outcome of whatever you do, but also take any necessary actions to ensure your success.

Effective positive thinking that brings results is much more than just repeating a few positive words, or telling you that everything is going to be all right. It has to be your predominant mental attitude. It is not enough to think positively for a few moments, and then letting fears and lack of belief enter your mind. Some effort and inner work are necessary.

Are you willing to make a real inner change? Are you willing to change the way you think? Are you willing to develop a mental power that can positively affect you, your environment and the people around you?

Here are a few actions and tips to help you develop the power of positive thinking:

- Always use only positive words while thinking and while talking. Use words such as, 'I can', 'I am able', 'it is possible', 'it can be done', etc.
- Allow into your awareness only feelings of happiness, strength, self improvement and success.
- Try to disregard and ignore negative thoughts. Refuse to think such thoughts, and substitute them with constructive happy thoughts.
- In your conversation use words that evoke feelings and mental images of strength, happiness, satisfaction, dominating outlook and success.
- Read at least one page of inspiring book every day.
- Watch movies that make you feel happy.
- Associate yourself with people who think positively.
- Walk, swim or engage in some other physical activity. This helps to develop a more positive attitude.
- Think positive and expect only favorable results and situations, even if your current circumstances are not as you wish them to be. In time, your mental attitude will affect your life and circumstances and change them accordingly.

## TOP 60 SOFT SKILLS

The Workforce Profile defined about 60 "soft skills", which employers seek. They are applicable to any field of work, according to the study, and are the "personal traits and skills that employers state are the most important when selecting employees for jobs of any type."

1. Math.
2. Safety.
3. Courtesy.
4. Honesty.
5. Grammar.
6. Reliability.
7. Flexibility.
8. Team skills.
9. Eye contact.
10. Cooperation.

11. Adaptability.
12. Follow rules.
13. Self-directed.
14. Good attitude.
15. Writing skills.
16. Driver's license.
17. Dependability.
18. Advanced math.
19. Self-supervising.
20. Good references.
21. Being drug free.
22. Good attendance.
23. Personal energy.
24. Work experience.
25. Ability to measure.
26. Personal integrity.
27. Good work history.
28. Positive work ethic.
29. Interpersonal skills.
30. Motivational skills.
31. Valuing education.
32. Personal chemistry.
33. Willingness to learn.
34. Common sense.
35. Critical thinking skills.
36. Knowledge of fractions.
37. Reporting to work on time.
38. Use of rulers and calculators.
39. Good personal appearance.
40. Wanting to do a good job.
41. Basic spelling and grammar.
42. Reading and comprehension.
43. Ability to follow regulations.
44. Willingness to be accountable.
45. Ability to fill out a job application.
46. Ability to make production quotas.
47. Basic manufacturing skills training.
48. Awareness of how business works.

49. Staying on the job until it is finished.
50. Ability to read and follow instructions.
51. Willingness to work second and third shifts.
52. Caring about seeing the company succeed.
53. Understanding what the world is all about.
54. Ability to listen and document what you have heard.
55. Commitment to continued training and learning.
56. Willingness to take instruction and responsibility.
57. Ability to relate to coworkers in a close environment.
58. Not expecting to become a supervisor in the first six months.
59. Willingness to be a good worker and go beyond the traditional eight-hour day.
60. Communication skills with public, fellow employees, supervisors, and customers.

**CONCLUSIONS**

Soft skills create opportunity for the personnel in the advancement of the career. The personnel with soft skills are more empowered than others and create opportunities for themselves. Soft skills not only improve academicians' career but they also offer personal growth.

Soft skills are vital as they help to grow beyond money motivation. They help in the development of professional ethics which for academicians career. An academician who has soft skills will show better performance, have more satisfaction and better quality of his working life. Presence of soft skills will have a direct impact on organizational total quality management, institutional effectiveness and innovation synergies.

# 12. Communication Skills

The essential ingredient in a dynamic society is communication. Indeed a society is people in communication. In an enlightened society the people are in touch with each other and are freely communicating important ideas.

Everyone has some thoughts, ideas, feelings etc., which he wants to share with others. This he does through gestures or language or some other means. Basically this process of sharing thoughts, ideas, feelings etc., with other, is called communication. The need for communication arises because man lives with his fellow beings. If he lives alone there is no necessity for communication. Even animals communicate with one another through gestures, cries etc.

Communication is the sharing of the ideas and feelings in a mood of mutuality. Communication involves interaction – "the give-and-take" – that provides feedback to persons involved in exchanging ideas. John Deway emphasizes shared experiences as a key element in communication. In his book, "Democracy and Education", he notes that communication is a process of sharing experience till it becomes a common possession. It modifies the disposition of both the parties who partake in it. Wilburn Schramm of Stanford University says..."Communication research is concerned with all the ways in which information and ideas are exchanged and shared.

Everyday we are facing with the problem of communication, whether it is in our classroom or outside. We are confronted with many difficulties while communicating ideas. The main difficulty is that many times the people to whom we communicate our ideas do not catch them properly. Sometimes they miss our point entirely.

Normally we use word spoken or written, to communicate our ideas. The person who wants to communicate has got a mental picture of the ideas to be communicated. He then translates that mental picture into verbal picture. Very often this translation itself does not take place effectively. So much as only part of that mental picture is translated into verbal picture. Another person listens to these words and imagines a mental picture of the ideas communicated by these words. The words he listens not convey the same meaning to him which the person who uses those words puts into them. The same word may give different meaning to different persons, each depending upon the experiences of those persons had with those words. That is why Edgar Dale points out, "When we read a book, we do not take meaning out of the printed page, but put meaning into the printed page".

## DEFINITION OF COMMUNICATION

The word "Communication" has been derived from the Latin Word "Communis" meaning common. Hence communication is having common experiences with people. The word communication means a wide variety of things to different people. The following are some of the widely accepted definitions for communication.

- Communication means sharing of ideas and feelings in a mood of mutuality.
- Communication is a process of sharing of experiences till it becomes a common possession.
- Communication involves interaction which encourages give and take. This provides feedback to persons involved in exchanging ideas.
- Effective communication is a two-way process, including feedback and interaction.

Thus, in short, communication is:

a) Passing of information;
b) Exchange of ideas; and
c) Sharing ideas with one another.

## OBJECTIVES OF COMMUNICATION

The objectives of communication are to motivate, inform suggest, warn, order, to change behaviour, establish better relations with other to make learning meaningful and understood.

It is rather difficult if not increasingly impossible to provide children with actual first-hand experiences as the world becomes increasingly complex. Obviously, some substitute experience must be evolved and used to enable children to understand and conceptualise their world. This is the essence of communication as an integral part of teaching.

A communicator is effective when he is competent, sincere and dynamic. The message that the communicator wants to communicate is communicated when it is acknowledged, understood, reacted, responded and shaped into learning behaviour.

## FORMS OF COMMUNICATION

These may be written, spoken, signs, gestures, actions or silence.

## COMPONENTS OF COMMUNICATION

Communication Involves Three Components:

1. Verbal Messages - the words we choose
2. Para verbal Messages - how we say the words
3. Nonverbal Messages - our body language

## COMMUNICATION SKILLS

Communication skills are skills that facilitate people to communicate effectively with one another. Effectual communication engages the choice of the best communications channel, the technical know-how to use the channel, the presentation of information to the target audience, and the skill to understand responses received from others. Self development, interpersonal skills, mutual understanding, mutual cooperation and trust is also important to set a complete channel of most effective and winning communication skills.

There are mainly three types of communication skills, expressive skills, listening skills and skills for managing the overall process of communication. The basic fundamental of all these types of communication is emotional skills.

Expressive skills are required to convey message to others through words, facial expressions and body language. Listening skills are skills that are used to obtain messages or information from others. These help to clearly understand what a person feels and thinks about you or understand the other person closely. Skills for managing the overall process of communication help to recognize the required information and develop a strong hold on the existing rules of communication and interaction.

## IMPORTANCE OF COMMUNICATION SKILLS

*"We all use language to communicate, to express ourselves, to get our ideas across, and to connect with the person to whom we are speaking. When a relationship is working, the act of communicating seems to flow relatively effortlessly. When a relationship is deteriorating, the act of communicating can be as frustrating as climbing a hill of sand."* -

**Chip Rose (attorney and mediator)**

The importance of communication skills cannot be overemphasized. Whether it's written or verbal, the ability to communicate a message accurately is extremely important. Whether or not the receiver understands what was intended by the speaker will have an effect not only on the conversation but also the relationship. Individuals that have mastered the art of communicating are often able to develop deeper, more meaningful relationships on a personal level. Professionally, they are able to communicate more effectively with both their colleagues and clients.

The modern world today, calls for high scale effective communication skills in order to win the heavy competition in all spheres of life. For effective communication, a sender transmits his or her message in a clear and organized form to maintain and promote the need and interest of the receivers. Receivers or listeners show interest only if the person communicating is loaded with confidence, gestures and softness. Apart from management professionals, good communication skills are also required at all stages of life.

## LIST OF COMMUNICATION SKILLS

The ability to communicate effectively is a trick learnt by many, but practiced perfectly by not too many. This is because for most communicating is simple process. However, it is not so, it a rather simple-complex-networking system that has varied undercurrents flowing between the speaker and listener/s.

Given here is an interesting list of communication skills that one should be aware of in order to better their ability to convey their valuable messages...

- Taking responsibility for one's messages
- Claiming ownership for one's messages
- Preparing to listen
- Encouraging the speaker to speak more
- Reflecting on what the speaker has to say
- Adapting to difference of opinions
- Being open minded
- Acknowledging differences
- Assessing without being judgmental
- Accepting feedback
- Being assertive
- Ability to share one's thoughts
- Sharing one's feelings
- Conveying to others a message without commanding or dictating terms
- Being aware of the information coming in
- Maintaining a communication wheel of conclusions, sense data, emotions, impact and desire
- Calm repetition to drive in a message
- Addressing people by their name
- Ability to explain a concept differently so that all those present understand it at their level
- Ability to resolve conflicts so that it is a win-win for all
- Ability to be concise and clear
- Ability to convey thoughts in a focused and concrete manner
- Ability to confront a situation when faced with reputation crises using techniques of reputation management
- Ability to convey with and empathetic statement

- Ability to explain objectively without evaluating
- Ability to provide specific details supported by concrete examples
- Ability to monitor emotional reactions and filter out irrational thoughts
- Ability to project oneself into the audience's point of view

# 13. Employability Skills

## EMPLOYABILITY SKILLS

Employability skills are technical and non-technical skills and competencies which have always been an important part of an individual's effective and successful participation in the workplace. Their explicit inclusion in Training Packages represents the progression of competency based training into a system which develops the full range of transferable skills, attitudes and behaviour required for successful participation in the workplace.

Employability skills have been developed from a business and industry need for a broader range of skills beyond the Mayer Key Competencies that were developed in 1992. The 2002 report, *Employability Skills for the Future*, published by the Business Council of Australia and the Australian Chamber of Commerce and Industry, outlined an 'Employability Skills Framework' which identifies eight employability skills. They are:

9) Communication
10) Teamwork
11) Problem solving
12) Initiative and Enterprise
13) Planning and Organizing
14) Self-management
15) Learning
16) Technology

## TOP TEN SKILLS THAT EMPLOYERS WANT

Based on a number of surveys on the skills required by graduates undertaken by Microsoft, Target Jobs, the BBC, Prospects, NACE and AGR and other organisations, here is summary of the skills which were most often deemed important.

| S. No. | SKILL | |
|---|---|---|
| 1 | Verbal Communication | Able to express your ideas clearly and confidently in speech |
| 2 | Teamwork | Work confidently within a group |
| 3 | Commercial Awareness | Understand the commercial realities affecting the organisation. |
| 4 | Analysing & Investigating | Gather information systematically to establish facts & principles. Problem solving. |
| 5 | Initiative/Self Motivation | Able to act on initiative, identify opportunities & proactive in putting forward ideas & solutions |
| 6 | Drive | Determination to get things done. Make things happen & constantly looking for better ways of doing things. |
| 7 | Written Communication | Able to express yourself clearly in writing |
| 8 | Planning & Organising | Able to plan activities & carry them through effectively |
| 9 | Flexibility | Adapt successfully to changing situations & environments |
| 10 | Time Management | Manage time effectively, prioritising tasks and able to work to deadlines. |

### OTHER IMPORTANT SKILLS

| S. No. | SKILL | |
|---|---|---|
| 1 | Global Skills | Able to speak and understand other languages. Appreciation of other cultures. See · Study and work placements outside the UK· Working Abroad |
| 2 | Negotiating & Persuading | Able to influence and convince others, to discuss and reach agreement. |
| 3 | Leadership | Able to motivate and direct others |
| 4 | Numeracy | Multiply & divide accurately, calculate percentages, use statistics & a calculator, interpret graphs & tables. |
| 5 | Computing Skills | Word-processing, using databases, spreadsheets, the Internet & email, designing web pages etc. |
| 6 | Self Awareness | Awareness of achievements, abilities, values & weaknesses & what you want out of life. |
| 7 | Personal Impact/ Confidence | Presents a strong, professional, positive image to others which inspires confidence & commands respect. |
| 8 | Lifelong Learning | Continues to learn throughout life. Develops the competencies needed for current & future roles |
| 9 | Stress Tolerance | Maintains effective performance under pressure |
| 10 | Integrity | Adheres to standards & procedures, maintains con- |

| | | |
|---|---|---|
| | | fidentiality and questions inappropriate behaviour. |
| 11 | Independence | Accepts responsibility for views & actions and able to work under their own direction & initiative. |
| 12 | Developing Professionalism | Pays care & attention to quality in all their work. Supports & empowers others. |
| 13 | Action Planning | Able to decide what steps are needed to achieve particular goals and then implement these. |
| 14 | Decision-Making | Determines the best course of action. Evaluates options based on logic & fact & presents solutions |
| 15 | Interpersonal Sensitivity | Recognises & respects different perspectives. Open to the ideas & views of others |
| 16 | Creativity | Generates & applying new ideas & solutions |

## NEED OF EMPLOYABILITY SKILLS

Graduate youth come out of college, polished in academic skills. But as we all know working for a Corporate is a different ball game altogether. While their academic skills definitely count, various other skills such as spoken and written English, interpersonal skills, the art of communication, situational behavior, and so on play a pivotal role in helping the student or candidate fit into the workplace. Lack of these skills may hamper the candidate's prospects at the interview stage itself. So a powerful program that aims to impart these skills in a candidate, implemented while the student is pursuing his graduation should make him/her completely employable by the time he is out of college and into the job hunt.

## PROGRAMME FOR INDIAN YOUTH

Skill Bridge is a program that aims at making Indian youth employable. The skills imparted through Skill Bridge will make them confident, and help them face the corporate with more than just an academic degree. The Skill Bridge curriculum covers written and spoken English, business communication, resume writing and interview skills, pronunciation, etiquette, leadership skills and more, making it a comprehensive training on employable skills.

## HOW TO IMPROVE EMPLOYABILITY SKILLS?

The job market is getting competitive, especially since there is a decline in jobs. The small percentages of jobs that are available are given to anyone who shows exceptional employability skills. You, too, can be a part of that small percentage. There are many resources available to anyone who would like to increase their chances of being employed.

## EMPLOYABILITY SKILLS FRAMEWORK

| Communication | Teamwork | Problem Solving | Initiative and Enterprise | Planning and Organising | Self-management | learning | Technology |
|---|---|---|---|---|---|---|---|
| Listening and understanding | Working an individual and a team member | Developing practical situations | Adapting to new situations -including changing work conditions | Managing time and priorities | Evaluating and monitoring own Performance | Using range of mediums to learn | Having a range of basic IT skills |
| Speaking clearly and directly | Applying teamwork a range of situations | Solving problem in teams | Indentifying opportunities not obvious to others | Collecting, analyzing and organizing information | Taking responsibility | Applying learning to technical issues and operations | Having the OHS knowledge to apply technology |
| Reading and interpreting documentation | Working with people of different ages, genders, races, religions or political Persuations | Showing independence and initiative in identifying problems and solving them | Being creative | Indentifying contingency situations | Having knowledge and confidence in cwn vision and goals | Being open to new ideas and change | Having appropriate physical capacity |
| Using numeracy effectively | Coaching, mentoring and giving feedback | Resolving customer concems in relations to complex projectissues | Generating a range of options | Implementing contingency Plans | Articulating ownideas and vision | Contributin g to the learning Community at the workplace | Operating equipment |
| Sharing information | knowing how to define a role as part of a team | Using mathematics, including budgeting and financial management. to solve problems | Translating ideas into action | Being resourcefull | | | Using IT to organize data |
| Being assertive | Identifying the strengths of team members | Testing assumptions, taking the context of data and circumstances into account | | Allocating resource allocations to cope with contingencies | | | Applying IT as a management tool |

## EMPLOYABILITY SKILLS FRAMEWORK (Continued)

| Communication | Teamwork Solving | Problem Enterprise | Initiative and Organising | Planning and management | Self- | learning | Technology |
|---|---|---|---|---|---|---|---|
| Writing to the needs of the audience | | | | Adapting resource allocations to cope with contingencies | | | |
| Empathizing | | | | Participating in continuous improvement and planning processes | | | |
| Negotiating responsively | | | | Planning the use of resources including time management | | | |
| Persuading effectively | | | | Developing a vision and a proactive plan to accompany it | | | |
| Establishing and using networks | | | | | | | |

- Enroll in a career center that offers skills to improve employability. Career centers offer career advice and classes that teach skills that are needed to be successful in the job market. The skills will also help to lead each individual down the right career path.
- Search the Internet for useful information and tips to help improve employability skills. There are many great resources online for free. Online courses are also available.
- Go to the library and choose books that cover the different types of marketable skills. Reading as much information as possible will help to improve the skills that are needed for employment success.
- Read business literature with the most updated information of the types of skills that employers are looking for. The more skills a person has, the greater possibility of his being hired.
- Search for popular interview questions. Go in front of a mirror and practice the questions and answers until you feel confident. The other option is to have someone pretend to be the interviewer.
- Take a typing course to improve your typing speed. Many jobs require some typing skills. Improving typing skills can increase productivity on the job.

# 14. Personality

Contrary to what you may think, you can improve your personality. Until quite recently it was believed that personality is permanent. In 1890 William James, the famous Harvard psychologist, wrote in his influential work The Principles of Psychology, that personality was "set in plaster" by early adulthood. This view prevailed for over a century; however, the idea that personality is more fluid has gained ground over time. We are now at the point where we realize that we have influence and control over which traits and characteristics we want to develop or refine.

**PERSONALITY**

- The "personality" is the typical pattern of thinking, feeling, and behaviors that make a person unique.
- When we say that someone has a "good personality" we mean that they are likeable, interesting and pleasant to be with.
- Everyone wants to be attractive to others. To that end, having a good personality is vital - probably even more so than good looks. In fact, approximately 85 percent of your success and happiness will be a result of how well you interact with others. Ultimately, it is your personality that determines whether people are attracted to, or shy away from you.

- While we can only enhance our looks to a certain extent, we have the ability to improve the personality as much as we want. We can develop or integrate any trait we deem fitting and agreeable.

Here are some ways we can accomplish this:

### 1. Be a better listener

Jacqueline Kennedy Onassis was considered one of the most charming women in the world because she cultivated the skill of being an exceptional listener. She was known for the way she would look a person in the eyes, hang on their every word, and make them feel important. There is nothing more appealing than having someone listen to you intently making you feel like you're the only person in the world.

### 2. Read more and expand your interests

The more you read and cultivate new interests, the more interesting you are to others. When you meet new people it gives you the opportunity to share what you know and to exchange your views with them.

### 3. Be a good conversationalist

This relates to how much you read and know. Once you have much to contribute, learn how to talk about it with others. No one can read about or know everything, so it's refreshing to learn from others those things we don't have the time to about read ourselves. If you happen to be shy, join a group like Toastmasters that encourages you to talk about what you know.

Enjoy the article on The Art of Conversation!

### 4. Have an Opinion

There is nothing more tiresome than trying to talk to someone who has no opinion on anything. A conversation has nowhere to go if you have nothing to expound on. If, however, you have an uncommon point of view or differing opinion, you are more interesting and stimulating to be with socially (unless you're a know-it-all, of course). A unique outlook expands everyone's perspective.

**5. Meet New People**

Make the effort to meet new people especially those unlike you. It not only exposes you to different cultures and alternative ways of doing things, it broadens your horizons.

**6. Be yourself**

The next most tiresome thing after having no opinions is trying to be something you're not. Molding yourself in order to fit in, or be accepted, usually backfires. Since each of us is unique, expressing that uniqueness is what makes us interesting. Attempting to be a carbon copy of someone else not only falls flat, but reveals a lack of authenticity.

**7. Have a positive outlook and attitude**

Who wants to be around people, who are negative, complain a lot, or have nothing good to say? In fact, most of us run when we see them coming. Instead, be the kind of upbeat person who lights up a room with your energy when you enter it. Do it by looking for the best in people and things. Smile warmly, spread good cheer, and enliven others with your presence.

**8. Be fun and see the humorous side of life**

Everyone enjoys the company of someone who makes them laugh, or smile, so look for the humorous, quirky side in a situation - there always is one. Comic relief is a much welcome and needed diversion at times. When you can add fun and lightheartedness to an otherwise dull or gloomy setting, others will naturally be attracted to you, not to mention grateful.

**9. Be supportive of others**

Being supportive is probably the most endearing quality you can integrate into your personality. Just as you yourself welcome it, be the support for others when they need it. We all love a cheerleader in our corner; someone who is encouraging believes in us and helps pick us up when we're down.

**10. Have Integrity and treat people with respect**

Being honest and true to your word will bring you the admiration, respect and gratitude of others. Nothing improves a person's personality more than integrity and respect - respect for others, as well as respect for yourself.

We humans have the power and ability to shape our personalities however we wish. When we develop ourselves to be all that we can be, we contribute to our own, as well as the happiness of others.

# 15. Moral Values in Ramayana

## INTRODUCTION

Since time immemorial the RAMAYAN has been accorded the undisputed status of one of the greatest epics ever. The epic is a virtual encyclopedia encompassing within its pages, our ancient history, culture, geography and philosophy. Ramayana offers valuable guidance in all the aspects of life. The story of Sri Ram has touched millions of hearts in the nook and corner of the globe.

The relevance of Ramayana as an epic of the great human and moral value is confined not only to India but to the entire universe. Ramayana is the saga of Lord Sri Ramchandra's life. His reign is known as Ram Rajya. Ram Rajya means the establishment of an ideal state where contentment, peace and prosperity reign, where there is no strife and bloodshed, where people live in amity and fraternity, cooperating with one another and helping each other. It is a state where there is no want, where people's basic needs of food, clothing and shelter are met and everyone lives happily.

## VALMIKI RAMAYANA

Valmiki Ramayana contains 24,000 verses which have been grouped into 500 Chapters and that again into seven Kandas or sections, viz., Bala, Ayodhya, Aranya, Kishkindha, Sundara, Yuddha and the Uttara Kandas. It contains genuine classical Sanskrit poetry. Rama's young sons, Kusa and Lava, were the first reciters to the world, who sang to music this reputed work. They came in the garb of ascetics from the hermitage of their teacher Valmiki, and sang the wonderful poem in the presence of their father Rama and other heroes of the story.

The *Ramayana* of Valmiki is perhaps the most ancient and glorious epic in the world. It is known as the Adikavyam,—the first poem. *Ramayana* exercises a great moulding power on the life of man. It contains object lessons for husbands and wives, parents and children, brothers and sisters, friends and enemies.

Valmiki once asked Narada, "O Venerable Rishi! Please tell me whether there is a perfect man in this world who is at once virtuous, brave, dutiful, truthful, noble, steadfast in duty, and kind to all beings".

Narada replied, "There is such a one, a prince of Ikshvaku's line named Rama. He is virtuous, brave, gentle, and wise. He is a great hero. He loves his subjects immensely. He is a protector of Dharma. He is firm and steadfast. He is just and liberal. He is well-versed in the Vedas and in the science of arms. He is unique in the possession of virtues and matchless in beauty. He is an obedient son, a kind brother, loving husband, a faithful friend, an ideal king, a merciful enemy, and a lover of all living beings. All people adore him".

The *Ramayana* is a marvelous and it contains the essence of all Vedas and all sacred scriptures. It is a treasure for man. It is a reservoir which contains the nectar of Immortality. It delineates the character of a son who kicks off the throne and the pleasures of the senses and the world to fulfil the words of his father and lives in the forest for a period of fourteen years. It depicts the character of a father who sends even his most beloved son in exile in order to keep up his word. It delineates the character of an ideal, chaste wife who is devoted to her husband till the end of her life, shares his adversities, and serves him untiringly in the forest, and who also regards her husband as God. Above all, it also points out the character of a brother, who places brotherly affection above everything else in this world and follows his brother in the forest leaving all pleasures of the palace and leading the way to ward off all dangers. The description of nature in *Ramayana* is most sublime and beautiful. Poetry and morality are charmingly united. There is loftiness of moral tone. The *Ramayana* has a historical basis. It is not a mere allegoric poem. It is a marvelous inspiring story for all times, that has loomed large for centuries over the destinies of millions of people and will certainly continue to do so for ages to come.

Modern society needs to follow the *dharma* that is contained in the epic *Ramayana*. The *Ramayana* teaches the importance of moral values. Today we are facing many problems viz., poverty, illiteracy, alcoholism, terrorism and corruption. Corruption is rampant in all fields such as business, education, and politics. Under these circumstances, the principles of the *Ramayana* are very important to solve all these problems. In the present paper an attempt has been made to observe the moral values in Ramayana for healthy and wealthy lives of all human beings.

## IMPORTANT MORAL VALUES IN RAMAYANA

The following few MORAL VALUES are identified in Ramayana:

- Self-independent
- Self-respect
- cleanness
- Proficient
- Brave
- Good character
- Single thought, deed and word
- Pure behaviour
- Chastity
- Pure heart
- Punishing innocent is sin
- Give Respect to Gurus, Elders and Parents
- Ideal character
- Righteousness
- Ultimate truth, Supreme Truth (Brahmajnana)
- Sthitha prajna (Oneness of the Absolute)
- Place and time is important to act
- To change oneself with time.....that alone is wisdom
- Ardent devotee, Endless devotion, Endless service (Hanuma)
- Praiseworthy (Bharat devotion, Sugriv friendship)

## KUSA, LAVA – MORAL VALUES

- Immature talks are not good
- Don't waste time
- Anger and pride are the qualities of failure
- Don't underestimate to kids
- 1) A scorpion is very small, but can even kill a camel with its poison.
- 2) A small ant can defeat an elephant.
- 3) A small mantra can bring God under our control.
- Brave men never attack secretly
- Using mantras and charms is not right for brave men
- Only a truly brave man himself can respect another
- Kshtriya duty is ready to take the challenge
- Kshtriya duty is fighting with weapons

## VALMIKI – MORAL VALUES

- The first and greatest Guru is the Mother.
- Be brave, be unique men.
- Keep practicing you knowledge.
- Keep practicing Yoga. So that you stay healthy. So that your mind and body becomes strong.
- You will grain the trust of the world, first trust in yourself.
- The world worships the brave. The power sleeping within you awaken them.
- A king is responsible for protecting Women, the old and children. Even though they are wrongdoers, a key does not punish them.
- Picking weapons against king is against principle
- A tree bears fruits for others. A river flows for others. A cow gives milk for others. So make your body live for others.
- A complete Guru's complete knowledge.

## SITA-MORAL VALUES

- Environmental value- *Vruksho rakshathi rakshitah.*
- Sita teaches her children about tree. It is a friend of man and many such beings. We are children of earth. Trees are children of earth. When it bears fruit, it does not eat it. It gives it to

others to eat. It purifies air. It gives birds and insects a place to stay. So we must salute a tree.

- A woman is truly recognized when she does all her housework by herself. Then even if she is Goddess.
- Those who are really brave do not praise themselves.
- You must not be afraid of other beings, nor scare them.
- When we love everyone; everyone will love us
- All are children of the earth. We all have to live here with love.

## SUNETRA – MORAL VALUES

Sunetra advising to her four daughters (Sita, Urmila, Mandavi and Srutakirti) how to behave in your in-law's how and them...your father has given you so much... all the world is filled by its splendor. But I can only give you precepts of a queen's dharma. At every stage of life these precepts will show you the path of duty.

- First of all remember a woman has no higher God than her husband. Besides her husband no ascetics, saints or deities or even God need be worshiped.
- Her ultimate duty is only this....to sacrifices her selfishness and do only what adds to her husband's glory and welfare.
- A virtuous wife who's chaste in thought, heart and deed does not need anyone's blessing even deities fear her and even God is bound by her commands.
- When man performs his duty a wife must help him as his true other half.
- She must honour her husband's parents and serving them is her higher dharma.
- The worship of her parents-in-law's lotus feet is a woman's dharma, that none else equals.
- The code of ethics advises: king or husband, first see their mood and then talk. Even if you speak the right thing at the wrong time it will not have good results.
- The final precept is, regard your husband's home your home. And never praise your natal home there or show off your parent's greatness. And give all your love there so you forget the natal home.

## RAMA – MORAL VALUES

- The duty of Kind:

An ordinary man's duty is to protect his wife, children, brothers, sisters, parents and close relatives; to keep them happy and in difficult times to support them. But when that same man wears a crown and becomes king his prime duty is not to care for his or close relatives happiness or sorrows. That is the only difference between a king's duty and an ordinary man's duty.

A king's duty is only to ensure the happiness of his subjects. All his deeds are dependent on the opinion of his subjects. Then whether at a personal level, he is happy, or sad. His duty lies in doing everything for the welfare of his subjects for their happiness, and according to their opinion. This is his prime and his final duty. That's a king duty.

- A king is like a father.
- An offender must be punished
- Kid is pure and equal to God
- Reward to brave, virtuous and knowledgeable persons
- Dharma and honour are more dear then life itself.
- Don't misuse power.
- The elder brother, the father and the guru all three are to be revered. In the same way a younger brother, son and disciple are deemed to be sons.
- A sister, the wife of a son or a younger brother must be treated like one's own daughter. Whoever looks upon these with a lustful eye may be slain without any sin. This is the familial, social and ethical duty.

## MORAL VALUES IN RAMAYANA FOR PRESENT SOCIETY

What was Lord Ramchandra like? What is the significance of values like adherence to truth, respect for others, tolerance, purity, patience and devotion to God? Today, in the twenty-first century, enmeshed as we are in the IT revolution, we are pursuing knowledge. This is the information age. Innovations through research seek to bring happiness to humanity and claim to do so all the time. But happiness is not necessarily contentment. And hence it is imperative to usher in Rama Rajya, which will ensure all-round happiness, peace and contentment. It was with this end in view that Lord Sri Ramchandra willingly went into exile to fulfill His father's solemn oath. By doing so, he set a shining example of upholding the perennial value systems. He demonstrated to us how to fully marshal and utilize one's faculties to attain one's goals. He showed us how to boldly approach and overcome difficult situations. Lord Sri Ramchandra proved that even God could be attained through perseverance.

The Ramayana is an unlimited source of these and several other truths. A daily study and reflection on the values propounded in the Ramayana will be a source of inspiration, guidance and a panacea for all the worries confronting us in this jet age. Short stories, attractive visuals and the messages derived from these are the highlights of the Ramayana. There is no alternative to the Ramayana to help us overcome the troubles and problems in the present day topsy-turvy scenario. Not only children but also teenagers and youth love the stories in the Ramayana and will benefit immensely from delving into the various aspects of the epic. In today's fast changing world, it is no longer surprising to see brothers become foes. The saga of love and affection between Sri Ram, Lakshman, Bharat and Shatrughna will inspire them to better fraternal relations. Sita's character provides an outstanding example of a chaste, loyal and devoted wife; Hanuman's unshakable faith in Lord Sri Ram provides us an example of unparalleled devotion to the Lord. Devotion, strength, strategy and faith find unparalleled confluence in the Ramayana. The events narrated in the epic will definitely have a positive and beneficial impact on the minds of children. The chapters like the meeting of Sri Ram with Bharat, the battle between Jatayu and Ravan, building of the transoceanic bridge to Sri Lanka and the slaying of Kumbhakarn and Ravan are very engrossing. The story of building the bridge across the sea to Lanka highlights the importance of faith and is very popular with children. The story of the squirrel's help in building the ocean bridge is an objective lesson on faith for children. It also provides them a lot of joy. This assures that immense benefits will be derived from the study of the Ramayana. However, we must be able to make children take to it in a meaningful way. The Ramayana is also an ideal medium to encourage reading habits among children. Children imbibe their culture and value systems through their parents, grandparents and teachers. Every child has to read and reflect on the Ramayan. Only then will the dream of establishing Rama Rajya come true. The responsibility of encouraging the reading habit is by no means restricted to parents and teachers solely, but also to those officials, bureaucrats and functionaries connected with education. Let us pledge ourselves to propagate the message of the Ramayan in every home and school.

## CONCLUSION

The Ramayana is a reservoir of moral values. We are living in the society of value crisis. It is our foremost duty of teacher to teach the story of Ramayana to all the children. Present children will become the citizens of tomorrow. It is necessary to take care of them. It is the duty of parents to inculcate important moral values in the children. Mother is the first teacher. First educate women then the family will be educated. Our foremost duty is to watch our actions at moment to moment and to follow moral values of Ramayana for human wellbeing.

## REFERNCE

1. Valmiki Ramayana.

# 16. Lifelong Learning

*For our people to benefit from new employment opportunities, we must ensure that every Indian is skilled and educated. Education alone is the foundation on which a prosperous and progressive society is built. I wish to see a revolution in education and skill development in the next five years. We will make India a nation of educated people, of skilled people, of creative people".* **...Manmohan Singh, Prime Minister of India, Red Fort, Aug 15$^{th}$, 2007**

*Anyone who stops learning is old, whether this happens at twenty or eighty. Anyone who keeps on learning not only remains young, but becomes constantly more valuable regardless of physical capacity.*

**...Harvey Ullman**

## INTRODUCTION

The concept of lifelong learning as an educational strategy emerged some three decades ago, through the efforts of the OECD, UNESCO and the Council of Europe. It was a response to the anomaly that while individuals learn throughout life, the provision of education opportunities was limited largely to the early phase of life, dominated by formal education. There was a perceived need to provide a "second chance" to those who did not benefit from educational opportunities available during childhood and youth.

Lifelong learning is far broader than the provision of second-chance education and training for adults. It is based on the view that everyone should be able, motivated and actively encouraged to learn throughout life. This view of learning embraces individual and social development of all kinds and in all settings: formally, in schools, vocational, tertiary and adult education institutions; and non-formally, at home, at work and in the community.

India is a developing country. We live in a society where diversity of background, culture, knowledge and skills should be valued and nurtured. We want a society where people actively engage in their communities, local and national, and learning can enable people to do that. Lifelong learning contributes to the development of society through the achievement of other social goals such as civic participation, sustainable development, improved health and wellbeing, reduced crime and greater social cohesion. The availability of opportunities to learn throughout life is crucial to the well being of any society, to strengthen its economy, enrich its culture and liberate its citizens. In the present paper an attempt has been made to know the importance of Lifelong Learning in India for happy and wealthy life of all people.

## WHY IS LIFELONG LEARNING NEEDED?

It is generally agreed that education has become one of the most significant vehicles in the development of human life in general and woman life in particular. Education can contribute toward personal well-being and happiness. To lead a happy life in society, one should be involved in education throughout life. Education is a tool for human beings to use for solving daily problems, or adjusting to the environment: in other words, "education for life and life for education". In this regard, education does not only mean learning through the formal school system or "formal education." The concept of "education" includes formal education, non-formal education and informal education, and the combination of all three is referred to as "lifelong education".

At present, the educational system that serves the majority of people all over the world including India emphasizes formal education, which is basically a classification system of formal performance, involving rigid curricula. The formal school system is usually classified into the primary or elementary, the secondary, high school and university levels. The second type of educational system is known as non-formal education, which educational planners are using as a substitute to the formal system for out-of-school youth and adults. Non-formal education is less formal in terms of its performance criteria and is more concerned with daily life problems. This includes adult school programs and other short-training courses. The last type of educational system is informal education, which is truly a lifelong process where every individual acquires attitudes, values, skills and knowledge from daily experience. It includes any kind of education besides formal and non-formal and any method of learning using various sources of knowledge. For example, knowledge may be acquired during conversation and travelling; attending shows or movies; reading books and newspapers; listening to the radio or watching television. It indicates that lifelong learning takes place in every life of human beings.

Considering the potential reach and the effectiveness of these three types of educational systems (formal, non-formal and informal), it is apparent that informal education is the most efficient and effective means to reach the rural adult population. Most rural people have little time for formal schooling due to the exigencies of meeting their personal, familial, occupational and societal needs. Each individual and society is unique in terms of its educational needs. It has been demonstrated that formal education is unable to serve individual needs since its curriculum is directed to respond to the needs of the majority target group. Moreover, the present formal school curriculum stresses general knowledge, while skills and experiences for living are left to the learners to acquire by themselves outside the school system. Through lifelong learning it is possible to acquire up to date knowledge and skills in the globalized world.

In the sociological aspect majority of married women are house wives. They are depending on theirs' husbands. Even though they have good educational qualifications and skills, they are wasting theirs' time with chit-chat. They have good capacity to do any work. They want only proper guidance and training. Lifelong learning is the correct platform for the empowerment men and women.

ASER (Assessment Survey Evaluation Report) surveys of 2005 and 2006, conducted by Pratham, give us a snapshot of learning achievements among children at elementary education level. In 2006, about 38.4% of all children in grade 1 could not read anything, 67.5% of grade 2 children could not read words, in grade 3, only 28% of all children could read grade 1 level text, and in grade 5 about 47% of children were unable to read grade 2 level texts. In arithmetic, 53.8% of children of grade 1 did not know anything, almost half of children in grade 2 could not recognise numbers, only 45.3% of children of grade 5 could do simple division, and only 24.2% of grade 8 children could do it. Thus, the ASER survey of 2006 shows the grim reality and illustrates the nature and magnitude of the problem. Unless concerted efforts are made to improve the quality of education, sustainability of literacy among children with low level of educational attainment would be problematic. Lifelong learning is the only solution to overcome this problem (by educating illiterate parents and adults).

## IMPORTANCE OF LIFELONG LEARNING

*The illiterate of the 21st century will not be those who cannot read and write but those who cannot learn, unlearn and relearn."*

**...Alvin Toffler (Futurist)**

The importance of Lifelong Learning/Education has been repeatedly stressed in several educational policy documents and discourses in India. While the *Report of the Education Commission* (1964-66) observed that *education does not end with schooling but is a lifelong process;* the *National Policy on Education in India - 1986* (modified in 1992) considered *Lifelong Education as the cherished goal of the educational process which presupposes universal literacy, provision of opportunities for youth, housewives, agricultural and industrial workers and professionals to continue the education of their choice at the pace suited to them.* It observes that the critical development issue is the continuous upgradation of skills so as to produce manpower resources of the kind and the number required by the society. Although these policies were translated into practice and a number of Lifelong Learning programs were implemented by governmental, non-governmental organizations and universities in the country during the last three decades, the bulk of the programs continued to focus on adult literacy and continuing education mainly due to the massive number of non literates (300.14.million ) and neo literates(110millions) as estimated by the National Literacy Mission (NLM-

*Literacy Facts At A Glance* ,2007) .With the formulation the Eleventh Five year Plan (2007-20012), the Government of India put forward the idea of expanding the scope of the Continuing Education Program by developing it as Lifelong Education and Awareness Program (LEAP).This may be partly influenced by the global discourse on Lifelong Learning and partly due to the socio economic changes taking place within and outside the country.

The role and importance of Lifelong Learning in India have increased in recent times due to several socio economic factors. In a technology driven knowledge based competitive economy; the landscape of learning is fast changing in India. According to Economic Survey 2006-07; the growth of Indian economy at an average rate of 9.2% per annum during 2006-07 (*The growth rate has been 8.6 per cent in 2010-11 and is expected to be around 9 per cent in the next fiscal year)* tremendous expansion of Information Communication Technology and the rapid globalization have all been instrumental in bringing about changes in the job skills so that the workforce keeps on learning and updating their skills to be globally competitive. The country's economic performance depends critically on access to and the adoption of new technology and improving the skills of the labor force. Since 92.4% of India's workforce is in the unorganized sectors (*National Sample Survey, 61st Round, 2004-5),* they need regular upgrading of skills to compete in the globalize economy. Equipping the labor force with relevant skills implies the need for creating a variety of learning and training opportunities. In this process, the university system in India will have to play an important role.

**Four key factors determine people's participation in learning:**

- Individual disposition and attitudes towards learning
- Social environment
- Economic and financial context
- Institutional factors

The various aspirations and motivations of future learners vary according to their personal situations and may change over time. The decision to undertake some form of learning after school or to interrupt a period of employment is variously dependent on personal, social and economic circumstances.

## BENEFITS OF LIFE LONG LEARNING

We live in a society where diversity of background, culture, knowledge and skills should be valued and nurtured. We want a society where people actively engage in their communities, local and national, and learning can enable people to do that. Lifelong learning contributes to the development of society through the achievement of other social goals such as civic participation, sustainable development, improved health and wellbeing, reduced crime and greater social cohesion. *The availability of opportunities to learn* through*out* life *is crucial to the well being of any society, to strengthen its economy, enrich its culture and liberate its citizens. The following are the main benefits of lifelong learning:*

- Lifelong learning leads to an enriching life of self-fulfilment.
- Lifelong learning helps us make new friends and establish valuable relationships.
- Lifelong learning keeps us involved as active contributors to society.
- Lifelong learning helps us find meaning in our lives.
- Lifelong learning helps us adapt to change.
- Lifelong learning makes the world a better place.
- Lifelong learning increases our wisdom.
- Lifelong learning creates a curious, hungry mind.
- Lifelong learning opens the mind.
- Lifelong learning helps fully develop natural abilities.

## REFERENCES

1. *OECD* (1996). "*Lifelong Learning for All*", Organization for Economic Co-operation and Development, Paris.

# 17. Introduction

Stress has been acknowledged inherent in the process of teaching. Most teachers, howsoever bright, well read, experienced and well prepared experience some amount of stress while going to lecture in front of the student, but manage to handle it. It is also true that some feel more stressed than others and face occasional difficulty in coping with it. Some teachers find it quite heavy on them and extremely difficult carry on the work, as they are not able to either structure the work environment or exercise control over the factors underlying the stress, or to enhance their capability to cope. It then threatens to adversely impact their physical health reduces their teaching commitment and effectiveness to the extent of their needing professional help. Prolonged periods of intense stress, if not taken care of, can produce feelings of emotional exhaustion, reduce personal accomplishment, induce a sense of professional failure, and even a tendency to act with the clientele in a depersonalized manner, the symptoms which define burnout. Stress and burnout among teachers found directly influence their functioning and survival in the system, and quality of educational and related services offered to all students, and without exception for those with special needs.

## STRESS AND BURNOUT IN INDIAN CONTEXT

As stated in the introduction and other subsequent places in the book, although the definitional complexities in the assessment of stress and burnout are enormous and difficult to be resolved in general. An additional problem has been confronted by researchers in the understanding and assessment of stress and burnout in educational institutions of south Asia because of the specific cultural values of obedience of authority, nurturance of the young, etc. The socio-cultural situations have though, undergone gradual changes in the post independence period, and the difficulty of such unmet unconditional expectations now characterize the numerous interpersonal problems at all levels from administrative heads to students. The emotional strains of interpersonal emotional distances and the non-reciprocal relationships among different sections often operate at the latent level, and camouflage the severity of stress effects.

Like many of the educational institutions in south Asia, teachers in contemporary Indian schools are confronted with the reality of diverse social groups of educators and pupils, large size of class and raised expectations , leaving for them little scope and time for personal interaction with students and colleagues. Over the years, as social power and money have become important personal and social values, and the new professions have emerged, the teaching profession has got devalued. Teachers do not have the desired social respect, nor do they get adequate financial rewards/support for their work. Teachers expected to confer knowledge, and make every child the best achiever in every domain of activity. The task is challenging and demanding, but the teachers represent a mixed lot, with varied levels of skills, capabilities, resources, etc. Teachers who are capability and good, generally respected and appreciated, but instances are uncommon, when parents and students alike so not give a hot to the teachers, and blame them for any shortcomings observed in children/ school. Many parents do not wish their child to be a teacher. Many (parents, husbands and in-laws) view teaching as an ideal profession for women, as they can finish their work by the afternoon and take care of their home and children (a part time employee on full salary).

There has been little research in the Indian schools in areas of teacher concerns, stress and burnout. The first and School Surveys of Research in Education (Buch, 1974, 1979) did not include any study on teacher stress and burnout. A later bibliography (Dave and Murry, 1933) included three studies, each emphasizing a different aspect of burnout. As the pressures to perform from various quarters continue to rise, despite the adverse conditions of functioning of teaching institutions, teachers need familial and social support in differentiating across variety of stresses and in handling the day to day stresses, and thus prevent burnout.

## INTRODUCTION: SETTING THE SCENE

Stress, burnout and coping researches have been confining for years to clinical areas, and the terms have acquired negative connotations, with which the inflicted struggled in a bid to find relief, and in the process depleted and/or exhausted the resources under their control. This indicates an unquestionable acceptance of the underlying assumption of persons going through the stressful experiences, having no control/volition or an alternative path out, and thus the need of therapy. The common experience as well as the evidence from research does not validate it. There neither is adequate logical ground to argue and suggest that all types of stress are necessarily negative and unhealthy for ones functioning, nor are the stress and burnout equivalents. A distinction been made in the literature between positive and negative stress, and between stress and burnout. Positive stress called eustress, and negative stress labelled distress. In fact, the positive affect has not been entirely neglected in the classical models of stress either. It has been discussed in relation to the (a) primary appraisal of stressful situations as challenges, which signal the probability of makings gains and characterized by positive emotions, like eagerness, excitement, and confidence. (b) Appraisal of the resolution of a stressful encounter as successful leading to emotions of happiness and pride. (c) Cessation of aversive conditions, when people are likely to experience an offsetting positive emotion, such as relief, and (d) Examining of the other positive outcomes of stressful events, even if the events have not been favorably resolved. The positive outcomes may include perceived benefits of stressful encounters, newly acquired skills and resources that may help in coping, and spiritual/ religious transformation in thinking and attitudes.

## MEANING OF STRESS

Stress is a condition stream on ones emotions, thought processes and physical conditions. When it is excessive, it can pretend once ability to cope with environment. (Hans Selye, 1976) "Stress is the general term applied to the pressures; employs developed various symptoms of stress as, "an adjective demand placed on the organism".

From the above definitions, it may understand that stress pretends the wellbeing of the organism; conditions that tend to because stress called pressure. In this age of anxiety, stress considered as an inevitable aspect of human life, forcing him to cope up with it for successful and happy life. The main factors of creating stress in individual are Biological, Psychological and Socio-Cultural. Biological factors influence all aspects of our behavior including our intellectual capabilities, basic temperament, primary reaction tendencies and stress tolerance. Psychosocial factors of stress also influence the well-being of the individual in contemporary life. Stress due to failure, losses, personal limitations, guilt and loneliness leads to self-deviation. Modern living is a bundle load of pressures acting on individuals. Each individual experience his own unique pattern of pressures such as competing with others, meeting educational, occupational, and marital depends and coping with the complexity and in rapid pace of modern life . There are other socio-cultural factors creating stress on modern man such as problems of war and violence, group prejudice and discrimination, economic and unemployment problems, rapid social change existential anxiety.

## JOB STRESS

In this last decade of twentieth century, many people are unable to cope up with stress generated because of circumstances forcing them to adopt fact-paced life styles. This position is highly significant when people are at work. A rational and logical inference one can make, now basing on the above premises is that working styles are also subjected to change in accordance to the fast changing life styles, mat be a presupposition for work stress or job stress. Therefore, job stress has received an increasing concern to the researchers in the areas of organizational behavior and social psychology, who have been undertaking evidences about the effects of stress on the organization, worker output, and the physical and emotional well-being of the worker.

## TEACHERS STRESS

Job stress is the most common psychological phenomena that are prevalent among people who are in different jobs and professions. The stress studies are initially directed toward industrial organization. With the private sector. Researchers have come to believe that stress may be especially prevalent among human service professions, particularly the teaching profession, (Kryacou and Suteliffe 1977-78; Pettigrew and Wolf 1982, Cherniss 1980; and Cooper and Marshall 1980). As teaching is a human service profession, stress with in the teaching profession is considerable and may have far-reaching consequences on the entire education system. Teaching is a complex process were in teacher is expected to exhibit many skills. This makes a teacher to experience stress in the profession.

Further Pettergrew and Wolf (1982) opined, "Teacher stress has a Nation-wide concern and relatively new area of empirical research". Concerns regarding stress among schoolteacher have been raised for over 40 years (Tunk, Meeks and Turk 1982) stress is considered very significant in any educative process much attention is not drawn towards this. Teacher behavior and his performance, classroom interactions, school and classroom climate may consider as the important components of any educative process.

It is not easy to ascertain sources of teacher stress, as its ambit is unlimited. However, several attempts are made to identify the sources that possible, create stress among teachers. Factors prepared by teachers as being troublesome or stressful have included students displine, negative student attitudes towards school, physical violence, is adequate preparation time, lack of clear role definition and heavy workloads".(Bearly, Myette and serna, 1983;Chichen and Koff, 1978;Gollady and Noel 1978;Olanderand Ferrel, 1970).

Further Kaiser and Polezynsky (1982) identified factors within educators themselves as a potential source of excess stress. Quick and Quick (1979) proposed four groups of factors creating work stress. They are 1) Role factors, 2) Job factors, 3) Physical factors and 4) Interpersonal factors. A heap of literature available on job stress identified main sources such as job setting, organizational, situational, lack of control over work, co-workers etc.

Teacher is subjected to stress due to incoherent social life, widening social distance, segregation, lack of social support, corruption, nepotism, unnecessary societal involvement in day-to-day activities, high degree of social indiscipline, deterioration of values, lack of social security etc.

Besides the potential stress that occurs outside the school, there are also those associated with the school itself. Teaching as a profession demands continuous growth, but teachers while discharging time for further studies, unable to utilize the training the salaries, lack of opportunity for reading training, less change for further promotion etc. are acting as source of stress on teachers.

Teaching as an occupation, present certain situation where in the teacher has to adjust to unhealthy school atmosphere, lack of recognition, for effective teaching. Teaching the subject is which he is not interested, lack of support for innovative approaches, lack of enthusiasm in staff meeting, monotonous working conditions, difference of opinions with head of the institution etc., are the situations acting as sources of stress.

Student behavior is also a major component in the teaching learning process. Continuous misbehavior or certain students, non-acceptance of teacher's authority indiscipline in the class, lack of interest on outsides. Threat from the students, lack of attention in the class, unable to estimate the student, lack of positive responses from the student etc., are some of the significant sources of stress on teachers. Thus, student as a group can be a significant source of teacher stress. Similarly lack of group cohesiveness in school, lack of social support and interpersonal conflicts create teacher stress.

So far, extra organizational, organizational and group stressors are discussed; teacher is the ultimate consumer of stress due to previously mentioned stressors. Thus individual dispositions such as role conflict and ambiguity at organizational and group levels, causes stress. Teachers have to play multiple roles and these often make conflicting expectation. In the present education system heavy expectation are there on teachers. Hence, teachers are supposed to undertake high magnitude of work.

Now teachers are experiencing stress as they are supposed to teach more periods a day without rest between periods, excess correction work, undertaking institutional work like censes lack of time for completing syllabus, conduct of co-curricular and extra curricular activities etc.

## EFFECTS OF TEACHER STRESS

As job stress effect organizational performance, teacher stress impedes teacher performance in teaching. Infect it is assumed that mild stress can even enhance performance but high level of stress can create physical, Psychological and behavioral problems among teacher. There are several research studies, which observed that, a high level of stress accompanied by physical illness such as high blood pressures, ulcers and even cancer. Similarly high level of stress may be accompanied by psychological problems such as anger, anxiety, depression, nervousness, irritability, tension and boredom. Excessive stress may also result in behavioral problems such as sleeplessness, under eating or over eating, increased smoking and drinking and drug abuse. Many researches of teacher studies have established some strong correlates of teacher stress. From these researches, it has found that teacher stress related to job dissatisfaction (Rudd and Wiseman 1962; Krysacon and Suteliff 1979). Absenteeism, (Bridger 1980; Kaiser and Polezynsky 1982); greater intention to leave profession (Kryiacon and Suteliff 1979), Physical Distress (Coats and Thoresen, 1979) and teacher performance (Kkryiacon and Sutcliffe 1977-79, Pettegrew and Wolf 1982, Kaiser and Polezynsky 1982, Soloman 1960).

However, teaching competency has been recognized as important component of teaching learning process, relatively little effort is made to define the term. A peep in into the literature of teacher effectiveness as one finds many related terms such as teaching success; successful teacher, teaching efficiency, teacher performance, teacher competency etc.

"As one looks through heap of investigations in this field" Writes Barr (1961), "One finds various terms used to designate or describe the successful teacher. Frequently the word 'efficiency' is used one will not that the terms are sometimes applied to teacher as in teacher efficiency and sometimes in the teacher behavior as in the teaching efficiency.

Donald M. Medley (1982) States that the teacher competency as those of knowledge, abilities and beliefs on teacher processes and brings to the teaching situation. Teaching competency differs from teacher performance and teacher effectiveness in that it is a stable characteristic of the teacher that does not change appreciably when the teacher moves from one situation to another.

By this, it is evident that the knowledge of subject matter, teaching skills, beliefs and feelings of teacher may be considered as the components of teaching competent that a competent teacher is supposed to process.

Biddle (1964) advocates that "disagreement and ambiguity with respect to the description of teaching competence are to be expected and cannot entirely be avoided because competent teaching as undoubtedly a relative matter. Some investigators to refer to training process, properties of teachers, behavior exhibited by teacher and effects produced by teachers, have used the term competence. The same variable have been termed by other investigators as effectiveness, criteria of competency, ability in reach and a host of other terms-teacher success, teacher effectiveness, teacher efficiency, teacher performance, teacher competency etc., are used synonymously by investigators.

Researchers study teacher effectiveness in three component, presage, process and product. Here the presage component refers to thought processes, training aspect and personality factors of the teachers. The process component effects produced by teachers, the same variable have been termed by other investigators as effectiveness, criteria of competency, ability in reach and a host of other terms-teacher success, teacher effectiveness, teacher efficiency, teacher performance, teacher competency etc., are used synonymously by investigators.

Ryan (1960) States, "What constitutes effective teaching?" What are the distinguishing characteristics of competent teacher? are provocative and running questions unfortunately, no universally acceptable definite answers can be given to these complex queries-embarrassing as it may be for professional educators to recognize relatively little progress has been made."

Similarly, Biddle and Ellena accepted in 1966 that nobody knows what a competent teacher was. They said, "Probably no aspect of education has been discussed with greater frequency with as much deep concern or by more educators and citizens. The teacher effectiveness-How to define it, how to identify it, how to measure it, how to evaluate it, and how to detect and remove obstacles to its achievement-finding about the competence of teachers are inconclusive and peace meal and little is presently known for certain about teacher excellence.

Researchers study teacher effectiveness in three components; presage, process and product. Here the presage component refers to thought processes, training aspects and personality factors of the teachers. The process component to the teacher's action or classroom practices and the product component refer to the quality of the products i.e. students predicted.

Jangira (1979) states, "teacher's effectiveness has been considered into its three separate components for convenience of presentation. It should be taken that these components are watertight compartment. It also fallow that there are no clear-cut lines to distinguish one component from the other.

## TEACHER COMPETENCY AND STRESS

The study is about teacher competency in relation to stress. Teacher competency, in general sense impedes, when teacher suffers from stress. In this chapter, a discussion is made about teacher competency, stress, and the development of this type of study in the world.

## TEACHER COMPETENCY

One of the most difficult problems in educational research is that of recognizing teacher competency of discriminating between more and less effective teachers. The role of the classroom teacher in educational is central. The teacher is, after all, the point at contact between the educational system and the pupil. The impact of any educational programme or innovation on the pupil operates through the pupil's teacher. It is therefore quite accurate to say that a school's competence depends on the competence of its teachers. Maximizing teacher competence is a major goal of education.

"Teacher competency" refers to the behavior of a teacher while teaching a class (both inside and outside the classroom).Teacher performance differs from teacher competence. It is defined in terms of teacher behavior, of what the teacher does, teacher performance resembles teacher competence in that it is a product of interaction between certain teacher characteristics and the teaching situation-teacher performance is often used as a basis from which teacher competence can be inferred.

"Teacher competence" refers to the set of knowledge, abilities and beliefs a teacher process and bring to the teaching situation Teacher competence differs from teacher performance and teacher effectiveness in that it is a stable characteristic of the teacher that does not change appreciably when the teacher moves from one situation to another. It resembles teacher performance in that it has also been proposed as a basis from which teacher effectiveness can be inferred.

Early Research: The first recorded study of teacher competence (Kratz, 1896), one of the earliest pieces of educational research of any kind to appear, set a design precedent that was to be followed for many years. A large group of elementary school pupils was asked to try to remember the best teacher each of them had ever encountered to write down what made that teacher different from others. Their descriptions were then collated and compared and from them was derived a list of characteristics that supposedly distinguished effective teachers from in effective ones. For the next half-century of so this kind of study was repeact6e again and again with groups chosen in various ways; sometime the task was performed by pupils currently attending schools sometimes by persons considered to be exports, educators, or teacher educators. Perhaps the most extensive and sophisticated example of this was the monumental common wealth teachers training study. (Charters of Waples 1929), which is used exhaustive and meticulous procedures to produce a number of lists of lengths. Typical of the characteristics listed were the following, which were the top six on a list of twenty-five.

1. Adaptability
2. Considerateness

3. Enthusiasm
4. Good judgment
5. Honesty
6. Magnetism

Pupil learning is a direct outcome of pupil learning experiences; learning is after all, something that pupils do not something teachers do. When a teacher "teacher' what she or he really does is try to provide certain learning experiences for the pupils that all expected to bring about desired learning out-comes.

Whatever the nature of the teachers performance, different pupils will have different learning experiences and will make different amounts of gain. Since the unit of study in the process-product model of the class, not the pupil, learning outcomes must me measured in terms of class mean gain before they can be correlated with teacher performance, and variations in gain made by different pupils with the same class must be related as errors that attitude the correlations obtains.

## DISSATISFACTION, STRESS AND BURNOUT

Do schools personnel have high moral and are they satisfied in their work setting? Newspaper headlines that emphasize teacher strikes, teacher burnout and stress on school employees suggest that many teachers are not satisfied. A number of studies conducted throughout the 1970s and into the 111980s indicate a gradual reduction in teacher satisfaction (for example, Fuller and Miskel (1972) found that about 89 percent of the teachers participating in this study were satisfied or very satisfied with their job. However, Bentzen, Williams and Heckman (1980), in an investigation conducted in the late 1970s, reported that slightly more than 75 percent of the teachers were satisfied with their jobs. In the later study, important difference in job satisfaction was discovered at the various levels of teaching, with elementary teachers expressing more satisfaction with their jobs than secondary teachers do. A nation wide pole of teachers conducted by the National Educational Association (NBA) in 1980 ("Teachers opinion poll: job satisfaction "1980) found that 35 percent of all public schoolteachers were dissatisfied with their current jobs. Two-fifths of the teacher said they would probably not become teachers if they had it to do all over again; one teacher in ten was planning to leave teaching as soon as possible, and another two teachers in ten were undecided about how long they would remain in teaching. These studies suggest a moderate trend in the direction of increasing dissatisfaction on the part of teachers-although a majority of school personnel continues to express satisfaction with this work.

## SYMPTOMS AND CAUSES OF STRESS

Symptoms of teacher dissatisfaction and low morale vary. They include questioning and criticizing of school goals and polices, lack of enthusiasm for teaching rejection or lack of follow- up on administrative directives (Cook, 1979), absenteeism (Educational Research Service, 1980) and fragmentation, that is, a general feeling of being pulled in different directions (Klugman, Cartes &Israel, 1979). Some of these symptoms are also reported in a study by Staplenton, Craft and Frankiewicz (1979).

These researches found a positive relationship between teacher job satisfaction and teacher brink man ship, which they defined as teacher behavior that attempts to challenge the authority structure of the school while attempting to avoid its negative sanctions.

The causes of teacher stress and burnout are not easy to as certain nor are they easily distinguishable from the symptoms, although there is no shortage of suggested causes. With regard to teacher stress, quick and quick (1979) believe that four group of factors create work stress. 1) Role factors 2) job factors 3) physical factors and 4) interpersonal factors. They recommended a number of techniques for reducing the stress related by the various factors. The New York State United Teachers Organization that the most important factors contributing to stress is the effect of disruptive children, incompetent administrators are identifies as the second most important cause of stress ("Urban teachers report more stress", 1980).

In the New York stud, urban teachers reported more stress than did sub urban or rural teachers. Cichon and Koff, (1980) found in their research on Chicago teachers that the more important causes of teacher stress are problems of disruption and threats to the teacher's, physical professional and personal well being. In this connection, in NEA survey of its membership in 1980("teacher opinion poll attacks on teacher",1980)estimated that 1,13,000 of the country's 21,84,000 public school teachers were physically attacked by students during a recent twelve month period. Suggested causes of teaches burnout are usually believed to those associated with stress (block, 1978;weiskopt,1980).In a personal account of teacher burnout, Bardol (1979) has described several symptoms and perceived causes.

A number of investigations into the causes of teacher dissatisfaction have been conducted. An NEA survey ("teacher opinion poll; job satisfaction", 1980), found that a majority of teachers felt that the following factors, listed in order of frequency of identification had agentive of feet on their job satisfaction. 1. Public attitudes toward the school.2.treatment of education by the media.3.Student attitudes toward learning. 4. Salary and 5. Status of teachers in the community. In addition, 49 per cent of the teachers indicated that student behavior had negative effect upon their job satisfaction.

Ford (1979) believe that variables faculty work loads may be related to teacher dissatisfaction between class size and teacher satisfaction is investigated (Glass, et al., 1979,Pages and price (1980)discovered in their study of 130 teachers that the factors contributing most to job dissatisfaction are in order of important.1.lack of planning time. 2. Tedious paper and clerical work 3.On out of tough and autocratic administration.4. Disruptive and unmotivated student's 5.Non teaching activities, such as faculty meeting and "time wasting" workshop 6.Uncooperative parents 7.Lack of autonomy to prescribe curriculum 8.Feeling of failure and 9.Low occupational prestige.

Thus, a brief discussion and outline is presented in the chapter about matters relating to teacher competency and stress. Thus, this kind of analysis gave the investigator. Some clues on the subject on the hand.

# 18. Reviev of The Related Literature

The investigator reviewed the available related literature pertaining to teacher stress and teaching competency for the present study and presented as follows.

1. Studies related to Teacher stress.
2. Studies related to Teaching competency.

**MOHOLICK'S (1969), MASTACH AND JACKSONS (1980)**

**STUDIES RELATED TO TEACHER STRESS**

A study of meaning in life, Stress and Burnout in Teachers of Secondary Schools in Calcutta.

**OBJECTS OF THE STUDY**

1. To study if teachers varied in the degree of overall meaning in life and if they showed a trend low or high meaning.
2. To identify important sources of meaning in the personal and professional life of teachers and to investigate if teachers varied in the degree of meaning derived from these sources.
3. To find out the relationship, if any among the different measures of meaning in life.
4. To identify the main sources of stress in teaching and to investigate if teachers varied in the extent of experienced stress.
5. To study if teachers varied in the extent of perceived.
6. To study the relationship between stress and burnout meaning

The tools used for data collection were Moholick's (1969) purpose in life Test, Mastach and Jackson (1981) inventory for study of burnout and a scale and interview schedules prepared by the investigator for measurement of stress and other background variables. The sample comprised 345 teachers from 15 secondary schools and an in service teachers Population of three teacher training institutions in Calcutta. Survey and case study techniques were followed in the conduct of the study. Descriptive and non-parametric statistical techniques were used for analysis of data.

## FINDINGS THE STUDY

1. Meaningfulness of life of the teachers was quite high according to their own perception.
2. Meaning in professional life was derived primarily from psychic reward obtained from task related outcomes and relationship with the student.
3. All the measures of meaning in life namely self reported meaning in life, source of meaning in life and sources of meaning in teaching had a political relationship with meaning of life.
4. The relationship between stress studied through test and stress reported by teachers was highly significant.
5. Age difference was significant with regard to stress of teachers.
6. The sample teachers had a lower degree of burnout.
7. Sex difference was significant on the burnout variable.
8. Stress was positively related to burnout with regard to emotional exhaustion and depersonalization.
9. There was negative relationship between meaning in life and stress variables measured by tests as well as self – reporting items.
10. A comparatively low level of meaning in life was identified among the sample teachers.

## STUDIES RELATED TO TEACHING COMPETENCY

### L.S.VERNE.M.R.,L.V.C.U.1985

A STUDY OF SOME OF THE PERSONALITY COMPONENT OF CREATIVE STUDENT TEACHERS IN RELATION TO THEIR COMPETENCE TOWARDS TEACHING.

The study was designed to compare high, medium and low creative student teachers on three dimensions of creativity and total creativity in terms of certain personality components sex, Teaching competence and achievement levels.

The sample consisted of 210 B.Ed., students randomly select from our educational instructions in Lucknow. Data regarding creative were collected with the help of tolerance Test of creative thinking. For assessment personality characteristics, the multivariate personality inventory and 16PF were administered to the student teachers. A teacher effectiveness scale was administered to get an idea about their effectiveness as teachers and division scored by them in practice teaching was taken as the criterion of their performance as teachers.

**Main findings of the study**

1) The F ratio for the effect of fluency was significant for dominance-reserved vs. outgoing, humble vs. assertive and tough-minded vs. tender minded.
2) The F ratio for the main effects of flexibility were significant for ego ideal, dominance, sober vs. happy-go-luck and group-dependent vs. self-sufficient.
3) The F ratio for the effect of originality was significant for self-confidence humble vs. assertive and sober vs. happy-go-lucky.
4) The F ratio for the effect of total creativity were significant for empathy, self confidence, reserved vs. outgoing sober vs. happy-go-lucky and taught minded vs. tender minded.
5) The F ratio for the interaction of sex and total creativity was significant for neuroticism, self confidence and reserved vs. outgoing
6) Personality factors distinguishing the low total creativity group from the medium total creativity group were self-confidence, thought minded vs. tender minded and sober vs. happy-go-luck.

**NATARAJAN.S. MADRAS-U**

A competency based Program in Teacher Education Curriculum:

The major objectives of these investigations were;

1. To study the relative efficiency of competency based teacher education in the pre-service education program of secondary school teachers.
2. To identify factors influencing competency achievement such as social status, economic status and level of education and.
3. To find out the relationship between an individual's self-esteem and competency achievement.

**MAJOR FINDINGS OF THE STUDY**

1. Competency-based instruction proved suitable for teaching selected units in institutions, planning and administration.
2. The seminar method seemed to be an effective method as it compared favourable with the competency-based approach.
3. The lecture method was effective as a group method.
4. Directed self-study did not compare well with other methods.
5. There was a significant relation between self-esteem and acquisition of competencies.
6. Attitude towards teaching methods had a favorable correlation with acquisition of competencies.
7. The study proved that teacher education programme could be made more effective through a competency-based approach.

**BHALWANKARA.G.**

**SNDT COLLEGE OF EDUCATION-PUNE-1984**
**SIE MAHARASTRA FINANCED**

A STUDY OF RELIABILITY AND VALIDITY OF THE PROCESS-PROCESS APPRAISING SCALE OF TEACHER OF EFFECTIVENESS.

**THE MAJOR OBJECTIVES OF THE STUDY:**

1. To determine the reliability of the process-process appraising scale of teacher.
2. To determine criterion related to and the content validity of the PASTE.
3. To determine the relationship between various component scores of PASTE teacher effectiveness scores on PASTE.
4. To study the effect of increase or decrease in number of components of PASTE on reliability and

5. To determine the relationship between presage variables and teacher effectiveness scores of student teacher.

**THE MAJOR FINDINGS OF THE STUDY**

1. The reliability of PASTE by four-way analysis of variance was 0.72; the reliability of PASTE was quite satisfactory.
2. PASTE had satisfactory content and criterion related validity.
3. All the components correlated positively with the total teacher 3effectiveness score some skills were significant related to total teacher effectiveness.

**SINGH.R.S.,GOR.-1987**

A STUDY OF TEACHER'S EFFECTIVENESS AND ITS CORRELATES AT HIGHER SECONDARY STAGE IN EASTERN.

**MAJOR OBJECTIVES OF THE STUDY**

1. To compare teacher effectiveness of Male and Female teachers of Urban and Rural area.
2. To compare their intelligence, socio-economic status, attitude towards teaching profession and adjustment.
3. To find out the relationship between teacher effectiveness and
4. To determine the combined effect of the correlates on teacher effectiveness.

The sample comprised 330 teachers of Urban and Rural areas from 22 intermediate colleges of Varanasi, Gorekhpur and Jaunpur districts. The tools used were teacher attitude inventory. Teacher adjustment inventory, SES Scale, Samoohik, Mansik Yogyata, Prakash (1/61) and teaching effectiveness rating scale.

**THE MAJOR FINDINGS**

1. No significant difference in the mean scores of male and female teachers in their effectiveness was observed.
2. The difference in the mean intelligence scores of male and female teachers was not significant.
3. It was revealed that the rural female teachers had secured comparatively better scores than the rural male teachers in teacher effectiveness.

4. The difference in the mean scores of urban male and female teachers was found to be non-significant on the SES scale.
5. There was no-significant difference in the mean scores of male and female teachers belonging to rural and urban area in their attitude towards teaching.
6. There was no-significant difference in the mean scores of adjustment of male and female teachers.
7. The scores of male and female teachers in teaching effectiveness appeared to be correlated significantly with only two variables-intelligence and attitudes towards the teaching profession.
8. A low relationship between intelligence and socio-economic status was observed. It was however not significant.
9. The teacher effectiveness scores of rural male and female teachers appeared to significantly relate with intelligence, socio-economic status and adjustment.
10. Intelligence showed a moderate and significant relationship with socio-economic status and adjustment of the urban teachers irrespective of sex.

SUSHILA SINGHAL; Stress in Education Indian Experience, Rawat publication, New Delhi, 2004, pp. 294-334.

**THE MAJOR FINDINGS**

The personal profiles of teachers are not much important, as most of them show mild to moderate levels of stress and burnout, yet the older and those having higher educational qualifications seem to be more stress prone. Those having higher socio-economic status are more involved with students and feel more responsible, but become less idealistic over the tears. In the regular as well as in special schools, teachers experience different levels of stress. So do the males and females, and the more vs. less experienced teachers. The negative perceptions of work-setting can induce negative feelings in teachers resulting in subsequent stress and burnout. Female teachers tend to perceive the work-setting as more positive than males. The special schoolteachers rate their work load higher; their contacts with students more frequent and intense feel more socially isolated and have more role conflicts. More experienced teachers have fewer interpersonal interactions, yet lower social isolation and fewer conflicts in regular as well as special schools. The work-setting of regular schools emerges as the necessary condition, and the stress as the sufficient condition for the onset of burnout. All teachers experience moderate levels of burnout, indicating something more can activate it to be a matter of concern. Males and females both experience it evenly. Teachers in the middle range of experience are more susceptible to stress and burnout than those with a few years or long experience. The finding of work-setting dimensions explaining a higher percent of variance in burnout is interesting to indicate that neither stress is independent of work context, nor all stress gets converted into burnout. Absence of adequate interpersonal interactions and positive feedback, bureaucratic hindrances, greater role conflicts, and difficult and problematic students are good predictors of burnout. Lack of proper training is a good predictor of burnout in special school teachers. The work overload, inadequate orientation few interpersonal interactions, and more role conflicts are associated with greater self-interest. Higher social isolation leads to reduced work goals. Those facing more role conflicts tend to become emotionally detached. The improvements in work-setting need to be initiated to suit the needs of the teachers so that they can efficaciously deliver instruction to their pupils and derive satisfaction from their performance.

# 19. Methods of Investigation

The present study is titled "A study of the Factors Influencing Teachers Stress among the School Teachers in Chittoor".

## NEED FOR THE STUDY

Accomplishment of educational goals and the objectives of teaching is possible only with teachers those who are competent in teaching and free from any type of stress. Teacher stress directly or indirectly influences the competency of teachers in teaching. So the teacher who is subjected to stress may not be possible to teach properly which in term competency in teaching.

Theoretically, the teacher stress may be heard to perform teaching in a competent way. But in practice how far teacher stress is influencing on teaching competency and to what extent teacher stress and teaching competency are related-are the questions waiting for answer. Hence, this study has taken up to find out how teacher stress and teaching competency are inter-related to each other in the context of high school education.

The present investigator has surveyed the available researches on teacher stress and teaching competency and presented in chapter-111.

Design is the heart of research. The following aspects have been discussed in detail, which are concerned with the design of the present study. The present chapter is set apart for making a brief discussion of the objectives of the study, the research procedure includes the operational definitions of the different terms used the various hypotheses that were framed for verification in the present study and the rationale of these hypotheses. The selection of sample includes the sampling techniques used, the reasons for selection of a particular sampling technique and the selection of the sample according to different variables. The selection of suitable tool for collection of data and the procedure followed in administering the tool to collect the data required for the present study.

## PROBLEM OF THE SUDY

In the view of the previous chapter, the investigator titled the problem in the following manner.

"A study of factors Influencing Teacher's Stress among the School Teachers in Chittoor"

## OBJECTIVES OF THE STUDY

1. To test the teacher stress and teaching competency scales to be use by the teacher himself.
2. To find out the relationship between teacher stress and teaching competency.
3. To find out the effect of demographical variables in respect of teacher stress.
4. To find out the effect of demographical variables in respect of teaching competency.

## ITEM ANALYSIS

For the purpose of determining the degree to which each item is effective in discriminating between high and low teaching competency and item analysis of the data obtained from above sample is undertaken by taking two extreme groups (High and Low) All the fifty two responses of the 200 subjects are scored and scores are arranged in an order from highest score to lowest score. Then the upper 27 per cent of the responses and lower 27per cent of the responses are taken into consideration for measuring significance of difference of means to know the item validity. A.M.S. and S.D.S for the 46 items of upper half and lower half are calculated for all the 46 items between upper and lower half using the following formula.

If the value of the critical ratio 0 the item is greater than 1. 96 (significant at 0.05 level of significant). Then the item is found valid and accepted. If the value of critical ratio of item is less than 1.96 then the item is found invalid and rejected.

## RE-TESTING OF TEACHER STRESS SCALE

In the present study, the investigator adopted the Rama's teacher stress self-rating five-point scale developed and standardized by. Dr. Krishnan Raju (1994) because it is more appropriate to measure the teacher stress related to the areas of 1.Professional growth, 2. Work load 3). Occupational Hazards 4).Student behavior 5). Family 6), Societal

The present investigator re-tested this scale on a tryout sample of 200teachers to minimize the error in the tool.

There are 46 items under six different areas of teacher stress scale of Dr. Krishnan Raju. The distribution or 52 items is as fallows. The items are given in appendix-2.

1. Items under professional growth area of teacher stress are 8 i.e., from 1to 8.
2. Items under workload area of teacher stress are 9 i.e., from 9 to 17.
3. Items under occupational Hazards area are of teacher stress are 9 i.e., 18 to26.
4. Items under student behavior area of teacher stress are 9 i.e., 27 to 35.
5. Items under family area of teacher stress are 8 i.e., 36 to43.
6. Items under society area of teacher stress are 3 i.e., 3.

**Table-1 Showing the number of items and percentage of items in teachers stress.**

| | Professional Growth | Work Load | Occupational Hazards | Student Behavior | Family | Societal | Total |
|---|---|---|---|---|---|---|---|
| No.of Que | 8 | 9 | 9 | 9 | 8 | 3 | 46 |
| % | 16.9 | 15.2 | 16.9 | 16.9 | 16.9 | 16.9 | 99.7 |

**ADMINISRRATION**

This tool I administered to a try out samples of 200 teachers of Chittoor. Instructions to the teachers are given on the title page of the scale. Care is taken to reduce bias in rating. This is done by clearly stating the purpose of study.

**SCORING**

The responses are scored according to the key. The scoring procedure, which was followed in the teacher competency scale, is followed to this teacher stress also. Total number of items is 46. The maximum is 230 and the minimum possible score is 46 the high score indicates high teacher stress; the low score indicates low teacher stress.

**ITEM ANALYSIS**

For the purpose of determining the degree to which each item is effective in discriminating high, low stress of teacher an item analysis of the data obtained from the above sample is under taken by taking two extreme groups (High and low) All the 46 responses of the 200subjects are scored and total scores are arranged in an order from highest score to lowest score. Then the upper 27per cent of the total response and lower 27 per cent of total responses are taken into consideration. For measuring significance of the items retained after item analysis for the final student in teacher difference of means to know item validity A.M.S and SDS for all the 46 items of the upper half and lower half are calculated. Critical ratio is then calculated for all the items between upper and lower halves. If the value of critical for ratio of the items is greater than 1.96 (significant at 0.05 level of significance). Then the item is found valid and accepted. If the value of the critical ratio of the item is less than 1.96 then the item is found as invalid and rejected. The scale with all the accepted items used for final study is given in appendix 4.

**COLLECTION OF DATA**

After retesting the two tools of the study, fresh and final scales are prepared for the final study with personal data pose. There two standardized tools of the resent study are administered to 200teacher of different schools in Chittioor of A.P. for collecting the data the investigator visited each school and administered the scales to the teachers personally. They are advised to put their name, sex, qualification, designation, experience etc. against the place provided in the personal data sheet of each scale.

Instructions are given in the first page of each scale. The investigator requested the teacher to fallow the instruction while responding the tools. Most of the teachers filled the tools on the spot and returned to the investigator. These two tools collected and scored according to the scoring procedure explained in the development and standardization of tools.

## SAMPLE

The sample selected for the present investigation consist 200 teachers of different Schools in Chittoor of A.P. The age of the teachers up to 35 and above 35 years, both male and female teachers are found in the sample. Teachers having 2 slabs experience i.e. above15 years, below 15 years are found in the sample. Teachers of two cadres of P.G. and graduate teachers. Another sample Government teacher. Thus, it is found to be a satisfactory sample and the sample is believed to be adequate to test the hypothesis.

The sample distribution of the study is shown in below

| AGE IN YEARS | ABOVE 35 | BELOW 35 |
|---|---|---|
| | 121 | 79 |
| SEX | MALE | FEMALE |
| | 88 | 112 |
| GENERAL | GRADUATES | P.G |
| QUALIFICATION | 100 | 100 |
| TEACHING | ABOVE 35 | BELOW 35 |
| EXPERIENCE | 84 | 116 |
| MANAGEMENT | GOVT. | PRIVATE |
| | 99 | 101 |

## ANALYSIS OF DATA

The following statistical techniques are used to analyze the data.

Mean and standard deviations of all the distributions are calculated.

To find out the relationship between teaching competency and Teacher stress "r" values are computed.

Co-efficiency of co-relation for the entire dimension was also calculated.

Critical ratios are calculated for testing the subsidiary hypothesis.

## HYPOTHESES OF THE STUDY

1. There is no significant difference between Above 35 years age of teachers and Below 35 years age of teacher towards teacher stress.
2. There is no significant difference between Male and Female teachers towards teacher stress.
3. There is no significant difference between Graduate teachers and post Graduate Teachers towards teacher stress.
4. There is no significant difference between Above 15 tears, and Below 15 years teaching experience towards teacher stress.
5. There is no significant difference between Government School Teachers and Private school Teachers towards teacher stress.
6. There is no significant difference between Male and Female Teachers towards teacher stress in Professional growth.
7. There is no significant difference between Male and Female Teachers towards teacher stress in Work Load.
8. There is no significant difference between Male and Female Teachers towards teacher stress in Occupational Hazards.
9. There is no significant difference between Male and Female Teachers towards teacher stress in Student Behavior.
10. There is no significant difference between Male and Female Teachers towards teacher stress in Family.
11. There is no significant difference between Graduate teachers and Post Graduate Teachers towards teacher stress in Professional Growth
12. There is no significant difference between Graduate teachers and Post Graduate Teachers towards teacher stress in Work Load
13. There is no significant difference between Graduate teachers and Post Graduate Teachers towards teacher stress in Occupational Hazards.

14. There is no significant difference between Graduate teachers and Post Graduate Teachers towards teacher stress in Student Behavior
15. There is no significant difference between Graduate teachers and Post Graduate Teachers towards teacher stress in Family.

## LIMITATIONS OF THE STUDY

1. The study is limited to only teachers of different primary and secondary schools in Chittoor of A.P.
2. Of the three criteria of teaching competency, only two criteria i.e. presage and process are covered in this study.
3. To measure the teaching competency and teacher stress teacher self –rating scales are used in this study.
4. Of many dimensions of teaching competency, planning presentation, closing evaluation, and managerial dimensions are considered in this study.
5. Of many dimensions of teacher stress professional growth, work load, Occupational hazards, Students behavior, family and societal dimensions are considered in this study

## PROCEDURE

In order to test the Hypothesis the investigator planned and executed in three steps

1) Measurement of teacher stress with the help of standardized teacher stress,
2) Measurement of teaching competency with the help of Rama's teaching competency scale.
3) Using appropriate statistical procedures to find out relationship between teacher stress and teaching competency.

## RE-TESTING OF RAMA'S TEACHER STRESS SCALE

In the present study, the investigator adopted the Rama's teacher stress self rating five point scale developed and standardized by Prof. R. Rama (2004) because it is more appropriate to measure the teacher stress related to the areas of

1. Professional Growth 2. Workload 3. Occupational Hazards 4. Student Behavior 5. Family 6. Societal.

There are 46 items under 6 different areas of teacher stress scale of Prof. R. Rama.

Items under professional growth area of teacher stress are 8 i.e., from 1to 8.

Items under Work Load area of teacher stress are 9 i.e., from 9 to 17.

Items under Occupational Hazards area of teacher stress are 9 i.e., from18 to 26.

Items under Student Behavior area of teacher stress are 9 i.e., from 27 to 35.

Items under Family area of teacher stress are 8 i.e., from 36 to 43.

Items under Societal area of teacher stress are 3 i.e., from 44 to 46.

**Table – 2 Variable wise distribution of the Sample**

| Variable | Categories | Size | Grand Total |
|---|---|---|---|
| Sex | Male | 85 | 200 |
| | Female | 115 | |
| Age | Above 35 | 129 | 200 |
| | Below 35 | 71 | |
| Qualification | Graduate | 92 | 200 |
| | Post-Graduate | 108 | |
| Management | Government | 99 | 200 |
| | Private | 101 | |
| Teaching | Above 15 | 92 | 200 |
| Experience | Below 15 | 108 | |

## SELECTION OF THE TOOL

A research tool plays a major role in any worthwhile research as it is the sole factor is determining the sound data and in arriving at perfect conclusions about the problem or study on hand, which ultimately, helps in providing suitable remedial measures to the problem concerned.

The progress of making depends upon well-conducted research programme. Well conducted research programmes postulate sufficient, reliable and valid facts such facts are obtained through a systematic procedure, which involves various devices. Each rehear tool is appropriate in a given situation to accomplish a particular purpose. It may be stressed that these tools may be used in combination. They supplement the work of each other.

John Best observes, "Like the tools in the carpenter box, each research tool is appropriate in a given situation to accomplish a particular purpose". Each data gathering –device has both merits and Hazards of limitations.

Different tools are used to collect various kinds of information for different purposes. The investigator should familiarize themselves with nature, merits and limitations of these tools and should attempt to learn how to construct and use them effectively.

The following are some of the tools generally employed for the purpose of research.

a) Inquiry forms:

1. Questionnaire
2. Schedule
3. Check-list
4. Rating scale
5. Score card
6. Attitude scale

b) Observation
c) Interview
d) Sociometry
e). Psychological tests:

1. Achivement test
2. Aptitude test
3. Intelligence test
4. Interest Inventory
5. Personality measures

Inequity forms are class of data gathering devices which make use of properly prepared Performa or forms for enquiring into and securing information about certain phenomena under study. Out of number of such inequity forms, perhaps the most used and the most abused of tools is the questionnaire.

Keeping in view the desirability and suitability for the collection of the data, the investigator adapted the questionnaire in case of the present investigation.

## ADMINISTRATION OF THE TOOL

The investigator personally went to each institution and has taken permission from the respective head of the institutions and personally administered to 200 teachers in the various schools. The investigator first explained to the teachers about the importance of the investigation and attitude of teachers towards teacher stress in relation to teaching competency in school teachers. As stated earlier, the present investigation is intended to the attitudes of schoolteachers.

## ANALISIS OF THE DATA

The following statistical techniques are followed to analyze of the data.

1. Mean and Standard Deviation of all the distributions are calculated.
2. To find out the relationship between teacher stress and teaching competency 'r' values are computed.

The analyze and interpretation of the present data is presented in proceeding Chapter

## SCORING PROCEDURE

The responses are scored in stress according to key, for all the items scores from five to one for the five responses i.e. N. S. (No stress), Mi. S (Mild stress), Mo. S (Moderate Stress), M. S.(More Stress), S. S. (Sevier Stress) total No. of items 46 in teacher stress scale.

**Table-3: The weightage given to responses**

| KIND OF RESPONSES | MARKS |
|---|---|
| No Stress (N.S) | **5** |
| Mild Stress (Mi. S.) | **4** |
| Moderate Stress (Mo. S.) | **3** |
| More Stress (M. S.) | **2** |
| Sevier Stress (S. S.) | **1** |

**STITISTICAL TECHNIQUES USED**

The above-mentioned hypotheses, which were framed keeping the variables like age, sex, teaching experience, medium of teaching, Qualification Type of management were taken into consideration. The collected data analyzed and the results are interpreted and statistical aspects like means, standard deviation and critical ratios are taken as the statistical techniques to study and analyze the variables. Co-efficient of co-relation with the help of scatter diagram was made use of to study the reliability of the test scores. The technique of the significance of the difference between means is used. Here technique only large samples in different categories considered for comparison so that use was made only of the formula for large samples. It was further assumed that the means were uncorrelated.

Where
A.M =Arithmetic mean
A.A.M = Assumed arithmetic mean
S.D = Standard deviation
C.R = Critical Ratio
1,2 = Standard deviation of two samples
M1, m2 = Means of the two samples
N1,N2 = The size of the two sample

# 20. Analysis and Interpretation of the Data

## INTRODUCTION

Data analysis is the heart of any social science research. Using questionnaire or any inventory the researcher collects the information. Until and unless, it is proposed through statistical treatment, it serves no purpose. The researcher using the standardized procedure that tool so constructed collected data from various variables. The he collected information is given numerical scoring and scores are tabulated. The mean, median, mode, quartile deviation, standard deviation, kurtosis etc. are also obtained. Basing on the responses of the individuals the the researcher tabulated the item of the tool according to their scoring order presented findings and calculations. Finally, the researcher presented suggestions for the teacher stress in relation to teaching competency scope for further research.

## ANALYSIS

The analysis and interpretation of data involves the objectives material in the processions of the research and his subjective and desires to derive from the data, the inherent meaning in their relation to the problem. To avoid making conclusions are interpretations from insufficient are invalid data, the final analysis must be anticipated in detailed when plans are being made for collecting information.

J. C. Agarwal, has explained thus:"However values, reliable and adequate the data may be, it does not serve any worthwhile purpose unless it is carefully edited. Systematically analyzed intelligently interpreted and rationally concluded".

Analysis of data means studying the tabulated material in order to determine inherent facts of meaning. It involves breaking down existing complex factors into smaller parts and putting the together in new arrangements for purposes interpretation.

## THE FOLLOWING ARE THE METHODS MOST COMMONLY USED IN STATISTICAL ANALYSIS

1. Calculating frequency distribution (usually in percentage) of items under study.
2. Testing the data for morality of distribution-Skewness and Kurtosis.
3. Calculating methods of central tendency –Mean, Median, Mode and establishing norms.
4. Calculating percentile and percentile ranks.
5. Calculating measures of dispersion –Standard deviation, Mean deviation, Quartile deviation and Range.
6. Calculating measures of relationship-Coefficient of correlation reliability and validity.
7. Graphical representation of data –Frequency Polygon curve, Hectograph, Cumulative frequency, Polygon and Ogive etc.

In the process of analysis of the data, the investigators usually make used of us many of the above simply statistical devises as necessary for purpose of their study. There are some other complicated devices of statistical analysis which researches use in particular experimental or complex casual comparative studies investigation.

## INTERPRETATION

"The process of interpretation is essentially one of the stating what the results (findings) show, what do they means What is their significance What is the answer to original problem

Interpretation is thus by no means a much of process. Its uses of scientific examination of the results of one's analysis in the light of all the limitations of the data gathering, Interpretation means the application of deductive and inductive logic to the research process.

Interpretation is the most important step in the total procedure of research, it is purely subjective and many errors are made at their stage.

An adequate knowledge not only of techniques of research, but also of one's field of study and a capacity to do carefully and critical thinking are very essential to safe guard against misinterpretation of facts collected.

The analysis and interpretation of the data represent the application of deductive and inductive logic to the research process. Interpretation calls for a critical examination of the result of one's analysis in the light of all the limitation of the data gathering and his subjective attitude to avoid subjectively, one must be critical on one's own thinking.

Good, Barr and Scats the following characteristics of good generalizations.

1. Education generalization should be conceivable and in agreement with facts.
2. They should not conflict with the known laws of nature of previously established generalization.
3. They should be stated in the simplest possible terms.
4. They should be amenable to deductive reasoning.

In this part the result of present study are analyzed and interpreted. The results are presented and all the hypotheses are tested and verified in the present study, the results are analyzed and presented in three parts.

1. The first part deals with related to significant relationship between the teacher stress and teaching competency.
2. The second part deals with testing the hypotheses pertaining to teacher stress.
3. The third part deals with testing the hypotheses pertaining to teaching competency.

## TESTING OF HYPOTHESES-1

There is no significant difference between above 35 years age of teachers and blow 35 years age of teachers towards teachers stress.

To test the validity of the above hypothesis, the following calculations are made. Table showing the significant difference between above 35 years age of teachers and below 35 years age of teacher in respect of teachers stress.

**TABLE -4**

| AGE | N | MEAN | SD | 't' VALUE |
|---|---|---|---|---|
| 1.00 | 129 | 161.66 | 35.70 | 0.56 |
| 2.00 | 71 | 158.87 | 29.49 | @ |

From the above table the calculated 't' value is 0.56 found to be less than the table value (1.96) at 0.05 level. Hence, the hypothesis-1 is accepted. Hence, there is no significance difference between above 35 years age of teachers and below 35 years age of teachers towards teacher stress.

## TESTING OF HYPOTHESES - 2

There is no significant difference between male and female teachers towards teacher stress.

To test the validity of the above hypothesis, the following calculations are made. The table showing the significant differences between male and female teachers in respect of teacher stress.

**TABLE -5**

| SEX | N | MEAN | SD | 't' VALUE |
|---|---|---|---|---|
| 1.00 | 85 | 28.41 | 6.02 | 1.54 |
| 2.00 | 115 | 29.78 | 6.33 | @ |

From the above table the calculated 't' value is 1.54 found to be less than the table value (1.96) at 0.05 level. Hence, the hypothesis-2 is accepted. Hence, there is no significance difference between male and female teacher towards teacher stress.

## TESTING OF HYPOTHESES - 3

There is no significant difference between graduate teachers and post-graduate teachers towards teacher stress.

To test the validity of the above hypothesis, the following calculations are made. The table showing the significant differences between graduate teachers and post-graduate teachers in respect of teacher stress.

**TABLE -6**

| EDUCATIONAL QUALIFICATION | N | MEAN | SD | 't' VALUE |
|---|---|---|---|---|
| 1.00 | 92 | 164.22 | 37.00 | 1.386 |
| 2.00 | 108 | 157.63 | 30.20 | @ |

From the above table the calculated 't' value is 1.386 found to be greater than the table value (1.96) at 0.05 level. Hence, the hypothesis-3 is accepted. Hence, there no is significance difference between graduate teacher and post-graduate teachers towards teacher stress.

## TESTING OF HYPOTHESES - 4

There is no significant difference between above 15 years, and below 15 years teaching experience towards teacher stress.

To test the validity of the above hypothesis, the following calculations are made. The table showing the significant differences between teaching experience of above 15 years and below 15 years towards in respect of teacher stress.

**TABLE -7**

| TEACHING EXPERIENCE | N | MEAN | SD | 't' VALUE |
|---|---|---|---|---|
| 1.00 | 92 | 159.78 | 36.488 | 0.344 |
| 2.00 | 108 | 161.42 | 31.044 | @ |

From the above table the calculated 't' value is 0.344 found to be greater than the table value (1.96) at 0.05 level. Hence, the hypothesis-4 is accepted. Hence, there is no significance difference between experience of above 15 years and below 15 years towards teacher stress.

## TESTING OF HYPOTHESES - 5

There is no significant difference between govt. school teachers and private school teachers towards teacher stress.

To test the validity of the above hypothesis, the following calculations are made. The table showing the significant differences between govt. school teachers and private school teachers towards in respect of teacher stress.

**TABLE -8**

| TYPE OF MANAGEMENT | N | MEAN | SD | 't' VALUE |
|---|---|---|---|---|
| 1.00 | 91 | 161.67 | 32.47 | 0.419 |
| 2.00 | 108 | 159.68 | 34.76 | @ |

From the above table the calculated 't' value is 0.419 found to be greater than the table value (1.96) at 0.05 level. Hence, the hypothesis-5 is accepted. Hence, there is no significance difference between govt. school teachers and private school teachers towards teacher stress.

## TESTING OF HYPOTHESES - 6

There is no significant difference between male and female teachers towards teacher stress in professional growth.

To test the validity of the above hypothesis, the following calculations are made. The table showing the significant differences between male and female teachers in respect of teacher stress in professional growth.

**TABLE -9**

| SEX | N | MEAN | SD | 't' VALUE |
|---|---|---|---|---|
| 1.00 | 85 | 28.41 | 6.02 | 01.544 |
| 2.00 | 115 | 29.78 | 6.33 | @ |

From the above table the calculated 't' value is 01.544 found to be less than the table value (1.96) at 0.05 level. Hence, the hypothesis-6 is accepted. Hence, there is no significance difference between male and female teacher towards teacher stress in professional growth.

## TESTING OF HYPOTHESES - 7

There is no significant difference between male and female teachers towards teacher stress in work load.

To test the validity of the above hypothesis, the following calculations are made. The table showing the significant differences between male and female teachers in respect of teacher stress in work load.

**TABLE -10**

| SEX | N | MEAN | SD | 't' VALUE |
|---|---|---|---|---|
| 1.00 | 85 | 30.20 | 8.22 | 0.939 |
| 2.00 | 115 | 31.32 | 8.44 | @ |

From the above table the calculated't' value is -.939 found to be greater than the table value (1.96) at 0.05 level. Hence, the hypothesis-7 is accepted. Hence, there is no significance difference between male and female teacher towards teacher stress in workload.

## TESTING OF HYPOTHESES - 8

There is no significant difference between male and female teachers towards teacher stress in occupational hazards.

To test the validity of the above hypothesis, the following calculations are made. The table showing the significant differences between male and female teachers in respect of teacher stress in occupational hazards.

**TABLE -11**

| SEX | N | MEAN | SD | 't' VALUE |
|---|---|---|---|---|
| 1.00 | 85 | 31.44 | 7.34 | 0.685 |
| 2.00 | 115 | 32.20 | 7.91 | @ |

From the above table the calculated 't' value is 0.685 found to be greater than the table value (1.96) at 0.05 level. Hence, the hypothesis-8 is accepted. Hence, there is no significance difference between male and female teacher towards teacher stress in occupational hazards.

## TESTING OF HYPOTHESES - 9

There is no significant difference between male and female teachers towards teacher stress in student behaviour.

To test the validity of the above hypothesis, the following calculations are made. The table showing the significant differences between male and female teachers in respect of teacher stress in student behaviour.

**TABLE -12**

| SEX | N | MEAN | SD | 't' VALUE |
|---|---|---|---|---|
| 1.00 | 85 | 30.87 | 8.51 | 1.386 |
| 2.00 | 115 | 29.26 | 7.81 | @ |

From the above table the calculated 't' value is 1.386 found to be greater than the table value (1.96) at 0.05 level. Hence, the hypothesis-9 is accepted. Hence, there is no significance difference between male and female teacher towards teacher stress in student behaviour.

## TESTING OF HYPOTHESES - 10

There is no significant difference between male and female teachers towards teacher stress in family.

To test the validity of the above hypothesis, the following calculations are made. The table showing the significant differences between male and female teachers in respect of teacher stress in family.

**TABLE -13**

| SEX | N | MEAN | SD | 't' VALUE |
|---|---|---|---|---|
| 1.00 | 85 | 28.01 | 7.266 | 1.305 |
| 2.00 | 115 | 29.417 | 7.72 | @ |

From the above table the calculated 't' value is 1.305 found to be greater than the table value (1.96) at 0.05 level. Hence, the hypothesis-10 is accepted. Hence, there is no significance difference between male and female teacher towards teacher stress in family.

## TESTING OF HYPOTHESES - 11

There is no significant difference between graduate teachers and post-graduate teachers towards stress in professional growth.

To test the validity of the above hypothesis, the following calculations are made. The table showing the significant differences between graduate teachers and post-graduate teachers in respect of teacher stress in professional growth.

**TABLE -14**

| EDUCATIONAL QUALIFICATION | N | MEAN | SD | 't' VALUE |
|---|---|---|---|---|
| 1.00 | 92 | 29.81 | 6.70 | 1.291 |
| 2.00 | 108 | 28.67 | 5.77 | @ |

From the above table the calculated 't' value is 1.291 found to be greater than the table value (1.96) at 0.05 level. Hence, the hypothesis-11 is accepted. Hence, there is no significance difference between graduate teacher and post-graduate teachers towards teacher stress in professional growth.

## TESTING OF HYPOTHESES - 12

There is no significant difference between graduate teachers and post-graduate teachers towards stress in workload.

To test the validity of the above hypothesis, the following calculations are made. The table showing the significant differences between graduate teachers and post-graduate teachers in respect of teacher stress in workload.

**TABLE -15**

| EDUCATIONAL QUALIFICATION | N | MEAN | SD | 't' VALUE |
|---|---|---|---|---|
| 1.00 | 92 | 32.4348 | 8.3827 | 2.518 |
| 2.00 | 108 | 29.4907 | 8.1166 | * |

From the above table the calculated 't' value is 2.518 found to be less than the table value (1.96) at 0.05 level. Hence, the hypothesis-12 is rejected. Hence, there is significance difference between graduate teacher and post-graduate teachers towards teacher stress in workload.

## TESTING OF HYPOTHESES - 13

There is no significant difference between graduate teachers and post-graduate teachers towards stress in occupational hazards.

To test the validity of the above hypothesis, the following calculations are made. The table showing the significant differences between graduate teachers and post-graduate teachers in respect of teacher stress in occupational hazards.

**TABLE -16**

| EDUCATIONAL QUALIFICATION | N | MEAN | SD | 't' VALUE |
|---|---|---|---|---|
| 1.00 | 92 | 32.3696 | 8.2405 | 0.832 |
| 2.00 | 108 | 31.4630 | 7.1662 | @ |

From the above table the calculated 't' value is 0.832 found to be greater than the table value (1.96) at 0.05 level. Hence, the hypothesis-13 is accepted. Hence, there is no significance difference between graduate teacher and post-graduate teachers towards teacher stress in occupational hazards.

## TESTING OF HYPOTHESES - 14

There is no significant difference between graduate teachers and post-graduate teachers towards stress in student behaviour.

To test the validity of the above hypothesis, the following calculations are made. The table showing the significant differences between graduate teachers and post-graduate teachers in respect of teacher stress in student behaviour.

**TABLE -17**

| EDUCATIONAL QUALIFICATION | N | MEAN | SD | 't' VALUE |
|---|---|---|---|---|
| 1.00 | 92 | 30.0109 | 8.7549 | 0.105 |
| 2.00 | 108 | 29.8889 | 7.6162 | @ |

From the above table the calculated 't' value is 0.105 found to be greater than the table value (1.96) at 0.05 level. Hence, the hypothesis-14 is accepted. Hence, there is no significance difference between graduate teacher and post-graduate teachers towards teacher stress in student behaviour.

## TESTING OF HYPOTHESES - 15

There is no significant difference between graduate teachers and post-graduate teachers towards stress in family.

To test the validity of the above hypothesis, the following calculations are made. The table showing the significant differences between graduate teachers and post-graduate teachers in respect of teacher stress in family.

**TABLE -18**

| EDUCATIONAL QUALIFICATION | N | MEAN | SD | 't' VALUE |
|---|---|---|---|---|
| 1.00 | 92 | 29.27 | 7.68 | 0.781 |
| 2.00 | 108 | 28.43 | 7.44 | @ |

From the above table the calculated 't' value is 0.781 found to be greater than the table value (1.96) at 0.05 level. Hence, the hypothesis-15 is accepted. Hence, there is no significance difference between graduate teacher and post-graduate teachers towards teacher stress in family.

# 21.Summary and Conclusion

It is high time to identify the problem of the teacher in particular his competency and his mental agony to make the teaching learning process useful to the present day condition. In the modern days teacher is loaded with so many sophisticated technological trends that were place in the modern human beings also confronted with many perplexing problems caused due to perpetually changing world resulting in frustration, Conflict, Anxiety, Stress and so on. Coleman in n1982 also observed that, "The 17$^{th}$ century has been called the age of enlightenment, the 18$^{th}$ century the age of reason, the 19$^{th}$ century the age of progress and the 20$^{th}$ century the age of anxiety". This emphasizes that a meaningful and satisfying way of life has become difficult in this age of anxiety the teacher of today is not exempted from the above age of anxiety.

Teaching is a sensitive weapon to achieve the expected educational goals through effective teaching learning process. The effective teaching is possible only with the teacher, those who are mentally sound. We should make the teacher away from the Anxiety, Stress and so on. So as to utilize all his teaching competencies to make the teaching learning processes in an effective way.

The modern research studies observed that the teacher performance and teacher behavior are strongly affected by stress. ARYACDU and SUTCLIFFE (1977) stated that," The stress with the teaching profession may affect the school as an organization, teacher performance, the physical and emotional well being of the teacher".

The modern research studies observed that the teacher performance and teacher behavior are strongly affected by stress. ARYACDU and SUTCLIFRE (1977) stated the, "The stress with the teaching profession may affect the school as an organization, teacher performance, the physical and emotional well being of the teacher".

## MEANING OF STRESS

Stress is a condition stream on one's emotions, thought processes and physical conditions. When it is excessive, it can pretend once ability to cope with environment. (Hans Selye, 1976) "Stress is the general term applied to the pressures; employs developed various symptoms of stress as, "an adjective demand placed on the organism".

Stress has been defined following Lazarus's model, as a state of imbalance when the demands made on the person in different areas of life exceed her / his capabilities and resources (Lazarus and Folkman , 1984)

Stress has been defined following Lazarus (1974) as a state arising from imbalance between the demands made and the coping resources at one's disposal.

Stress has been defined as a state of imbalance between one's personal resources and the environmental demands, and manifested in the form of a number of psychosomatic factor, such as Somatization, Obsessive-Compulsive interpersonal sensitivity, Depression and Anxiety.

## TEACHER STRESS

Job stress is most common psychological phenomena that is prevalent among people who are in different jobs and professions. The stress studies are initially directed toward industrial organizations within the private sector. Researchers have come to believe that stress may be especially prevalent among human service profession, particularly the teaching profession, (Kjyiacou and Suteliffe 1977-78; Pettegrew and Wolf 1982, Cherniss 1980: and Coorper and Marshall 1980). As a teaching is a human service profession, stress within the teaching profession is considerable and may have far-reaching consequences on the entire education system. Teaching is complex process were in teacher is expected to exhibit many skills. This makes a teacher to experiences stress in the profession.

Further, Pettergrew and Wolf (1982) opined that 'Teacher stress has a nationwide concern and relatively new area of empirical research".

Factors prepared by teachers as being troublesome or stressful have included students discipline, negative attitudes towards school, physical violence, is adequate preparation time, lack of clear role definition and heavy workloads". (Bearly, Myette and Serma, 1983; Chichen and Koff, 1978; Olander and Ferrel, 1970).

Teacher is subjected to stress due to incoherent social life, widening social distance, segregation, lack of societal support, corruption, nepotism, unnecessary societal involvement in day-to-day activities, high degree of social indiscipline, deterioration of values, lack of social security etc.

## EFFECTS OF TEACHER STRESS

As job stress effect organizational performance, teacher stress impedes teacher performance in teaching. Infect it is assumed that mild stress can even enhance performance but high level of stress can create physical, Psychological and behavioral problems among teacher. There are several research studies, which observed that, a high level of stress accompanied by physical illness such as high blood pressures, ulcers and even cancer. Similarly high level of stress may be accompanied by psychological problems such as anger, anxiety, depression, nervousness, irritability, tension and boredom. Excessive stress may also result in behavioral problems such as sleeplessness, under eating or over eating, increased smoking and drinking and drug abuse. Many researches of teacher

## TEACHER COMPETENCY AND STRESS-A BRIEFOUTLINE

The study is about teacher competency in relation to stress. Teacher competence, in general scene, impedes when teacher suffer from stress. In this chapter, a discussion is made about teacher competency, stress, and the development of this type of study in the world.

"Teacher competency" refers to the set of knowledge, abilities and beliefs a teacher possess and bring to the teaching situation. Teacher competence differs from teacher performance and teacher effectiveness in that it is a stable characteristic of the teacher that does not change appreciably when the teacher moves from one situation to another. It resembles teacher performance in that it has also been proposed as a basis from which teach effectiveness can be inferred.

## NEED FOR THE STUDY

Accomplishment of educational goals and the objectives of teaching is possible only with the teacher those who are competent in teaching and free from any type of stress. Teacher stress directly or indirectly influences the competency of teacher in teaching. So the teacher who is subjected to stress may not be possible to teach properly which in term Indus is competency in teaching. Theoretically, this teacher stress may be heard to perform teaching in a competent way. But in practice how for teacher stress is influencing on teaching competency and to what extent teacher stress and teaching competency are related-are the questions waiting for answer. Hence, this study has taken up to find out how teacher stress teaching competency are inter related to each other in the context of high school education.

## OBJECTIVES OF THE STUDY

1. To test the teacher stress and teaching competency scales to be use by the teacher himself.
2. To find out the relationship between teacher stress and teaching competency.
3. To find out the effect of demographical variables in respect of teacher stress.
4. To find out the effect of demographical variables in respect of teaching competency.

## HYPOTHESES OF THE STUDY

1. There is no significant difference between Above 35 years age of teachers and Below 35 years age of teachers towards teacher stress.

2. There is no significant difference between Male and Female Teachers towards teacher stress.
3. There is no significant difference between Graduate teachers and Post Graduate Teachers towards teacher stress.
4. There is no significant difference between Above 15 tears, and Below 15 years teaching experience towards teacher stress.
5. There is no significant difference between Government School Teachers and Private school Teachers towards teacher stress.
6. There is no significant difference between Male and Female Teachers towards teacher stress in Professional growth.
7. There is no significant difference between Male and Female Teachers towards teacher stress in Work Load.
8. There is no significant difference between Male and Female Teachers towards teacher stress in Occupational Hazards.
9. There is no significant difference between Male and Female Teachers towards teacher stress in Student Behavior.
10. There is no significant difference between Male and Female Teachers towards teacher stress in Family.
11. There is no significant difference between Graduate teachers and Post Graduate Teachers towards teacher stress in Professional Growth
12. There is no significant difference between Graduate teachers and Post Graduate Teachers towards teacher stress in Work Load
13. There is no significant difference between Graduate teachers and Post Graduate Teachers towards teacher stress in Occupational Hazards.
14. There is no significant difference between Graduate teachers and Post Graduate Teachers towards teacher stress in Student Behavior
15. There is no significant difference between Graduate teachers and Post Graduate Teachers towards teacher stress in Family.

## LIMITATIONS OF THE STUDY

1. The study is limited to only teachers of different schools in Chittoor of A.P.
2. Of the three criteria of teaching competency, only two criteria i.e. presage and process are covered in this study.

3. To measure the teaching competency and teacher stress teacher self –rating scales are used in this study.
4. Of many dimensions of teaching competency, planning presentation, closing evaluation, and managerial dimensions are considered in this study.
5. Of many dimensions of teacher stress professional growth, work load, Occupational hazards, Students behavior, family and societal dimensions are considered in this study

## CONCLUSIONS

From the present study only one factor that is Educational Qualification as significant impact on teachers stress. The male teachers Mean value is 32.4348, which is more than Female teachers mean value (29.4907). The other factors are viz.,

1. There is no significance difference between Above 35 year's age of teachers and below 35 years age of teachers towards teacher stress.
2. There is no significance difference between Male and Female teachers towards teacher stress.
3. There is no significance difference between Graduate teachers and Post-Graduate teachers towards teacher stress.
4. There is no significance difference between Experience of above 15 years and below 15 years towards teacher stress.
5. There is no significance difference between Govt. school teachers and private school teachers towards teacher stress.
6. There is no significance difference between Male and Female teachers towards teacher stress in professional growth.
7. There is no significance difference between Male and Female teachers towards teacher stress in Work Load.
8. There is no significance difference between Male and Female teachers towards teacher stress in Occupational Hazards.
9. There is no significance difference between Male and Female teachers towards teacher stress in Student behavior.
10. There is no significance difference between Male and Female teachers towards teacher stress in Family.
11. There is no significance difference between Graduate teachers and Post-Graduate teachers towards teacher stress in Professional Growth.

12. There is significance difference between Graduate teachers and Post-Graduate teachers towards teacher stress in Work Load.
13. There is no significance difference between Graduate teachers and Post-Graduate teachers towards teacher stress in Occupational Hazards.
14. There is no significance difference between Graduate teachers and Post-Graduate teachers towards teacher stress in Student behavior.
15. There is no significance difference between Graduate teachers and Post-Graduate teachers towards teacher stress in Family.

Hence, there is no significant impact on teachers stress. Teachers would give more importance for the quality of education. It is necessary to encourage teachers to study for the further education. The role of Government is also important to motivate the teachers towards higher education.

## SUGGESTIONS

**EXERCISE:** Physical exercise is accepted as the best antidote to stress. It keeps the body healthy, makes one emotionally strong, and eases nervous tension. It keeps the mind, body and action coordinated.

**RELAXATION:** Relaxation response is an innate physiological change elicited by some psychological means. Evidence indicates that the immune function in the body improves by relaxation training, and its regular practice can help maintain the cool. These can include hobbies like reading, listening to music, etc.

**VALUE EDUCATION:** Intervention for change in social and practical values can help them think and act rationally and proactively.

**MEDITATION:** It is a continuous scream of effortless concentration, on a single point, over an extended period. It is suggested that the concentration should be maintained unbroken. Psychologists have argued that meditation leads to better emotional and physical health.

**YOGA:** A stress management programme in the Indian setting may combine some elements of Gita and Yoga in the preventive plans. Srivastava (1981) concluded that persons coping more effectively with stress have more positive orientation to life in general, and employ a valuable mix of coping and defense response. Yoga is a holistic science, which gives to the person tools and techniques to expand conscious awareness into the unconscious In order to become aware of the patterns and tendencies that cause stress.

1. It is to be suggested that teachers effects teaching competency.
2. The stress creators harm the teacher effectiveness and teaching competency
3. The government or Private management of the institution should improve the conditions for better teaching by reducing the stress factors.
4. The main stress creators like lack of promotional opportunities lack of professional growth are to be tackled to improve the teaching competency.
5. Unless stress creators are reduced qualitative improvement teaching, learning process cannot be improved.

## SUGGESTIONS FOR FURTHER STUDY

1. The study may be extended to higher and primary education.
2. To measure the teaching competency presage, process and product variables may be compared.
3. Stress and psychological well-being Among Tribal and Non-Tribal primary school teachers.
4. Stress and burnout among teachers in Regular and special schools.
5. Stress and coping among college students.
6. Stress and Coping among Adolescents.
7. Relationship between teaching competency and teacher motivation may be studied.
8. Relationship between teacher stress and teacher adjustment may be studied.
9. An extensive study is needed for teacher stress and teaching competency.

# Bibliography


1. Bailkeri, K. N. (1983): Effect of self- Instructional Remedial Micro Teaching course on the Instructional Competency of in service secondary school mathematics teachers.
2. Bhalwankar, A. G. (1984): A study of Reliability and Validity of the process appraising scale of teacher effectiveness.
3. Balachandran, E. S. (1981): Teaching effectiveness and student evaluation of Teaching, Ph.D., Education, Madras University.
4. Coates, T. I. and Thoresen (1976 spring): Teacher anxiety, A review with recommendation, Review of educational research 49(2), pp.159-184.
5. Cooper, C. Marshal, J. (1976): Occupational sources of stress. A review of the literature relating to coronary heart disease and mental ill health Journal of occupational Psychology, pp.11-28.
6. Cox, T. Mackay, C. J. Cox, S. Watts, C. and Brockley (1978): Stress and wellbeing in schoolteachers psycho-physiological response to occupational stress. Paper presented to the Economic Society Conference, Nottingham University England.
7. Dohrenwend, D. et. al (1981): Stress in the community a report to the president's commission on the accidents at three-mile land. Annual of the New York Academy of Sciences 365, 159-174.
8. Dac, R.C. Passi, B K. and Singh, A. (1982): Effectiveness of different strategies of integration of teaching skills in deve-

loping general teaching competency of student's teachers department of teacher education, NCERT.

9. Davis, H. (1964): Evaluation of current practices in evaluating teacher competency, in B. J. Biddle and J. Ellance (Eds). Contemporary research on teacher effectiveness, New York, Holt, Rinehart and Winston.
10. Donald, M. Medley (1982): Teacher Effectiveness" Encyclopedia of Educational Research, Education Harold. E. Mitzel, Vol. 4. Mac millan publishing &Co., New York.
11. Fimian, M. J. and Santoro, T.M. (1983): sources and manifestations of occupational stress and reported by full item special education teachers. Exceptional children, pp. 540-543.
12. Gupta, N. and Beehr, T.A. (1973): "Job stress and employee behavior", Organization behaviors and human performance, pp. 373-387.
13. Girdano, D.E. and Everly, G. S. (1979): Controlling stress and tension, Englewood cliffs, N.J. Prinetice hall.
14. Greenwood, G.E. Olejuik, S. F. and Parkoy, F. W. (1990): Relationship between four teacher efficiency belief patterns and selected teacher characteristics. Journal of research and development in education,23 (2), 102-106.
15. Gupta, S. (1981): A comparative study of Socio-Economic background problems and professional behavior of men women teachers in co-education Institutions at different levels in the state of Haryana, Ph.D., Education, Kurnool University.
16. Gupta, U. (1981): job involvement and need patterns of primary school teachers in relation to teaching effectiveness Ph.D. Education, All Universities.
17. Hodge, J. and Marker (1978): assuring teacher stress; Beneficial task for administrator, American secondary Education, 8(4).
18. Joseph schwrzwaldet at stress reaction of school age children to the Bombardment by send missiles journal of Abnormal Psychology 1993, Vol. 102, No.3, 404-410.
19. Kaiser, J.S. and Polezynski, J. J. (1982): Educational stress sources, reaction, preventions. Poe body journal of education 10.

20. Kessler, R. C. Price, R.H. and Wortman, C. B. (1985): social factors in phycho pathology, stress support and coping process, annual review of psychology 36, 531-572.
21. Kryiacane and Suteliffe, J. (1977): Teacher Stress; A review educational review 29.
22. Kryiacau, C. and Sutclifee, J. (1978): Teacher stress; Prevalence, Source and Symptoms, British journal of educational psychology 48.
23. Lazarus, S. Folkman (1984): Stress appraisal and coping, New York springer publishing company.
24. Lislie Sovoy (1990): "Source of stress on trainee lectures for further and higher education". Journal for Higher education summer (1990).
25. Vene, M.R. (1985): A study of some of the personality components of creative student teacher in relation to their competency towards teaching.
26. Yogendra Kumar and Rattan Lai (1980): Use of micro-teaching in improving general teaching competency of in service teachers.
27. Arnett, J.J. (1999): Adolescent storm and stress, Reconsidered. American Psychologist, pp. 317-326.
28. Folkman, S. and Lazarus, R. S.(1985): If it changes it must be a prosess: Study of emotion and coping during three stages of a college examination. Journal of personality and social psychology, 48, 150-170.
29. Lazarus, R. S. (1993): Coping theory and research: Past, present and future. Psychosomatic Medicine, pp.234-247.

# Spiritual Development Through Education -swami Vivekananda

*Keep your thoughts positive because your thoughts become your words. Keep your words positive because your words become your behaviors. Keep your behaviors positive because your behaviors become your habits. Keep your habits positive because your habits become your values. Keep your values positive because your values become your destiny. ...M.K. Gandhi*

## Introduction

Swami Vivekananda (1863 – 1902), a great thinker and reformer of India, embraces education, which for him signifies 'man-making', as the very mission of his life. Vivekananda realizes that mankind is passing through a crisis. The tremendous emphasis on the scientific and mechanical ways of life is fast reducing man to the status of a machine. Moral and religious values are being undermined. The fundamental principles of civilization are being ignored. Conflicts of ideals, manners and habits are pervading the atmosphere. Disregard for everything old is the fashion of the day. Vivekananda seeks the solutions of all these social and global evils through education. With this end in view, he feels the dire need of awakening man to his spiritual self wherein, he thinks, lies the very purpose of education.

## Goal of Education

Vivekananda points out that the defect of the present-day education is that it has no definite goal to pursue. A sculptor has a clear idea about what he wants to shape out of the marble block; similarly, a painter knows what he is going to paint. But a teacher, he says, has no clear idea about the goal of his teaching. Swamiji attempts to establish, through his words and deeds, that the end of all education is man making. He prepares the scheme of this man-making education in the light of his over-all philosophy of Vedanta. According to Vedanta, the essence of man lies in his soul, which he possesses in addition to his body and mind. In true with this philosophy, Swamiji defines education as 'the manifestation of the perfection already in man.' The aim of education is to manifest in our lives the perfection, which is the very nature of our inner self. This perfection is the realization of the infinite power which resides in everything and every-where-existence, consciousness and bliss (satchidananda). After understanding the essential nature of this perfection, we should identify it with our inner self. For achieving this, one will have to eliminate one's ego, ignorance and all other false identification, which stand in the way. Meditation, fortified by moral purity and passion for truth, helps man to leave behind the body, the senses, the ego and all other non-self elements, which are perishable. He thus realizes his immortal divine self, which is of the nature of infinite existence, infinite knowledge and infinite bliss.

At this stage, man becomes aware of his self as identical with all other selves of the universe, i.e. different selves as manifestations of the same self. Hence education, in Vivekananda's sense, enables one to comprehend one's self within as the self everywhere. The essential unity of the entire universe is realized through education. Accordingly, man making for Swamiji stands for rousing mans to the awareness of his true self. However, education thus signified does not point towards the development of the soul in isolation from body and mind. We have to remember that basis of Swamiji's philosophy is Advaita which preaches unity in diversity. Therefore, man making for him means a harmonious development of the body, mind and soul. Education for him means that process by which character is formed, strength of mind is increased, and intellect is sharpened, as a result of which one can stand on one's own feet.

### Education of the Masses

According to Swami Vivekananda a nation's progress is depending on the spread of education among the masses. The bane of India's progress is that the whole education and intelligence of the land became the monopoly of a handful of men. Unless and until we care for the spread of education among the masses^ no progress will be achieved in this country. Priest power and foreign rule have exploited the poor people to such an extent that they don't even think they are human beings. In a sad situation like this we have to open their eyes and make them see what is happening in the world around. "Our duty is to put the ideas into their heads, they will do the rest." He contended.

Swami blamed 'the cruel society which is interested to shower blows upon the poor man instead of coming to his help in this terrible situation. Next he takes to task the educated of our country. "So long as the millions live in hunger and ignorance I hold every man a traitor who, having been educated at their expense, pays not the least heed to them', said Vivekananda. He regarded the neglect of the masses as a great national sin.

Vivekananda was fully convinced that only through education the lot of the poor can be improved here. Through education we should develop in them their lost individuality, once they become conscious of their human dignity, they would naturally try to rise up from their miserable state. But he was very much disappointed to see that nothing substantial has been done for educating the people. The germs of spirituality stored in our sacred books have to be brought to the common man. This can be done by spreading education among the masses through the medium of mother tongue. Ideas can easily be understood and assimilated even by the common-eat man if they are taught through their own mother-tongue. Our duty is to give those ideas and culture. "Without giving them culture, there can be no permanence in the raised condition of the masses", Vivekananda warned. Besides, they must be instructed in simple words about the necessities of -life and in trade, commerce, agriculture etc.

Once the poor man is made conscious of his strength, that he is the 'Omnipotent' and the 'Omniscient', the rest of the work becomes easy. The moment a fisherman thinks that he is spirit; he will be a better fisherman. Likewise a student becomes a better student, too. But so long as the novelty of the people is not banished, the hope of mass education remains a pious wish. For, even if free schools are opened in villages, the children would rather so to help their parents in their work or try to make a living than going to the school, if the poor bony cannot come to school for education, education must go to him.

## Spiritual Development through Education

There are different types of education for spiritual development viz., Religious Education, Yoga Education, Moral Education...etc.

## Religious Education – Spiritual Development

Hinduism is the world's oldest religious tradition; it goes back to the very dawn of history. The hymns composed some 5,000 years ago are still recited today.

Hinduism is the third largest of the world's religions, after Christianity and Islam. Nearly one-seventh of humanity calls Hinduism their spiritual home. Millions more in South and Southeast Asia and in the Far East trace their spiritual roots to Hinduism.

Hinduism is also the world's largest pluralistic tradition. A multiplicity of spiritual paths and ways are recognized as valid in Hinduism. Hinduism is not based on the teachings of a single Prophet or a single Book. The teachings of many different sages and saints find home within Hinduism. God may be worshiped both in male and female forms. Hinduism has much in common with the earth based religious traditions of the world.

Hinduism is not a creedal religion, based on dogma. Its emphasis is not on correct belief but on search for the Truth. The scripture describes several paths to spiritual development. The mountain peak may be reached by taking any of the several paths.

Sri Aurobindo (1872-1950), the great Indian seer of the first half of the twentieth century declared that Hinduism (also known as *Sanatan Dharma* or the eternal tradition) was rising not for India alone but for the world. Arnold Toynbee in his *A Study of History* was of the view that Hinduism will gain the status of a world religion in the new century.

Hindus believe that Reality is One – Ekam Sat. This Reality is everywhere, in everything, in every being. It is one and many at the same time and it also transcends them both. At the popular level, the One Reality is worshipped as the Trinity: Brahma the creator, Vishnu the preserver and Shiva the dissolver. Brahma, Vishnu and Shiva are not different gods, but they represent different faces of the One Supreme. Brahma, Vishnu and Shiva have their respective female consorts: Saraswati, Lakshmi and Durga. Even though God is One, Hindus worship God in a number of both male and female forms. Ram Swarup puts the matter this way:

Spiritual life is one but it is vast and rich in expression. The human mind conceives it differently. If the human mind was uniform without different depths, heights and levels of subtlety; or if all men had the same mind, the same psyche, the same imagination, the same needs, in short, if all men were the same, then perhaps One God would do. But a man's mind is not a fixed quantity and men and their powers and needs are different. So only some form of polytheism alone can do justice to this variety and richness. **- The Word As Revelation: Names of Gods, 1980.**

**FOUR PATHS**: Hinduism prescribes four ways of spiritual salvation, depending on the personality of the seeker.

1. For the active person, there is Karma yoga, the path of selfless works.
2. For the contemplative and intellectual person, there is Jnana Yoga, the path of Knowledge.
3. For the emotional person, there is Bhakti yoga, the path of love and surrender. Bhakti yoga is said to be similar to the Christian path of love.
4. Finally, Raja yoga is the path of meditative exercises including concentration and one-pointedness. This path focusing on meditation has become popular in the West

**Yoga Education – Spiritual Development**

**The Eight Limbs (Ashtanga) of Raja Yoga**

The eight "limbs" or steps prescribed in the second pada of the Yoga Sutras are: Yama, Niyama, Asana, Pranayama, Pratyahara, Dharana, Dhyana and Samadhi.

Ashtanga yoga consists of the following steps: The first five are called external aids to Yoga (bahiranga sadhana)

- **Yama** refers to the five abstentions. These are the same as the five vows of Jainism.
- **Ahimsa**: non-violence, inflicting no injury or harm to others or even to one's ownself, it goes as far as nonviolence in thought, word and deed.
- **Satya**: truth in word & thought.
- **Asteya**: non-covetousness, to the extent that one should not even desire something that is not his own.
- **Brahmacharya**: abstain from sexual intercourse; celibacy in case of unmarried people and monogamy in case of married people. Even this to the extent that one should not possess any sexual thoughts towards any other man or woman except one's own spouse. It's common to associate Brahmacharya with celibacy.
- **Aparigraha**: non-possessiveness

- **Niyama** refers to the five observances
    - **Shaucha**: cleanliness of body & mind.
    - **Santosha**: satisfaction; satisfied with what one has.
    - **Tapas**: austerity and associated observances for body discipline & thereby mental control.
    - **Svadhyaya**: study of the Vedic scriptures to know about God and the soul, which leads to introspection on a greater awakening to the soul and God within,
    - **Ishvarapranidhana**: surrender to (or worship of) God.
- **Asana**: Discipline of the body: rules and postures to keep it disease-free and for preserving vital energy. Correct postures are a physical aid to meditation, for they control the limbs and nervous system and prevent them from producing disturbances.
- **Pranayama**: control of breath. Beneficial to health, steadies the body and is highly conducive to the concentration of the mind.

- **Pratyahara**: withdrawal of senses from their external objects.
- The last three levels are called internal aids to Yoga (antaranga sadhana)
- **Dharana**: concentration of the citta upon a physical object, such as a flame of a lamp, the mid point of the eyebrows, or the image of a deity.
- **Dhyana**: steadfast meditation. Undisturbed flow of thought around the object of meditation (pratyayaikatanata). The act of meditation and the object of meditation remain distinct and separate.
- **Samadhi**: oneness with the object of meditation. There is no distinction between act of meditation and the object of meditation. Samadhi is of two kinds:

**Samprajnata Samadhi** conscious samadhi. The mind remains concentrated (ekagra) on the object of meditation, therefore the consciousness of the object of meditation persists. Mental modifications arise only in respect of this object of meditation. This state is of four kinds:

- Savitarka: the Citta is concentrated upon a gross object of meditation such as a flame of a lamp, the tip of the nose, or the image of a deity.
- Savichara: the Citta is concentrated upon a subtle object of meditation , such as the tanmatras
- Sananda: the Citta is concentrated upon a still subtler object of meditation, like the senses.
- Sasmita: the Citta is concentrated upon the ego-substance with which the self is generally identified.

**Asamprajnata Samadhi** supraconscious. The citta and the object of meditation are fused together. The consciousness of the object of meditation is transcended. All mental modifications are checked (niruddha), although latent impressions may continue.

Combined simultaneous practice of Dhâranâ, Dhyâna & Samâdhi is referred to as Samyama and is considered a tool of achieving various perfections, or Siddhis.

## Yoga and Religion

Yoga is not a religion. It has no creed or fixed set of beliefs, nor is there a prescribed godlike figure to be worshipped in a particular manner. Religions for the most part seem to be based upon the belief in and worship of things (God or godlike figures) that exist outside one-self. The core of Yoga's philosophy is that everything is supplied from within the individual. Thus, there is no dependence on an external figure, either in the sense of a person or god figure, or a religious organization.

The common belief that Yoga derives from Hinduism is a misconception. Yoga actually predates Hinduism by many centuries. Ancient seals unearthed in the Indus Valley provide clear evidence of widespread Yoga practice earlier than 3,000 B.C.E. The techniques of Yoga have been adopted by Hinduism as well as by other world religions. Yoga is a system of techniques that can be used for a number of goals, from simply managing stress better, learning to relax, and increasing limberness all the way to becoming more self-aware and acquiring the deepest knowledge of one's own self.

The practice of Yoga will not interfere with any religion. Many American Yoga Association students who have practiced Yoga intensively for many years continue to follow the religious traditions they have grown up in or adopted without conflict.

## Swami Vivekananda Spiritual Quotes

1. Anything that brings spiritual, mental or physical weakness, touch it not with the toes of your feet.
2. Be brave! Be strong! Be fearless! Once you have taken up the spiritual life, fight as long as there is any life in you. Even though you know you are going to be killed, fight till you "are killed." Don't die of fright. Die fighting. Don't go down till you are knocked down.
3. BY the study of different RELIGIONS we find that in essence they are one.
4. By the Vedas no books are meant. They mean the accumulated treasury of spiritual laws discovered by different persons in different times. Just as the law of gravitation existed before

its discovery, and would exist if all humanity forgot it, so is it with the laws that govern the spiritual world

5. External nature is only internal nature writ large.
6. Give up all desire for enjoyment in earth or heaven. Control the organs of the senses and control the mind. Bear every misery without even knowing that you are miserable. Think of nothing but spiritual freedom.
7. GOD is to be worshipped as the one beloved, dearer than everything in this and next life.
8. God is very merciful to those whom He sees struggling heart and soul for spiritual realization. But remain idle, without any struggle, and you will see that His grace will never come.
9. GOD of truth, be Thou alone my guide...
10. Let us put forth all our energies to acquire that which never fails—our spiritual perfection. If we have true yearning for realization, we must struggle, and through struggle growth will come. We shall make mistakes, but they may be angels unawares.
11. Never think there is anything impossible for the soul. It is the greatest heresy to think so. If there is sin, this is the only sin? To say that you are weak, or others are weak.
12. Our supreme duty is to advance toward freedom—physical, mental, and spiritual—and help others to do so.
13. Records of great spiritual men of the past do us no good whatever except that they urge us onward to do the same, to experience religion ourselves.
14. Renunciation is the background of all religious thought wherever it be, and you will always find that as this idea of renunciation lessens, the more will the senses creep into the field of religion, and spirituality will decrease in the same ratio.
15. Salvation is not achieved by inactivity but by spiritual activities.
16. Save the spiritual store in your body by observing continence.

17. "Seek ye first the kingdom of God, and everything shall be added unto you".This is the one great duty, this is renunciation. Live for an ideal, and leave no place in the mind for anything else. Let us put forth all our energies to acquire that which never fails—our spiritual perfection. If we have true yearning for realization, we must struggle, and through struggle growth will come. We shall make mistakes, but they may be angels unawares.

18. Take up one idea. Make that one idea your life - think of it, dream of it, live on that idea. Let the brain, muscles, nerves, every part of your body, be full of that idea, and just leave every other idea alone. This is the way to success that is way great spiritual giants are produced.

19. The animal has its happiness in the senses, the human beings in their intellect, and the gods in spiritual contemplation. It is only to the soul that has attained to this contemplative state that the world really becomes beautiful.

20. The first sign of your becoming religious is that you are becoming cheerful

21. The greatest help to spiritual life is meditation. In meditation we divest ourselves of all material conditions and feel our divine nature. We do not depend upon any external help in meditation. The touch of the soul can paint the brightest color even in the dingiest places; it can cast a fragrance over the vilest thing; it can make the wicked divine—and all enmity, all selfishness is effaced.

22. The more we come out and do good to others, the more our hearts will be purified, and God will be in them.

23. This is the great lesson that we are here to learn through myriads of births and heavens and hells—that there is nothing to be asked for, desired for, beyond one's spiritual Self (atman).

24. Tremendous purity, tremendous renunciation, is the one secret of spirituality. "Neither through wealth, nor through progeny, but through renunciation alone is immortality to be reached," say the Vedas. "Sell all that thou hast and give to poor, and follow me," says the Christ. So all great saints and

prophets have expressed it, and have carried it out in their lives. How can great spirituality come without renunciation?

25. We are what our thoughts have made us; so take care about what you think. Words are secondary. Thoughts live; they travel far.

26. What is material and what is not material? When the world is the end and God the means to attain that end, then that is material. When God is the end and the world is only the means to attain that end, spirituality has begun.

27. Where can we go to find God if we cannot see Him in our own hearts and in every living being.

28. You cannot believe in God until you believe in yourself.

29. You have to grow from the inside out. None can teach you, none can make you spiritual. There is no other teacher but your own soul.

## Conclusions

Inculcation of Spiritual values in each and every student is important. Today we are facing so many problems like terrorism, poverty, corruption, illiteracy, alcoholism and teenage pregnancy. Terrorism is the most dangerous problem in the modern world. The only cause for all these problems is lack of spiritual knowledge. We are giving priority or importance for external world. "*Brahma Satyam, Jagat Mithya, and Jivo Brahmaiva naparah*"...according this the ultimate reality is Brahman. There is no difference between self and Brahman. If any one loves God, definitely he loves fellow human beings. Love and affection towards fellow human beings, animals and plants is more important. Spiritual knowledge gives discriminative power- what is right? What is wrong? Which is good? Which is bad? What is right way? Etc. It is the duty of parents and teacher to develop spiritual values in the students. Education is power. Through Education it is easy to inculcate spiritual knowledge in the students. According to swami Vivekananda education means that character is formed, strength of mind is increased, and intellect is sharpened, as a result of which one can stand on one's own feet. It is the fore most duty of government to provide such type of education for all.

## References


1. Amareswaran, N. (2010). "*Moral Values of Intermediate Students*", Discovery Publication, New Delhi.
2. Amareswaran, N. (2011): "*Importance of Yoga for Human Wellbeing*", edited by Anjana Kaul, Discovery Publication, New Delhi.
3. Madan Lal Goel. "*Religious Tolerance and Hinduism*", unpublished article.
4. Sudipa dutta Roy (2001). "*Education in the Vision of Swami Vivekananda*", published in 'e-Samskriti: The Essence of Indian Culture', online article.

# The Mind and The Heart

In 1998, the National Basketball Association (NBA) owners initiated a 202-day lockout of players, resulting in a loss of about $1 billion for owners and about half a billion dollars in foregone salaries for basketball players. Fans were frustrated and disenchanted, and supporters and advertisers lost millions. In 1999, the members of the World Trade Organization met in Seattle, Washington to lower trade barriers. The members of the organization could not even agree on an agenda and the meeting was an utter failure.

During 1999, Belinda Clark handled about 200 job offers for nursing assistants, research scientists, and a number of other employees. All but about 10 of these candidates took the initial offer without attempting to negotiate for something extra or more. Clark was delighted, but puzzled. The job applicants apparently did not realize that the offers Clark made were just starting points. She says, laughing, "I don't say anything if they don't." (Clark 1999, 88)

These examples suggest that negotiating is not easy. This is a problem, considering that people negotiate in their personal and business relationships, within organizations, between companies, across industries, and among nations. Furthermore, negotiations occur between two people and, in other cases—such as the World Trade Organization—hundreds of people. The variety of negotiation contexts presents special challenges for managers, who are required to demonstrate competencies in all of these contexts.This book is designed to improve managers' and executives' negotiation skills across a wide variety of situations.

The working definition of **negotiation** used in this book is "an interpersonal decision-making process by which two or more people agree how to allocate scarce resources." By this definition, it is difficult to imagine how people can get through a single day without negotiating.

## NEGOTIATION AS A CORE MANAGEMENT COMPETENCY

Effective negotiation skills are increasingly important for executives, leaders, and managers in the business world. There are five key reasons for this.

## DYNAMIC NATURE OF BUSINESS

Mobility and flexibility are the dictates of the new world of work. The dynamic, changing nature of business means that people must negotiate and renegotiate their existence in organizations throughout the duration of their careers. The advent of decentralized business structures and the absence of hierarchical decision making provide opportunities for managers, but they also pose some daunting challenges. For example, most people do not stay in the same job that they take upon graduating from college or receiving their MBA degree; furthermore, most people will not have the same job as their predecessor. These realities mean that people must continually create possibilities, integrate their interests with others, and recognize that there will be competition both within companies and between companies (see Sidebar 1–1). Managers must be in a near-constant mode of negotiating opportunities.

## SIDEBAR 1–1. NEW BUSINESSES AND CAREERS

According to *Business Week* (Alderman, 1999), it is the "era of the employee," with the tightest labor market in 29 years. This means that employees are in a one-up position, and employers need to keep them happy. For example, Doug Ross, the owner of Evolution Film & Tape Inc., a television production company in North Hollywood, California, lets his employees create their own hours, dress as they please, and bring their children to work—all in order to stay competitive. Employees and companies are in positions to negotiate all kinds of things, such as opportunities for training, flex time, family leave, health insurance, and other benefits. Another example: The

California based Cheesecake Factory, Inc., pays salaries 20 percent above market rates. It also gives stock options to all its general managers, as well as new BMW 323s. This sounds expensive, but Cheesecake Factory says it has actually saved money, losing only two general managers in the last two years in an industry where a 38 percent turnover is the average (Conlin, Coy, Palmer, and Saveri 1999).

According to Linda Greene, associate vice-chancellor for academic affairs at the University of Wisconsin—Madison, "Many important events essential to professional success and professional satisfaction happen every day in the workplace and they are not always announced in advance" (Kalk 2000, 1E). In truth, negotiation comes into play when people participate in important meetings, get new assignments, head a team, participate in a reorganization process, and set priorities for their work unit (Kalk 2000). Ideally, negotiation should be second nature, but often, it is not.

## INTERDEPENDENCE

The increasing interdependence of people within organizations, both laterally and hierarchically, implies that people need to know how to integrate their interests and work together across business units and functional areas. This not only occurs within companies, as people from different departments and units integrate their knowledge to create a product or service, but it also occurs between people from different companies, as is the case with strategic alliances. The increasing degree of specialization and expertise in the business world implies that people are more and more dependent on others to supply the components for a complete service or product. It is unwise to assume that others have similar incentive structures, so managers need to know how to promote their own interests while simultaneously creating joint value for their organizations. This requires negotiation.

## COMPETITION

Business is increasingly competitive. In today's economy, a few large firms are emerging as dominant players in the biggest markets. These industry leaders often enjoy vast economies of scale and earn tremendous profits. The losers are often left with little in the way of a market, let alone a marketable product (Frank and Cook 1995). This means that companies must be experts in the vast fields of competition. Managers not only need to function as advocates for their products and services, but they must also recognize the competition that is inevitable between companies and, in some cases, between units within a given company. Understanding how to navigate this competitive environment is essential for successful negotiation.

## INFORMATION AGE

The information age also provides special opportunities and challenges for the manager as negotiator. Computer technology, for example, extends a company's obligations and capacity to add value to its customers. This must be accomplished in a way that also benefits the company. Further, with ever-improving technology making it possible to communicate with people anywhere in the world, managers need to be able to negotiate at a moment's notice. Thus, the ability to determine relevant information from irrelevant information is critical for successful negotiation in the information overload age.

## DIVERSITY

Increasing diversity means that managers need to develop negotiation skills that can be successfully employed with people of different nationalities, backgrounds, and styles of communication. Thus, negotiators who have developed a bargaining style that works only within a narrow subset of the business world will suffer unless they can broaden their negotiation skills to effectively work with different people across functional units, industries, and cultures (Bazerman and Neale 1992). It is a challenge to develop a negotiation skill set generalizable enough to be used across different contexts, groups, and continents, but specialized enough to provide meaningful behavioral strategies in any given situation. This book provides the manager with such skills.

## MOST PEOPLE ARE INEFFECTIVE NEGOTIATORS

Because negotiation is so important for personal and business success, it is rather surprising that most people do not negotiate very well—judging from their performance in realistic business negotiation simulations (for reviews, see Neale and Bazerman 1991; Thompson and Hrebec 1996; Thompson 1990a). For example, in a recent investigation of senior-level executives from major companies across the world, 95 percent reached suboptimal outcomes in a realistic business simulation; in practical terms, they "left money on the table."They are not alone. A voluminous body of evidence indicates that people consistently leave money on the table; walk away from profitable deals and in some cases, settle for something worse than they could otherwise obtain by pursuing a different course of action.

## THE MAJOR SINS OF NEGOTIATION

There are four major shortcomings in negotiation we have observed and documented in our research. They are:

**1. Leaving money on the table** (also known as "lose-lose" negotiation) occurs when negotiators fail to recognize and exploit win-win potential.

**2. Settling for too little** (also known as "the winner's curse") occurs when negotiators make too-large concessions, resulting in a too-small share of the bargaining pie.

**3. Walking away from the table** occurs when negotiators reject terms offered by the other party that are demonstrably better than any other option available to them. (Sometimes this is traceable to hubris or overweening pride; other times, it results from gross miscalculation.)

**4. Settling for terms that are worse than your alternative** (also known as the "agreement bias") occurs when negotiators feel obligated to reach agreement even when the settlement terms are not as good as their other alternatives.

This book teaches you how to avoid these errors, create value in negotiation, get your share of the bargaining pie, reach agreement when it is profitable to do so, and quickly recognize when agreement is not a viable option in a negotiation.

## *WHY* ARE PEOPLE INEFFECTIVE NEGOTIATORS?

The dramatic instances of lose-lose outcomes, the winner's curse, walking away from the table, and the agreement bias raise the question of why people are not more effective at the bargaining table if negotiation is indeed critical for business success. The reason is not due to a lack of motivation or lack of intelligence on the part of negotiators. Many of the managers who fall victim to the major sins of negotiation do so for three primary causes: absence of feedback, satisfying, and self-reinforcement.

## ABSENCE OF RELEVANT AND DIAGNOSTIC FEEDBACK

Most people have little opportunity to learn how to negotiate effectively. The problem is not lack of experience but a shortage of timely and accurate feedback. Even those people who have daily experiences in negotiation receive very little feedback on their negotiating effectiveness. The absence of feedback results in two human biases that further prevent negotiators from optimally benefiting from experience. The first problem is the **confirmation bias,** or the tendency for people to see what they want to see when appraising their own performance. The confirmation bias leads people to selectively seek information that confirms what they believe is true. Whereas the confirmation bias may seem perfectly harmless, it results in a myopic view of reality and can hinder learning. A second problem associated with the absence of relevant and diagnostic feedback is **egocentrism,** which is the tendency for people to view their experiences in a way that is flattering or fulfilling for themselves. This may increase a manager's self-esteem; however, in the long run, it does a disservice to managers by preventing them from learning effectively. For example, it was egocentrism and the corresponding inability to recognize her own shortcomings that lead to the removal of Jill Barad as chairperson/CEO of toy maker Mattel Inc. (Byrne and Grover 2000). According to analysts, Barad never assumed responsibility for earnings surprises or adverse announcements. Instead, she blamed her subordinates and sacked them.

## SATISFICING

The second reason why people often fall short in negotiation is due to the human tendency to satisfied (Simon 1955). **Satisfying** is the opposite of *optimizing:* In a negotiation situation, as we will argue later in this book, it is important to optimize one's strategies by setting high aspirations and attempting to achieve as much as possible; in contrast, when people satisfied, they settle for something less than they could otherwise have. Over the long run, satisfying (or the acceptance of mediocrity) can do one's self and one's company a disservice because there is a variety of effective negotiation strategies and skills that can be cheaply employed to result in dramatic increases in profit (we will discuss these strategies in detail in the next three chapters).

## SELF-REINFORCEMENT

The final reason why people perform poorly in negotiation is due to a principle known as **self-reinforcement,** which is the reluctance to try something new or change certain behaviors. It works like this: People are reluctant to change their behavior and experiment with new courses of action because of the risks associated with experimentation. In short, the fear of losing keeps people from experimenting with change. Negotiators instead rationalize their behavior in a self-perpetuating fashion. The fear of making mistakes may result in a manager's inability to improve his or her negotiation skills. In this book, we remove the risk of experimentation by providing several exercises and clear demonstrations of how changing one's behavior can lead to better results in negotiation.

## DEBUNKING NEGOTIATION MYTHS

Before we start on our journey toward developing a more effective negotiation strategy, we need to dispel several faulty assumptions and myths about negotiation. These myths hamper people's ability to learn effective negotiation skills and, in some cases, reinforce poor negotiation skills. In the following section, we expose the four most prevalent myths about negotiation behavior.

## MYTH 1: GOOD NEGOTIATORS ARE BORN

A pervasive belief is that good negotiation skills are something that people are born with, not something that can be readily learned. This is false because most excellent negotiators are self-made. In fact, there are very few naturally gifted negotiators. We tend to hear their stories, but we must remember that their stories are *selective,* meaning that it is always possible for someone to have a lucky day or a fortunate experience.

This myth is often perpetuated by the tendency of people to judge negotiation skills by their car-dealership experiences. Whereas purchasing a car is certainly an important and common type of negotiation, it is not the best context by which to judge your negotiation skills. The most important negotiations are those that we engage in every day with our colleagues, supervisors, co-workers, and business associates. These relationships provide a much better index of one's effectiveness in negotiation. In short, effective negotiation requires practice and feedback. The problem is that most of us do not get an opportunity to develop effective negotiation skills in a disciplined fashion; rather, most of us learn by doing. As the second myth reveals, experience is helpful, but not sufficient.

## MYTH 2: EXPERIENCE IS A GREAT TEACHER

We have all met that person at the cocktail party or on the airplane who boasts about his or her great negotiation feats and how he or she learned on the job (Bazerman and Neale 1992). It is only partly true that experience can improve negotiation skills; in fact, naïve experience is largely ineffective in improving negotiation skills (Thompson and DeHarpport 1994).There are three strikes against natural experience as an effective teacher. First, in the absence of feedback, it is nearly impossible to improve performance.

For example, can you imagine trying to learn mathematics without ever doing homework or taking tests? Without diagnostic feedback, it is very difficult to learn from experience. The second problem is that our memories tend to be selective, meaning that people tend to remember their successes and forget their failures or shortcomings. This is, of course, comforting to our ego, but it does not improve our ability to negotiate. Finally, experience improves our confidence, but not necessarily our accuracy. People with more experience grow more and more confident, but the accuracy of their judgment and the effectiveness of their behavior do not increase in a commensurate fashion. Overconfidence can be dangerous because it may lead people to take unwise risks.

## MYTH 3: GOOD NEGOTIATORS TAKE RISKS

A pervasive myth is that effective negotiation necessitates taking risks and gambles. In negotiation, this may mean saying things like

"This is my final offer" or "Take it or leave it" or using threats and bluffs. This is what we call a "tough" style of negotiation. Tough negotiators are rarely effective; however, we tend to be impressed by the tough negotiator. In this book, we teach negotiators how to evaluate risk, how to determine the appropriate time to make a final offer and, more importantly, how to make excellent decisions in the face of the uncertainty of negotiation.

## MYTH 4: GOOD NEGOTIATORS RELY ON INTUITION

An interesting exercise is to ask managers and anyone else who negotiates, to describe their approach to negotiating. Many seasoned negotiators believe that their negotiation style involves a lot of "gut feeling," intuition, and "in-the-moment" responses. We believes that this type of intuition does not serve people well. Effective negotiation involves deliberate thought and preparation and is quite systematic. The goal of this book is to help managers effectively prepare for negotiation, become more self-aware of their own strengths and shortcomings, and develop strategies that are **proactive** (i.e., those that anticipate the reactions of their opponent) rather than **reactive** (i.e., those that are dependent upon the actions and reactions of their opponent). Thus, excellent negotiators do not rely on intuition; rather, they are deliberate planners.

## LEARNING OBJECTIVES

This book promises three things: First (and most important), reading this book will *improve your ability to successfully negotiate.* You and your company will be richer, and you will experience fewer sleepless nights, because you will have a solid framework and excellent toolbox for successful negotiation. However, in making this promise, we must also issue a warning: Successful negotiation skills do not come through passive learning. Rather, you will need to actively challenge yourself. We can think of no better way of doing this than to supplement this book with classroom experiences in negotiation, where managers can test their negotiation skills, receive timely feedback, and refine their negotiation strategies on a repeated basis.

Second, we provide you with a *general strategy for successful negotiation.* This book explicitly does not support a contextual model of negotiation, which prescribes using different negotiation strategies with different types of people, situations, and industries. Rather, we believe that negotiation skills are transferable across situations.

In saying this, we do not mean to imply that all negotiation situations are identical. This is patently false because negotiation situations differ dramatically across cultures and activities. However, there are key negotiation principles that are essential in all of these different contexts. The skills in this book are effective across a wide range of situations, ranging from complex, multiparty, multicultural deals to one-on-one personal exchanges.

Finally, this book offers an *enlightened model of negotiation.* Being a successful negotiator does not depend on your opponent's lack of familiarity with a book like this or a lack of training in negotiation. In fact, it would be ideal for you if your key clients and customers knew about these strategies. This approach follows what we call a *fraternal twin model,* which assumes that the other person you are negotiating with is every bit as motivated, intelligent, and prepared as you are. Thus, the negotiating strategies and techniques outlined in this book do not rely on "outsmarting" or tricking the other party; rather, they teach you to focus on simultaneously expanding the pie of resources and ensuring the resources are allocated in a manner that is favorable to you.

## THE MIND AND HEART

Across all of the sections of this book, we focus on the *mind* of the negotiator as it involves the development of deliberate, rational, thoughtful strategies for negotiation. We also focus on the *heart* of the negotiator because it involves emotions, psychology, and the intuitive aspects of negotiation. This book strikes a balance between these two approaches to negotiation situations.

# Interpersonal Negotiation Skills

"Deep conflict requires a tremendous exertion of psychological and physical energy. ... Such conflict may be creatively transformed when adversaries come to learn, ironically perhaps, that they may fulfill their deepest needs and aspirations only with the cooperation of those who most vigorously oppose them." As we saw in Chapter 13, while discussing deep-seated interpersonal conflict, people are more willing to listen when they feel that they have been heard and have a sense of control over the outcome. In more traditional (or competitive) negotiations, instead, people often attempt to convince the other side of the merit or justice of their proposal. "If the other side understands our ideas," we reason, "surely they will agree with us." Merit and justice still play a role in interest-based negotiation, but so does exploring for solutions that meet mutual needs. Not everyone finds the interest-based concept easy to swallow, however. "Traditional negotiation techniques suggest you hide your true business needs and goals...," explains a grape grower who looks at the idea of interest-based negotiation with a certain amount of distrust. "Once the other side gets a hold of your real needs they will strangle you with that knowledge."

A little caution, if not cynicism, may well be necessary to survive. While we can attempt to model effective negotiation strategies when dealing with others, at times we may have to resort to a more traditional approach. Research has demonstrated, for instance, that those who are willing to "play to win," if so forced, yet prefer to attempt a mutually productive approach, may be more credible negotiators.

Daniela, a young employee in one corporation, had heard of the difficult reputation developed by John, one of the agricultural technicians, but she had never had any difficulties with this individual herself. Daniela approached John one day, and found him sitting with his feet up on a table, reading a magazine. She apologized for disturbing him, assuming that perhaps this might have been his break period. "John, when you can, could you please pick up some parts for me in town?" Daniela asked politely. John answered rather curtly, "Right now?" She was not going to be intimidated, and responded, "That will work great for me, thanks!" John continued to show difficult behaviors with other individuals, but from then on never showed Daniela any discourtesy. I am not suggesting that Daniela took the very best approach available, but it served her well on that occasion.

The catch is that once people get caught up in competitive negotiation, it is often hard to step back and see clearly enough to work through difficulties in a collegial manner. A third person to help mediate may be needed (see Chapter 13). Traditional negotiation approaches have sometimes been described as including competition, yielding, withdrawal, or compromise. No one approach is always right or wrong. Competing means one person gets his way. Or at least it seems so at first. In the long run both parties often end up losing. It does little good, for instance, to get a wonderful contract for your new swine facility, if the contractor is left with such a small profit margin that she goes out of business before completing it.

At one dairy, the incentive was to get done quickly. Employees were paid for the full shift even if they got done early. As one milker was washing his boots and preparing to go home, his supervisor asked if he could work into the next shift. When the milker got his paycheck, he was not given credit for the free time he had accumulated (as a result of quickly finishing his first shift). No amount of arguing helped convince his supervisor of how unfair this seemed. The milker refused any overtime work in the future. This is a perfect example of a win-lose outcome turning into a lose-lose scenario. Competition tends to focus on a particular episode, rather than on long-term viability; on the present goal rather than on the long-term relationship. I know a retired manager who brags that his subordinates soon learned "he was not always right—but always *the boss*."

Although this manager may have obtained worker compliance from his winning tactics, I doubt he got much in terms of employee commitment. Losers often hold grudges, and find ways of getting even.

Should not a farmer try to obtain a good price for her apricot crop? Or get the best possible deal when buying that new piece of farm machinery? What about one-time situations, where you will never see another again in your life? Hidden in these questions, I believe there are some deeper issues that we must answer for ourselves. Surely, there *are* times when we bargain with the idea of getting the best possible results. In some cultures, people are offended if you pay the asking price without bargaining. But I will say this, many times in life we think we are dealing with a one-time situation, only to find that we have to negotiate or interact with that individual again.

*Yielding* (unilateral concessions at the expense of the person doing the giving in). We are most likely to yield if we feel there is little chance of winning, or if the outcome is more important to the other person than to us. "An angry co-worker began to shout and push me trying to pick a fight, and I left," a dairy worker explained. "For some reason I let it go and just backed away and left." The milker reflected that in his more youthful times he was a hot head, and would have probably fought back. Instead, when the dairy farmer returned, the worker reported the abusive incident to the dairyman, who fired the co-worker. In some situations yielding can be a virtue, but not always. A person who continues to yield sometimes stops caring. I do not see any harm in the occasional business yielding, or a balanced yielding among spouses, or even the frequent yielding obedience of a child to a parent or teacher. There are two specific types of yielding that concern me: (1) if saying yes today means living with frustration or resentment tomorrow, yielding is not a virtue; and related to that, (2) when we repeatedly agree to go along with a weak solution, this is not appropriate yielding, either (e.g., because we want to avoid disagreement at all costs, or feel coerced). When we stop caring, we often withdraw physically or emotionally.

***Compromise*** (mutual concessions where both parties yield some). Some types of compromises involve an arrangement somewhere between two positions; others may mean alternating the beneficiary. An example of the former is paying 20 cents per vine pruned when management wanted to pay 18 cents and crew workers asked for a quarter. An instance of the latter may involve alternating who gets to use the computer when there is limited computer time. While some issues lend themselves well to compromise, many others really do not. Compromise takes a measure of goodwill, trust and maturity, but not much creativity. But why is it that finding a middle ground can provide so little long-term satisfaction? Compromise often involves lazy communication and problem solving. For many of us, the term compromise certainly has come to have a negative connotation. While mutual concessions may take place at any time in the negotiation process, all too often such compromising occurs before the challenge has been sufficiently understood, or more creative solutions considered.

Our human brain is incredibly capable, when it comes to taking a huge amount of data and quickly digesting it and coming up with the one best solution. This is good, when it comes to making quick decisions in emergencies, and under time pressures. Unfortunately, making quick decisions can often deprive us of arriving at more effective, long lasting determinations. We are often too ready to accept a solution that seems to work, rather than the truly creative solution. The latter provides a sort of exhilaration. It is contagious. Once employees are involved to this degree, it is hard to turn back. You may have heard the classic tale of two siblings who argued over who would get an orange. They compromised and split it in half. One ate half and threw away the peel; the other, who was involved in a cooking project, grated the peel and discarded the rest. Compromise is good, especially when one considers the alternative, but creative or interest-based negotiation can provide much greater satisfaction.

**Scenario 1:** We want a raise Seven tractor drivers walked into a farm manager's office. These men had worked for the farm enterprise for several years. "We are all here," one of them began, slowly gathering confidence as he spoke. "Because we want a raise." The farm manager, somewhat stunned, turned around to look at each of them in unbelief. "How dare these guys come here, all together, and try and intimidate me into giving them a raise," he thought, but no words came out of his mouth. Two of the tractor drivers did most of the talking, and insisted that the manager either give them a raise, or they would quit.

So, what happened? The manager called the tractor drivers on their bravado or bluff, or so he thought. Soon he found himself without a single equipment operator as they had all quit in masse. The farm foreman in that operation tells us that when he went to town to purchase some parts a few hours later, he saw one of the tractor drivers walking aimlessly through town. The worker explained that he had no idea how he would face his wife. How he would tell her he had lost a job he had held for over five years. The foreman acted quickly, and the situation was somewhat salvaged, as the farm manager was able to convince four of the tractor drivers to come back and work for him.

**Scenario 2:** Leading by example? A foreman forced his will on the crew, but did it for a good cause. "No harm," he thought, "I am just trying to maximize all of our efforts." One day the crew workers were hungry and wanted to stop for lunch. The foreman wanted to get just a little more work done before lunch, and kept them going for another hour before breaking to eat. He could tell that a few workers were mumbling a bit, but he thought, "I am hungry too, I can wait for another hour, so can they."

So, what happened? "We were all very upset about this," one of the crew workers explained, speaking of the resentment felt at not being able to stop for lunch at the appointed hour. "The next time the foreman tried to make us work past lunch time we all walked off and left him fuming. The foreman told us to never do that to him again, but from then on he respected our need to stop at noon."

How have these farm operations been affected? What challenges do you think they may face in the future? How did the idea of "saving face" enter each of these situations? Even though some of the tractor drivers came back to work for the grower, do you think they will stay with him, or will they be looking for other work? Is there anything the farm manager could do now to improve the situation with the tractor drivers? How about the foreman, what can he do to recover the respect that has been lost?

What makes for an effective negotiator? Trustworthiness, for one, plays a huge role in successful negotiation. Dependability, honesty, and consistency are all part of trustworthiness. I often hear individuals involved in negotiations say, "I don't trust that person." It has also been said, "It is more important to be trusted than to be loved." As we break down negotiation talent into more specific type of skills, we can see that trust plays a large role in many, if not all of them. When we lose trust for a person, we begin to discount them. In our mind they begin to become undependable and dishonest. Some of the remaining scenarios will be broken down into multiple parts before the final resolution is given. Consider each of these parts fully in terms of what you would do, before reading what happened next. Some scenarios do not have a follow up, and leave you with the issue to reflect upon.

**Scenario 3:** Housing arrangements *Part I.* A horse breeder was facing some stress related to an employee living in a ranch-provided home. Actually, *not living* in the home would be a better description. The employee's wife had kicked him out a few weeks ago, and he was now sleeping in his pickup. It was important for the horse breeder to get his employee back in the house. They would soon be leaving for an important equestrian competition, and he just did not want to leave the issue up in the air.

*So, what happened? Part II.* The first step the horse breeder took was to find out if there was anything he could do to help repair the marriage difficulties. He offered to pay for marriage counseling. The wife was surprised and grateful that the farmer cared enough and agreed to let him know the next day. When the next day arrived, she informed the horse breeder that she had opted against counseling, and had made up her mind that she was leaving her husband. While the horse breeder did not want to sound crass, he did want to know when she would vacate the home.

So, what happened? *Part III.* The breeder knew that if the worker's wife pushed the issue, she could stay in the housing for quite a while. After talking a bit, the opportunity was right, and so he asked, trying not to seem overly anxious, "What are your plans?" She explained that she would need to stay in this home for at least one month, "We need to get together some money for a rental, including one month's deposit."

So, what happened? *Resolution.* The horse breeder first researched the cost of rental housing. When he approached the woman again, he was well prepared. "I realize it will be hard, but if you can manage to leave in two weeks, I will pay for one month's rental up to $X," he explained. "I realize it will be even harder, but if you manage to vacate the home in only one week, I will pay for two month's rental for you, or up to $2X." She was out in three days, after the horse breeder agreed to give her the cash instead of the rental payment. How may this horse breeding farm scenario have changed if the farmer would have made the same bottom line offer to help with the rental, but would have inverted the sentences so that the offer for leaving in one week would have been brought up first? "I realize it will be hard, but if you manage to vacate the home in one week, I will pay for two month's rental for you, up to $2X. If you leave in two weeks, however, I will pay for one month's rental up to $X."

**Prepare**

To prepare effectively, one needs to know as much as possible about all aspects of the situation and the personalities involved. Cost comparisons are essential when dealing with economic issues. There has been much written about being a smart shopper. Sometimes the most unexpected issues may come up. You may, for instance, have to face a worker who has come asking for a loan to bury a family member. One worker was struck by the tragedy of his young wife's untimely death. He was going to have to pay $4,700 for the funeral (not including the graveside plot). With a little calling around, the farmer's wife discovered that the same service could be had for $1,024. Sure, the second funeral home was not providing caskets that were as fancy, nor flowers. She figured that for those savings, they could purchase their own flowers.

Being prepared, may also mean better understanding the style of the person one will be dealing with. For instance, if you are exporting your fruit to Asia, and are meeting with prospective buyers, you may want to know as much as possible about the proper etiquette and preferences of your guests. Should you plan to get right to the point, for instance, or take more time talking about other pre-negotiation issues? Is there a right or a wrong way to handle greetings? Even details, such as how to accept a business card, may play an important role in showing the potential buyers the proper respect. In some Asian cultures, for instance, the proper etiquette is to hold the card with both hands and take time to study it carefully. You keep the card before you throughout the meeting, rather than putting it away in your wallet. An effective way to prepare for very difficult or emotionally charged situations is to role play ahead of time. Role playing the opposite perspective can be particularly enlightening.

**Search for Clarity**

As negotiators, it helps to learn about other people's preferences and also make our own clear. One grower explained that it was hard enough to understand our own needs and preferences, let alone be able to concentrate on someone else's. And perhaps that is one of the reasons why we do not see as frequent a use of interest-based negotiation. It does take a certain amount of effort, especially at first. With time, it can begin to feel more natural.

In the 1980s, when the non-smoking movement had not yet reached Chile, I taught a graduate course on labor management. Perhaps as many as 80% of my students smoked. I was clearly in the minority. I did not want to be rude, but I also knew that tobacco smoke would give me a headache. "I want to encourage everyone who wishes to smoke, to do so whenever they wish," I began. "Nevertheless, I would ask that you just step outside the classroom to do so." This was taken positively, and several in the class even nodded their approval. Part of effective preparation is considering the worse possible scenario, or "best alternative to a negotiated agreement" (BATNA). I suppose that even not agreeing to negotiate is a form of negotiation. If we cannot come to an agreement, what is the worst possible outcome to this situation? If your neighbor has a dispute with you over water rights? If the only welding shop in town substantially raises their prices? If your son threatens to leave the dairy if you do not meet certain conditions?

**Show Patience**

Effective negotiation frequently calls for a great amount of patience. Logic is not the only thing that prevails in bargaining efforts. There is a lot that comes into play in the form of interpersonal relations. Allowing other people as well as ourselves the time to work out problems is essential. When dealing with someone of a dissimilar culture, we may also need to allot additional time to work out an agreement. Not coming across as *wanting something too much* is related to patience. When we become overly narrow as to the result we will accept, we put ourselves at a negotiation disadvantage. So it was when my wife and I bought our first home. We were so openly delighted with it, that we lost an opportunity to bargain much over price. Of course, there is a balance between being *desperate* and playing *hard to get*, neither of which is very positive.

**Maintain Integrity**

At a time when many decisions were made on a handshake, my parents invited all the children to a family conference. "Earlier this year," they explained, "we came to an agreement with the winery for a price. Since then, many vineyards were affected by a terrible freeze, one that has meant a huge decline in supply. Had we waited a few more months before coming to an agreement on the price for our wine, we could have gotten a much better deal." My parents asked each of their five children for their opinions. The answer was a unanimous agreement to honor the oral agreement. At the time, I felt impressed that my parents would ask for our input. Since then I have come to the conclusion that they knew the answer all along, but wanted to teach us an important lesson about integrity. It is really impossible to have a discussion about *trust* and neglect the issue of integrity. Integrity in business and in every part of our lives is completely tied to our ability to be effective negotiators and be considered trustworthy.

**Avoid the Presumption of Evil**

"And she didn't even sign the E-mail!" the farmer complained. He had a bitter taste as a result of some dealings with a local government agency. In a world of increasing electronic correspondence, the possibilities for misunderstanding are ever increasing. When using E-mail, there is much we can do to become better communicators ourselves. Nevertheless, it is dangerous to assume that someone did not sign so she could offend us. This is especially so when the person's name already appears as part of the E-mail address.

E-mail etiquette is no different than any other type of good manners. There is a great variation in what people consider polite. For instance, in some cultures it is considered good manners to leave the toilet seat down. In others, the polite thing is to leave it up so it can stay clean. In some Hispanic sub-cultures it is rude for a man to greet the wife of a friend with a kiss on the cheek; in others, it is rude not to. While we want to make every effort to be polite ourselves, it is best to avoid being judgmental about other people's behavior. At one ranch operation, one of the partners tended to assume that the other two partners were talking about him when he saw them conversing. This is called negative attribution. It is all too easy to incorrectly interpret another person's innocent behavior and assume the worst. Contention breeds mistrust. It is good *not to be easily provoked*, especially when no offense was intended.

Some years ago I was asked to give a talk to a group of young adults. I noticed that as I spoke, a young man would lean toward the young lady beside him and whisper. I found this to be very distracting. I feel very strongly that only one person should speak at a time, and so it was that every time he began to talk, I stopped. When I stopped, he stopped, and so it went. I later found out he was interpreting for a foreign visitor. On another occasion, I attended a meeting where my supervisor was pointing out some problems. I began to defend myself. "We were not talking about you," the supervisor said calmly. It is embarrassing to run at "the sound of a shaken leaf" when no one pursues. It is good to avoid assumptions, or to become defensive. An effective tool, instead of assuming the worse when we do not know how to interpret something, is to describe what happened and let the other person explain. Such a description should avoid inferences as to why someone did something. We will often find out there was a good reason for what took place. Or at least give each party the opportunity to explain her perspective.

**Control Emotions**

Our emotions get in the way of effective negotiations regularly. Nothing kills creativity quicker than anger, pride, embarrassment, envy, greed, or other strong negative emotion. Anger is often an expression of fear, or lack of confidence in our ability to get what we think we want. Emotional outbursts tend to escalate rather than solve a conflict. If we can improve our ability to manage our emotions and respond without getting defensive, we have gone a long way toward creative negotiation. A friend once said, "When we permit negative emotions, such as anger, to take control of us, this is a sure sign we are about to step into a trap." It is extremely difficult to hide our emotions, especially when we feel there is much in the balance. Our body language, particularly our facial gestures and voice tonal qualities, often give us away. We are not emotionless robots, nor is it advantageous to completely hide our emotions. However, it is better to *describe* our emotions (e.g., a feeling of disappointment) rather than to *show* them.

**Scenario 4:** I won't work for that foreman *Part I.* A peach grower hired a foreman who was very effective. The man was kind, but firm. Some of the equipment operators, accustomed to work without supervision, highly resented having a foreman. "We just do not want a foreman," some of the employees had told the grower. The farmer noticed that jobs that used to take much longer to accomplish were being completed in a much more timely fashion.

*So, what happened? Part II.* The grower wanted to make sure the foreman was respectful of the employees, was giving them their proper breaks, providing them with cold water, and doing all the things a thoughtful foreman should do. This seemed to be so in every way, but it had not been a week since the grower started to investigate the situation, when one of the most outspoken workers came to speak to him. Most of the other workers had adjusted to having a foreman, especially after the grower went out of his way to explain what the duties of the foreman would be, and how having a foreman would allow the grower to spend more time taking care of other orchard duties. The worker seemed agitated, and upset, and soon set out the ultimatum, "I will not work here with *this* foreman," he blurted out his feelings. So, what happened? *Part III.* Fifteen years ago this peach grower would have fired the crew worker for insubordination. Now, as he was getting older, the grower had mellowed out considerably. He knew the importance of listening to others. "What's the matter?" he inquired solicitously. "Well, it's just not right," the crew worker responded, still upset. "The man does not have a foreman's license!"

So, what happened? *Part IV.* The grower wanted to laugh at this response. He had heard almost every story in the book during his years in farming, ever since he started working alongside his dad as a youngster. But this one was a new one. While the grower knew that there was much about the law he did not know, he was clear on this point. There was no law that required foremen to have a supervisor's license. But then, he looked at it from the worker's perspective, and realized that there really was not anything funny about the employee's concerns. "Did you know that here in California a foreman does not need a license?" he began. As far as the grower knew, there was no state that required a license, but he wanted to make sure that the employee did not lose face or feel foolish. "What you say is important, maybe foremen *should* be required to have a license, just like farm labor contractors," he added in an effort to further validate the employee. "Tell me, now that you know that a foreman's license is not required in California" the grower eventually asked, "how do you feel about working for me?" "I just don't know," the worker spoke now much more calmly, but was shaking his head somewhat. The grower tried to find out if there was something else that was the matter, but made no discovery that cleared up the situation.

So, what happened? *Part V.* The grower felt his own options narrowing, and was about to tell the crew worker that he was fired if he could not work for the foreman. Then he remembered that the worker had asked for additional time off for the Thanksgiving holiday weekend. It was now the day before Thanksgiving. The grower was amazed when he heard himself asking, "Would you like some time to think about it? You had asked for time off during the Thanksgiving weekend. Would Tuesday of next week work for you?" The crew worker agreed and seemed satisfied, and began to leave. "Wait a moment," the grower stopped him. "Do not forget to take the turkey I bought for you," he said cheerfully, pretending there was nothing wrong as he handed over the big bird. As he watched the worker disappear with the turkey, what amazed the grower the most about himself was that he had stayed calm through the whole situation, never getting angry at the employee. So, what happened? *Resolution.* The grower knew that despite his own calm, there was still something wrong. As he stood there watching the worker leave, the grower saw the employee put the turkey in a co-worker's pickup. The worker did not wait until Tuesday to come back and talk to the grower. Friday morning he showed up asking, "You do not have work for me?!" In reality, it sounded more like a statement rather than a question. "Actually, we *do* have work for you," the grower answered. "No, you do not understand," the worker continued apprehensively. "You do *not* have work for me!" "But we *do* have work for you," the grower repeated. Finally, the worker clarified, "You see, now I cannot collect Unemployment Insurance!" The worker had wanted to be fired, because those who quit are not eligible for Unemployment Insurance in California.

**Understand Time Pressures**

Deadlines are often self-imposed. How often do we feel obligated to respond right away when facing a difficult situation? People can ask for a little more time to study out a matter, or to accomplish a task. Do not be afraid to ask, "This is a tough one, can you give me until 3 p.m. tomorrow to get back to you?" Or, "It is now 7:15 a.m., and I am tied up for the next two hours. If I call you between 10 and 10:30 a.m., will that work for you?" This type of detail only takes a few minutes longer to negotiate. "I will call you back as soon as I can," on the other hand, leaves much to be desired. As a recipient of that message we may wonder, does that mean I will receive a call in the next half hour, two hours, or week? Although not intended as such, this may well come across as an avoidance tactic. To be credible, then, it is important to agree on a specific time wherein we will get back to a person. We also need to be specific about exactly what it is that we have agreed to accomplish.

If we can build a little cushion for the unexpected, that is helpful. Most people do not mind having to wait a little longer if they know what the real situation is. Armed with such knowledge, each individual can plan her own time more effectively, rather than wait for another person who may or may not come through. If a deadline seems hard to meet, ask to re-negotiate an extension *before* the time for the deadline is up. An effective negotiator will ask the other party to suggest or take a role in establishing a deadline, rather than arbitrarily impose one. Furthermore, it is good to give others the time they need to make a decision with which they are comfortable. To do what we say we will do, and do so in a timely fashion, builds trust. People who can be counted to follow through with what they say they will do are invaluable.

**Break Down Bigger Issues Into Smaller Ones**

An effective negotiator is constantly looking for ways to break down challenges into smaller, more easily solvable issues. For instance, if a farm foreman is resisting the introduction of an electronic gadget to help keep track of each crew member's performance, it helps to talk it over, and find out specific concerns. There may be some apprehension about (1) the reliability of the system, (2) setup time, or even (3) staying on top of production data right in the field. Each of these concerns can be addressed separately.

**Separate Problem from Self-Worth**

Without a doubt, the worst type of intermixing issues is that of combining some problem that is important to us with our own self-worth. It is ineffective and manipulative, for instance, to imply that disagreement with our idea is equivalent with a vote of no-confidence against us. Such an approach, will sooner than later result in our feeling reject.

A member of a dairy's corporate board (who also happened to be one of the founders of the original dairy), made the mistake of suggesting that a vote against the incentive pay program she was suggesting for the milkers was equivalent to a vote against her. After the meeting, she confronted a member of the board who voted against the proposal as it presently stood. She was fortunate that this individual was willing to stand up to such pressure. He explained that as long as he was a member of the board he would vote for what was best for the dairy. And furthermore, the board member told the founder that he did not appreciate being pushed into doing anything short of voting his conscience. The founder apologized.

**Avoid Threats and Manipulative Tactics**

Threats also reduce our negotiating ability. Such threats may entail a directed consequence—towards ourselves or someone else. Any type of threat can greatly undermine our long-term negotiating ability. This is even more so, when an individual does not follow through. Threats do not engender trust or liking. Even inconsequential threats can be annoying. At a family game, one player repeatedly threatened to quit. After a half dozen threats, his mother told him, "The first time you threatened, I was concerned, by the last threat, I was just ready for you to quit and let the rest of us enjoy the game." Sometimes we may not realize that sharing some of our discouragement may come across as a threat. My research shows that people in deep seated interpersonal organizational conflict, more often than not, are seriously contemplating bailing out the organization. Yet, these individuals have seldom told others at the farm that they are contemplating withdrawal. And that is good!

One farm manager, who would continually threaten those around him with comments about leaving the farm operation, began to quickly lose the support of others around him. The respect that this individual so much wanted from his colleagues began to vanish, and even his loyalty to the organization was questioned. While people often feel a great need to share their feelings with someone who can be supportive, we need to choose such a person with care. If the individual always agrees with us and validates our perspective, such a person may not be doing us a favor. People who feel validated elsewhere may put less effort into improving a failing relationship. A positive relationship, is one where the listener can help us identify where we may have contributed to the problem. We all need people who can help us see the *blind spots* in our personalities and behaviors.

## Focus on the Problem Rather than the Solution

The suggestion of focusing on the problem rather than the solution may sound counter intuitive. Yet for a number of reasons, it is one of the keys to effective negotiation. The more complex the situation, the more important this principle. When someone comes with the solution, even when that solution is a good one, it gives the other stakeholder the feeling of not having any control. Research has shown that people often prefer an outcome that is not as beneficial, yet one where they sense greater control over possible outcomes. Even if a stakeholder has gone out of his way to find a fair solution for all involved, when such a solution is presented as firm, it tends to put other stakeholders on the defensive. In one such case, a rancher who was presented with such a stance (i.e., given the solution) felt coerced to do all the compromising. What this stakeholder did not realize until later, is that the solution being presented was already a huge concession and compromise on the part of the other stakeholder who presented it. The timing and approach had been ineffective, however.

An individual with an excellent idea needs to wait until the predicament that has brought everyone together has been carefully discussed, and until the needs of all the stakeholders are understood. Only then can the solution be presented, and this needs to be done in a very tentative fashion. "Would such and such an idea meet your needs, or can we play with the concept and twist it a bit so it does?"

Where there is an emotionally charged atmosphere, or when there is much riding in terms of consequences for individual stakeholders, this approach may make a difference between success and failure. An effective negotiating technique, then, is to come to the bargaining table with the idea of studying the problem and individual needs, rather than imposing a solution. This approach of coming right out with a fair solution, but doing away with all the bargaining, is known to most of us as the "take it or leave it" tactic. In collective bargaining, it is called *Boulwarism*, named after former General Electric (GE) Vice President Lemuel R. Boulware. What management would do was to propose a final offer to the union right up front. Management went out of their way to study all the facts that could pertain to the contract, and to make it fair for all involved, "trying to do right voluntarily." They refused to budge from their position, however, unless any "new facts" of sufficient strength were presented. Such an approach was highly resented by the union, who felt undermined. Two "new facts" played key roles against Boulwarism, (1) the practice was found to some degree, to constitute bad-faith bargaining by the National Labor Relations Board (NLRB) and the courts; and (2) the union also made a very strong point against the tactic through a successful strike.

When we are the ones being presented with a possible solution, it is good to be slow to find fault. If someone's proposal is quickly followed by our counterproposal, the other individual is likely to feel slighted. Two key reasons for avoiding quick counterproposals include (1) the other stakeholder is least receptive to hear another proposal after setting hers on the table, and (2) such counteroffers are often perceived as disagreement, or an affront to "face."

At the very least, then, efforts should be made to let the other stakeholders feel that their proposal is being taken seriously, and has been understood. If a counterproposal builds on the other stakeholder's proposal, and credit is so given, then the chances for negative feelings are further curtailed.

**Scenario 5:** Poor quality pack A greenhouse manager has had terrible results this year in terms of tomatoes being picked outside of the acceptable color range. He asked both the assistant production manager and the foreman to work on the difficulty. The foreman insisted that the problem was caused by the incentive pay program. In his opinion workers were paying little interest to quality issues, as there was no negative consequence for poor quality. The assistant manager, on the other hand, felt that a return to hourly pay would greatly reduce productivity. Plus, she remembers that last year, when workers were paid by the hour, they still had problems with quality.

Who are all the possible individuals that can be affected by this challenge? Do they have any common needs? What might these be? Are there some hidden challenges here? How could we be more sure that the correct problem was understood?

### Try for Interest-Based Solutions

In traditional negotiations (i.e., focused on competition, yielding or compromise), we are inclined to focus exclusively on our needs and assume it is the other stakeholder's responsibility to worry about having her needs met. Yet, by showing a sincere interest in the needs of others we increase the chances of having our needs met. While talking about our needs may have been considered a selfish thing in traditional negotiation, here in creative negotiation it is not selfish by definition, as it is not only our needs that are being considered, but also the needs of the other stakeholders. We frequently fail to explore beyond the obvious solution—like the sisters who split the orange in half. It helps to validate the other stakeholder's needs as a starting point in exploring creative solutions and as a way to reduce negative emotion. "Hmm...you need to get home by four today. Let's think of how we can do that and get the animals fed, too." Integrative negotiation seeks to carefully understand the true nature of the problem, and genuinely attempt, where it is possible, to provide solutions that meet the respective needs of all who are affected.

In recent years there have been some very positive developments in the field of negotiation, including union-management relations. The past has offered a frequently adversarial, turbulent and sometimes violent approach to collective bargaining and labor union-management relations. These positive changes, which have in no way been universally adopted, have come about as a result of an interest-based negotiation approach. Union representatives are becoming more conscious of the need to increase the competitiveness of unionized employers, while further enhancing job security and quality of life for all employees. Employers under a union contract are more likely to work with rather than against the union, to meet both worker and organizational needs. I have had the opportunity to watch representatives of union and management sitting side by side, and enthusiastically reporting success after success with the interest-based approach. At the very core of creative negotiation is the idea that it is possible for everyone to get more of what they need by working together. The foundation of effective problem-solving understands the problem itself. Otherwise, it is all too easy to build solutions on a false foundation. After such understanding, creative negotiation involves looking for the hidden opportunities presented by challenges.

Having said all this, it is not easy to be *creative*. It takes work. The following five-step process has been suggested to get the creative juices flowing: (1) actively consider all alternatives, (2) digest and re-arrange the data, and (3) set the challenge aside and wait. Wait for what? ... for a (4) sudden flash of inspiration, which needs to be (5) rigorously tested. These steps are important, as they recognize the importance of looking at a challenge from all angles, studying out a problem, and then putting it aside for a time. I suspect that sometimes steps one through three may need to be repeated several times until that inspiration comes. As we practice creative negotiation, faith in our ability to turn challenges into opportunities will increase. This self-confidence will help us focus on problem solving and reduce the chances of falling back on contention, negative emotion or competitive negotiation.

## Admit Error and Apologize

We mentioned earlier that strong negative emotion can lead us into psychological traps. So can over-investment in an idea. If the foundation is wrong, we may have to undo all our work and begin from scratch. Depending how far into a project we are, this can be quite painful and expensive. We have to first recognize that we *have been wrong* before we can *make things right.* If we notice that the concrete foundation to the dairy barn we are building is faulty, we can close our eyes and continue construction only at our own peril. As painful as it may seem now, the sooner we recognize our error and make the necessary expenditures to break up and remove the concrete so we can start over, the better off we are.

Sometimes we may feel over-invested in terms of an idea. It may be as hard to admit we were wrong as it was to break up that concrete. People who are willing to admit a mistake are more likely to be considered trustworthy. A proper apology is extremely powerful. So is sharing a goal we have in terms of a new approach to dealing with issues. If we have been extremely critical in the past, it helps to let people know we will be working to improve that negative pattern. To be genuine, an apology must not come across as a justification for what we have done wrong. A true apology is also accompanied with an offer to make restitution when that is possible. Furthermore, a sincere apology implies a willingness to make the appropriate changes commensurate with what we have done wrong. When I feel it is warranted, I like the idea of asking a person to whom I am apologizing, "Will you accept my apology?"

When someone expresses regret often for the same thing but makes no real efforts to change, this is hardly an apology. As powerful as an apology can be, when someone takes back that apology by word or deed, this puts such an individual in a position of greater disadvantage than if she had expressed no regrets at all. Such is the situation, for instance, in many cases of domestic violence (physical or verbal). It is not uncommon for a man to be contrite after beating his wife today. But by tomorrow he has begun to minimize the damage, and not long thereafter is striking her again. A person, who is willing to accept an apology, and forgive another, is likewise in a better position than one who is not. It is also hard to trust a person who will not acknowledge an apology. An individual who has truly forgiven another does not continually remind the other of that fact. Some comments and deeds are so hurtful in their nature, however, that it may take extensive time before a person can truly feel free of the associated pain.

**Reject Weak Solutions**

In traditional negotiation, as soon as we get close enough to the solution we want, we are often prone to accept someone's yielding their will to ours. While at times the motivation on our part may be selfish, in others we may truly believe that our solution will best serve all involved. Then again, earlier we said that (1) it was difficult for true caring to co-exist with frequent giving in; and (2) jumping to solutions before the problem is carefully understood, often yields weak solutions. Sometimes people will yield or pretend to yield out of frustration over the situation. By accepting their yielding, we have reduced our direct and indirect negotiation power. Instead, we not only get better solutions when we make sure the other person is completely satisfied with the solution, but we gain trust in their eyes and can thus improve our negotiation strength.

**Scenario 6:** Disagreement over the radio Two milkers had a disagreement over which radio station to listen to. "I don't know," one of them sighed as he lifted his hands in disappointment, "just choose whichever station you want." So, what happened? *Resolution.* The one milker accepted the defeat of the other, and began to walk towards the radio. But before the milker arrived to where the radio was located at the other side of the parlor, his co-worker protested, "That's just not right, why should you get your way." Their negotiation process had to begin anew.

Sometimes people give in easily. We should not be quick to accept such yielding. Taking extra time to consider alternatives can be very rewarding. We may often sense that another person is giving in, rather than agreeing that the solution that has been suggested is indeed the best possible alternative. If you read emotion or strength of conviction in another stakeholder (or the very opposite), you may want to step back and consider together what unmet needs may exist still, and work towards finding a solution that takes these into consideration.

**Sidebar 17-1:** Not so fast! Benie and Jennifer Matsuda were making some joint succession plans for their farm operation. They came to an agreement, but Benie noticed that his wife had only agreed hesitantly. Rather than just accepting Jennifer's agreement and moving on with his own plans, Benie said, "I notice that you are not totally pleased with our decision. It is really important to me that this is right, and that you are as happy with this decision as I am."

Jennifer said she was OK with the decision, but Benie still sensed otherwise. Benie had the perfect opportunity to move forward and do things the way he wanted to, but hesitated again. "I still sense there is something you are feeling, perhaps difficult to put into words, but nevertheless something important that makes you hesitate." Jennifer answered, "Actually, I think you may be right." She agreed to think over the matter some more. That night they had another chance to converse at length, and Jennifer was able to better articulate a fear she had. As a result they were able to make some small but important adjustments that left them both satisfied. Moreover, Jennifer was able to further build her trust on her husband, because he had honored her feelings, thoughts, and opinions.

## Be Tentative About Reading People's Feelings

Attributions should be neutral or tentative, such as "I sense there is something wrong here." Avoid attributing negative emotions to another person, such as "You are angry." Nor should one ascribe a reason along an attribution, "You must be hurt because we switched to 3x milking." Instead, just describe the emotion in more neutral ways, and with some degree of tentativeness, allowing the other stakeholder to either validate these feelings, or offer their own explanation: "I sense that something is still not right in our agreement, but I am not sure if I am reading that correctly."

## Summary

Each one of us negotiates our way through life. While there are no easy answers that will fit every negotiation need, there are some important principles that will help us become more effective. Creative negotiation skills at first seem different enough from how we may have reacted to challenges in the past, which reading a chapter and a book such as this one, only begins to plant some ideas in our minds. Some of the approaches may seem mechanical at first. I like to keep these thoughts alive from day to day by reading good books, or listening to audio tapes. Furthermore, I tend to analyze human interaction. There is much to be learned from both interpersonal success and failure.

There are many excellent books available on the topics of negotiation skills, listening skills, conflict management, interpersonal communications, and so on. Try your local library and you may find some real treasures. After I read a book or listen to a tape, I like to note the most important things I have learned from each. You may want to do the same, keeping special notes on the outcomes of your negotiations. As I grow older, *doing right* has become more important to me than *being right* (in the sense of winning). There is a great amount of satisfaction in being able to give the *soft answer* ("A soft answer turneth away wrath"). This is a journey that one embarks in, the challenge of which is so difficult, that one can never truly say, "I have arrived there." May your own excursion be filled with satisfaction and hope.

**A Final Note**

Your comments about this book will be greatly welcomed. I wish you prosperity in your farming enterprise and success in the management of people on your farm. I invite you to explore our Website and join the AG-HRnet or to receive our electronic newsletter People in Ag. If you have any comments, suggestions, or questions, please feel free to contact me.

The very thought of negotiating sounds intimidating, yet we are all experienced negotiators. Any time we come to an agreement on anything, we are negotiating. Some of it we may do somewhat subconsciously, such as deciding who says hello first, or holding a cattle gate open for another rider to pass through. Determining where to go out for dinner with your spouse, or asking your daughter for help in training a colt also involves negotiation. More traditional issues we associate with negotiation may include agreeing on (1) a pruning price with your vineyard crew, (2) how much you are going to pay to have your post-harvest cooling shed constructed, or (3) what you will get for your export cherries. One thing that these examples have in common is that they involve people. Many of us developed a love for agriculture based on our love for farm animals and plants. We may at first be surprised to see instead, what a large portion of our day involves interacting with people. Although negotiation can be downright hard at times, there are specific steps we can take to become more effective negotiators.

Negotiation skills include being well prepared, showing patience, maintaining integrity, avoiding the presumption of evil, controlling our emotions, understanding the role of time pressures, breaking down bigger issues into smaller ones, avoiding threats and manipulative tactics, focusing first on the problem rather than on the solution, seeking for interest-based decisions, and rejecting weak solutions. We shall visit these later on in the chapter. A fair portion of this book incorporates negotiation principles in one way or another. This chapter is presented as a way to help us think through challenging day-to-day situations, especially those for whom we may not find direct answers in the book. I find that it helps to keep a mental or written notebook on how we react to difficult situations. Certainly, we have lots of opportunities to practice. While still focusing on agricultural labor management, it is my hope in this chapter to expand to other *people issues* that affect us. Whatever improvements we make in one area of our lives, these tend to spill over to other areas, such as the home, ranch, business dealings, or sports. For those of you who operate a family farm, many such distinctions are already blurry.

Interspersed through this chapter, a number of scenarios are provided for you to practice negotiation skills. Set aside your reading after each one, and think through all the issues that may be involved. How do you think you would react to each case? Put yourself in the place of each of the players. Only after considering each scenario separately, move on to find out how they were resolved. While resolutions are provided for most scenarios, please note that these may *not* reflect the best or worst possible outcome. Furthermore, what is *best* for one stakeholder may not be for the other. You may want to ask yourself, in what ways could these individuals have arrived at a better solution. Finally, the scenarios are placed somewhat randomly throughout the chapter, and are not necessarily intended to reflect the topic discussed in that section.

**References**

1. Rothman, J. (1997). *Resolving Identity-Based Conflict in Nations, Organizations, and Communities* (pp. xii, xiii). San Francisco: Jossey-Bass Publishers.
2. Fisher, R., & Ury, W. (1981). *Getting to Yes: Negotiating Agreement Without Giving In.* New York, NY: Penguin Books.
3. Alavi, K. Personal conversations.
4. Swann, W. B., Jr. (1996). *Self-Traps: The Elusive Quest for Higher Self-Esteem* (p. 47). New York: W. H. Freeman and Company.
5. Sloane, A. A., & Witney, F. *Labor Relations* (4th Edition) (pp. 205-206). Englewood Cliffs, New Jersery: Prentice-Hall Inc.; and Peterson, W. (April 1991). "Ideas Have Consequences." Commencement Address to Harvard Business School Alumni. *The Freeman,* a publication of the Foundation for Economic Education, Inc., (Vol. 41, No. 4) in "Liberty Haven" Website.
6. Rackham, N. (1999). "The Behavior of Successful Negotiators," in Lewicki et. al. (Editors). *Negotiation: Readings, Exercises, and Cases* (3rd Edition) (p. 347). Burr Ridge, Illinois: Irwin.
7. Sperber, P. (1983). *Fail-Safe Business Negotiating* (pp. 10-21). Englewood Cliffs, N. J.: Prentice Hall, in Lewicki et. al. (Editors); *Negotiation: Readings, Exercises, and Cases* (1993) (2nd Edition) (p. 173). Burr Ridge, Illinois: Irwin.

# Index